A MAN
OF THE
WORLD

A MAN
OF THE
WORLD

MY LIFE AT
NATIONAL GEOGRAPHIC

GILBERT M. GROSVENOR
WITH MARK COLLINS JENKINS

WASHINGTON, D.C.

Since 1888, the National Geographic Society has funded more than 14,000 research, conservation, education, and storytelling projects around the world. National Geographic Partners distributes a portion of the funds it receives from your purchase to National Geographic Society to support programs including the conservation of animals and their habitats.

Get closer to National Geographic Explorers and photographers, and connect with our global community. Join us today at national geographic.org/joinus

For rights or permissions inquiries, please contact National Geographic Books Subsidiary Rights: bookrights@natgeo.com

Financially supported by the National Geographic Society.

ISBN: 978-1-4262-2153-8

Printed in the United States of America

22/MP-PCML/1

To the Geographic family: the people who made
this iconic institution what it is today

CONTENTS

HUBBARD-BELL-GROSVENOR
FAMILY

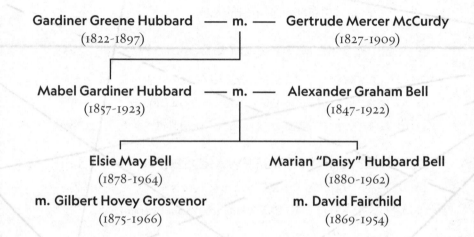

Gardiner Greene Hubbard —— m. —— Gertrude Mercer McCurdy
(1822-1897)   (1827-1909)

Mabel Gardiner Hubbard —— m. —— Alexander Graham Bell
(1857-1923)   (1847-1922)

Elsie May Bell   Marian "Daisy" Hubbard Bell
(1878-1964)   (1880-1962)

m. Gilbert Hovey Grosvenor   m. David Fairchild
(1875-1966)   (1869-1954)

MELVILLE BELL GROSVENOR
("MBG") FAMILY

Melville Bell Grosvenor —— m. 1st —— Helen North Rowland
(1901-1982)   (1902-1985)

m. 2nd Anne Elizabeth Revis
(1918-present)

                                        Helen "Teeny" Rowland
                                        Grosvenor
Edwin Stuart Grosvenor   (1925-1988)
(1951-present)

Sara Anne Grosvenor   Alexander "Alec"
(1956-present)   Graham Bell Grosvenor
                                        (1927-1978)

                                Gilbert "Gil" Melville Grosvenor
                                        (1931-present)

GILBERT HOVEY GROSVENOR
("GHG") FAMILY

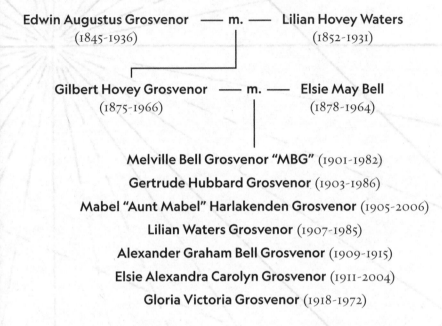

Edwin Augustus Grosvenor —— m. —— Lilian Hovey Waters
(1845-1936)   (1852-1931)

Gilbert Hovey Grosvenor —— m. —— Elsie May Bell
(1875-1966)   (1878-1964)

Melville Bell Grosvenor "MBG" (1901-1982)

Gertrude Hubbard Grosvenor (1903-1986)

Mabel "Aunt Mabel" Harlakenden Grosvenor (1905-2006)

Lilian Waters Grosvenor (1907-1985)

Alexander Graham Bell Grosvenor (1909-1915)

Elsie Alexandra Carolyn Grosvenor (1911-2004)

Gloria Victoria Grosvenor (1918-1972)

GILBERT MELVILLE GROSVENOR
("GIL" OR "GMG") FAMILY

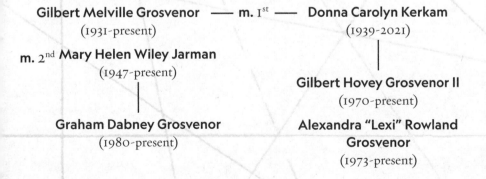

Gilbert Melville Grosvenor —— m. 1st —— Donna Carolyn Kerkam
(1931-present)   (1939-2021)

m. 2nd Mary Helen Wiley Jarman
(1947-present)

Gilbert Hovey Grosvenor II
(1970-present)

Graham Dabney Grosvenor
(1980-present)

Alexandra "Lexi" Rowland
Grosvenor
(1973-present)

PROLOGUE

You may not know my name. But chances are you have encountered my family legacy—perhaps in rows of neatly aligned yellow magazines, on television, or online, where our social media channels are followed by an audience of nearly 200 million. You might know some of our milestone accomplishments, which include funding the initial fieldwork of a young scientist named Jane Goodall studying chimpanzees in Africa and bringing the discovery of the *Titanic* to the world's attention.

I was born into this world—the National Geographic family—as the fifth generation fortunate enough to spend a lifetime searching out and celebrating the planet, pledged, in the words of our mission, "to increase and diffuse geographical knowledge."

My great-grandfather Alexander Graham Bell, inventor of the telephone, was an original member, with 165 like-minded scientists and explorers, of the National Geographic Society. My grandfather Gilbert Hovey Grosvenor was the first full-time editor of *National Geographic* magazine, a cherished institution and global "magazine of record." My father, Melville Bell Grosvenor, his successor, helped make scientists like Jacques Cousteau a household name.

But in the world of National Geographic, "family" meant something broader and deeper than my own forebearers. It encompassed writers, photographers, engravers, artists—in short, an entire staff at our fabled headquarters in Washington, D.C. Most of all, it meant our members— those who supported our efforts and, in turn, received our flagship magazine, books, globes, atlases, and more. For much of our history, in order to share in the National Geographic experience, one had to be a member of the Society.

The map of my life was charted by men and women curious about the scope of our planet who wanted to pass along that sense of wonder to anyone who ever marveled at an endless horizon, a velvet sky at night, or the ocean's deep azure. They inspired me to embrace this place we call home, and to inspire others to do the same.

"We see a good deal of the world," the photographer Margaret Bourke-White once said. "Our obligation is to pass it on to others." From its founding, the National Geographic Society met that obligation and continues to do so today.

This is the story of my family and the Society it helped create.

WHERE ALL LONGITUDES CONVERGE

n March 1979 I was in my office on the ninth floor of the National Geographic Society's headquarters in Washington, D.C., when I was told Al Giddings was on the line. Al was a longtime *National Geographic* contributor, and I was the magazine's editor. I picked up the phone.

"Hi, Al," I said.

"Want to go diving at the North Pole?"

I was about to make some crack about Santa Claus when I recalled that Al was filming a documentary in the Arctic.

"I'm serious. Joe MacInnis is on board, and the Canadians will let us use the LOREX floating ice station as our platform."

Joe, the world's leading specialist in diving medicine, was also the world's expert in under-ice diving. In 1973 he and four companions became the first humans to dive beneath the ice at the North Pole.

"Hardly anyone has done it since," Al said. "You can probably count them on your fingers. As editor of the *Geographic,* you should be the first journalist to do so!"

I could feel the barb of the hook setting within me.

"When do we leave?" I asked.

Arctic exploration was a legacy of the institution to which I was devoting my life, as it was to every geographical society founded in the 19th century. Each in turn had urged a renewed quest for the elusive Arctic grail, the North Pole. In 1909 the National Geographic Society had helped sponsor the first expedition that attained that goal, a source of deep-seated institutional pride. My grandfather Gilbert Hovey Grosvenor, the pioneering editor of *National Geographic* magazine, had championed that expedition's leader, Robert E. Peary.

My grandfather, and my father after him, also sponsored Richard E. Byrd, the "admiral of the ends of the Earth," who was the first to fly over the two antipodes. Others we'd been associated with, like Roald Amundsen, Ernest Shackleton, and Wally Herbert, made clear the poles were in our blood.

In mid-April, I flew to Resolute Bay on barren Cornwallis Island, not far from the fabled Northwest Passage, where I met Joe. We took an old DC-3 across the Canadian Arctic Archipelago—all gray rock, brown tundra, and ice-choked seas—to Alert, perched on the northern tip of Ellesmere Island. There we climbed aboard the de Havilland Twin Otter warming up for its supply run to the Lomonosov Ridge Experiment (LOREX) base camp.

The LOREX was Canada's effort to map its portion of an immense undersea mountain range—the Lomonosov Ridge—that spanned the 1,100 miles between Ellesmere Island and Russia. National Geographic had lent the services of its deep-water photographic expert, Emory Kristof, to the camp's scientists.

Aloft over the Arctic Ocean, I couldn't take my eyes off that endless expanse of whiteness beneath. Everything to the west had been marked "Unexplored" on a map my grandfather had published only a few years before I was born. Somewhere below was the track Peary had followed to the North Pole.

A floating island can be a challenge to find. But eventually the cluster of white tents and red Quonset huts loomed into view, and we set down on the improvised airstrip. For the next two days and nights we lived on a raft drifting at the stately pace of five miles a day.

That's where the 26 scientists were spending two months profiling the undersea ridge with echolocation instruments. What little free time they had was spent in one of three places: a sleeping bag, the plywood sauna marked by a barber pole (the "North Pole"), or the "LOREX Slum and Polar Bar" tent, where an invigorating dram could be found.

The camaraderie of the frozen north was flourishing when we arrived. I appreciated that fellowship when it came time to face that hole in the ice.

THE TIME CAME AND WITH IT a glorious high Arctic day: cloudless; cold but not bitter; winds calm; the silence broken only by the occasional crackle and groan of the shifting ice pack. The sun was low—where it would stay all day and all night—over the endless white ocean.

I caught only glimpses of it, waddling in my bulky red dry suit into the ghastly artificial light of the heated tent. In its center was the eight-foot-square, eight-foot-deep hole that Al and Joe had cut out of the ice with an electric auger and a shovel.

I squeezed into a neoprene hood that exposed only my eyes and lips, adjusted my face mask, pulled on booties and fins, added a weighted belt to control buoyancy, tested the regulator, and made sure air was flowing from my tank. Carefully, I tied the emergency rope to my dry suit and pulled on the bulky gloves.

"Remember, one tug on the rope means all's well," Al told me. "Two tugs, the diver is returning topside—either because his air supply is running low or there's a problem."

"Got it," I said.

Al had laid out some of the things that could go wrong diving under ice in 28°F water. Your lips could become so numb you might swallow seawater, which would paralyze your larynx. Frozen condensation crystals could choke off your air supply. In conventional scuba diving, you can always break through the surface for help and fresh air. But not here under a ceiling of ice.

Taking a deep breath, I put my regulator into my mouth and gingerly felt my way down the rough steps carved in the ice.

I braced myself for the shock as my legs entered the water. I slipped farther down; now I was up to my shoulders. Gripping the rope, I made the final plunge.

Excruciatingly cold water instantly numbed my exposed lips. A flutter of panic swept over me. After several seconds I was relieved to find the regulator still firmly planted in my mouth. I kicked tentatively away from the light of the hole.

Suddenly, I was enveloped in a blue-black universe. Thinner ice overhead was a delicate powder hue; older slabs, a darker Delft. Thicker blocks were cobalt. Everywhere else, indigo gave way to midnight.

I felt utterly alone, as if I were the first and only human being who would ever explore what I was exploring—an aquanaut hovering over an unknown world. Soon I was in a transcendent realm of pure form. I saw prisms of color and light that appeared at first glance to be dancing and at second to be as intricately structured as the magnificent stained-glass windows of Chartres. Waving my gloved hand through one formation, I watched it shatter, then reform into an even more spectacular composition. I swatted at another, mesmerized by a kaleidoscopic display of what must have been crystals of frozen freshwater. A jellyfish, translucent yet pale orange with long and fragile tentacles, pumped its way past.

Slowly, I descended farther, dazzled by massive ice blocks cut with canyons and fissures. I had known that six-sevenths of floating ice is underwater but didn't fully understand until I experienced it. I had become a human tuning fork, reverberating to the tremendous heartbeat that sets all flows and currents in motion, from the mightiest Gulf Stream to the tiniest rivulet.

Then I felt my lifeline snag.

My pulse rate shot up, and a cascade of bubbles rushed toward the surface. I counted to 10, then felt along the line, which had snagged on my knife handle. With one quick movement, I freed it.

I was running low on air but still had enough to ease down again. I dropped, foot by foot, until the lifeline tightened. I had literally reached the end of my tether. Time to turn back.

One more thing to do and—with a dwindling reserve in my air tanks— quickly. I pushed the weight belt as high on my chest as possible, so that my head would turn downward. Squeezing a small amount of air into my vest, I felt my body slowly rise. By inflating or deflating as needed, I obtained positive buoyancy, and my feet gently bumped up against the underside of the ice. Finally, my feet were flush. I slipped, readjusted, and—hanging upside down—took a single step. Then a second . . . a third . . . a fourth step. I had done it. I had walked underneath the North Pole.

Seconds later Al was helping me back to the surface.

SOMEONE OPENED A bottle of champagne, and I toasted my companions in the stifling warmth of the tent. I unpacked Robert E. Peary's small sledge flag, long housed in Geographic headquarters, symbolically returning it to the pole for the first time since 1909.

My elation persisted even when we got the bad news that a lead—a fissure in the ice—was opening, a sheet of dark Arctic water splitting the airstrip. Until that refroze, our flight would be delayed—for how long, nobody could guess. After closer inspection, however, the pilot thought it would freeze over in a couple of hours.

Two days spent cooped up with other men made me want to spend that time out on the ice, with only my thoughts for company. My boots crunched as I angled across the surface of the sea toward an uplifted ridge 150 yards away to experience the eerie solitude that featured so prominently in the old explorers' journals.

On my ridge of ice, I could survey a frozen kingdom. The pole at last! I thought, echoing Peary. I spun 360 degrees, swinging symbolically through every longitude on the planet in seconds. No better place for pondering than where all time zones merge and all geographic directions are south.

I was in a special place on Earth at a special time. I would soon be 48 years old, as close to a midpoint in my life as I would be. Too bad that being where all paths meet doesn't promise the benefit of seeing where all paths might lead.

In little less than a year, the National Geographic Society's president, Robert E. Doyle, would turn 65 and retire. Members of the board of trustees were already approaching me to take on the job when that time came.

My first impulse was to decline because it would entail surrendering the editorship of *National Geographic.* Who would give up the best job in journalism?

But there were other considerations I could not deny any more than I could avert my gaze from four portraits hanging in the Society's board-room. One of them depicted my great-great-grandfather Gardiner Greene Hubbard, one of the Society's principal founders, circa 1888, looking over a beard that must have been two feet long. The second was of my great-grandfather Alexander Graham Bell, his beard still as black as when he invented the telephone, who succeeded Hubbard, his father-in-law, as the Society's president in 1898.

The third was of my beloved grandfather Gilbert Hovey Grosve-nor—"GHG" around the office—Bell's son-in-law and the man who made

National Geographic a household name and ran the organization for over half a century as president and editor.

Finally, there was the portrait of my father, Melville Bell Grosvenor—"MBG"—who had retired as president and editor in 1967 and was still the most infectiously enthusiastic person you could imagine.

Four generations of National Geographic Society leadership—I was poised to be the fifth. As if I needed prompting, the board threatened that, should I not accede to the office, they would be forced to go outside the organization for a president.

Going outside could be fatal. Not tomorrow. Not next year. But fatal in the long run. Someone schooled in the academy of the bottom line could come in and kill what was unique about us. I could not let that happen. Not on my watch.

Sitting on that shelf of ice where all longitudes converge, I knew the path I would follow. I would exchange the editor's office for the more gracious space of the president's office.

A distant shout interrupted my musings. The tiny figure of Al was waving me in. I began my trek back.

PART ONE

CHARTING A COURSE

CHAPTER ONE

THE FORTUNATE ISLES

The wind screeches out of the northeast, ricochets off the steep slopes of Cape Smokey, and knocks *Elsie* on her beam-ends, burying the lee rail in salt spray. My father, youthful again in memory, spins the wheel of our family's boat to windward and exults, "Boys and girls, this is real sailing!" My mother and older siblings brace themselves, against my father's glee as much as the wind and cold spray.

I am three years old, sloshing around in the cockpit, constrained from venturing topside by a rope tied to a pedestal. What am I doing? I'm seasick, blowing my lunch all over the place. Grabbing a bucket, Dad scoops up salt water and splashes down the cockpit—including me.

That is my earliest memory, embellished in later years by my mother, who would laughingly recall the incident after I became a competitive sailor. The teasing never bothered me; I can't think of a better foundation for my life than the deck of a boat. I love that my first act of awareness is rooted in a setting I have returned to many times—the Cabot Strait between Cape Breton Island and Newfoundland.

The great conservationist Frank Craighead once said that "every individual is formed by his past environment, reflects his present one, and in turn shapes the environment of the future." The statement applies to my own life and career, symbolically rooted here on Cape Breton Island in the Canadian Maritimes, just over the ranges from Cape Smokey.

I'm sure I know the route we took that day. The Great Bras d'Or Channel slants southwest from the Cabot Strait into Cape Breton Island and leads to the lake country through a fjord-like passage. The deep indentation to starboard marking the entrance to Big Harbour is a sign the lakes aren't far and demarcates one end of a soaring anvil-shaped peninsula.

A few miles farther, near the southwest point of this peninsula, looms a promontory then called Red Head; my great-grandmother Mabel Bell stood on the heights and gazed at the Bras d'Or Lakes glittering in the sun. As she wrote to her mother, it was like "seeing the land stretching out on every side of you like a map." Her husband, Alexander Graham Bell, promptly bought that spot of ground. The couple eventually amassed 2,000 contiguous acres of the promontory and renamed the new estate Beinn Bhreagh (pronounced Ben Vreea), the Gaelic equivalent of "beautiful mountain." Those islands, those headlands, those encircling seas draw me back every summer.

In places, Cape Breton is as wild and steep as anything in the Scottish Highlands. But as the sailor rounds its tip and steers west by north for the village of Baddeck, he would see on the starboard quarter the dreamlike turrets, gables, porches, and chimneys of the Bells' summer mansion, Beinn Bhreagh Hall—known to us descendants as simply "The Point."

Beinn Bhreagh on a midsummer morning is a splendid place to anchor one's soul. From the deck of my summer log cabin, the village of Baddeck across the bay has changed little since I was a boy. The harbor lighthouse is still painted white and red; the harbor is still crowded with sloops, sporty outboards, and the occasional schooner. If I go down to The Point and stroll out onto the terrace, I can see the meadows on Washabuck, the headland across the water—still part of a well-kept farm from Bell's day, owned by the same family.

The spellbound character of the setting emanates from those waters. Cupped in a ring of highlands, the Great and Little Bras d'Or, described by a 19th-century traveler as "a passage to the Fortunate Isles," comprise one of the few tidal saltwater lake systems in the world. Small wonder that Bell—known as Alec to his family—felt at home in this windy, hilly country surrounded by a magical sea. It reminded him of his native Scotland.

What was once a working estate is now a family compound, where cousins, nephews, and nieces have their own summer cottages. Since my aunt Mabel died in 2006, no one lives in The Point, although the family does its best to maintain this historical place with 37 rooms and 17 fireplaces built in the late 19th century. One recent afternoon my wife, Wiley, and I made our way down there. Inside the entrance, the same stuffed bear greets us as he did years ago. The Chinese gong in the dining room emits the same sonorous tone each time I strike it. Pictures, furniture, and rugs seem untouched by time. All is quiet and enduring.

We've come down to thumb through the old guest registers. Wiley points out a favorite entry, a signature in a clumsy block print and dated in the late 1890s: Helen Keller. I see other names from the late 19th century: Samuel Langley, secretary of the Smithsonian Institution. George Kennan, the first American to explore Siberia and the Caucasus Mountains and another founder of the National Geographic Society. Wilfred Grenfell, a legendary doctor who provided medical care to scores of remote hamlets tucked into the bays and coves of Labrador. An entry in June 1897 marks my grandfather Gilbert H. Grosvenor's first visit to Baddeck.

Families, they say, are born in blood but made in the heart—and so it was with mine. My family history—and the Geographic's—began one dark winter during the Civil War with a case of scarlet fever that left a young woman named Mabel Gardiner Hubbard profoundly deaf for life.

Her father, a wealthy Boston attorney named Gardiner Greene Hubbard, hired a 26-year-old scruffy, bearded elocutionist recently emigrated from Scotland via Canada to teach the 15-year-old Mabel Hubbard to read lips. Young Bell, who was spending much of his earnings trying to create a "talking machine," needed the money. In the summer of 1875, the young inventor fell in love with his student, who initially was less than enthralled. When Bell asked to marry Mabel, he was rebuffed; Mabel, her family felt, was too young for marriage. When Bell perfected his invention the following year, Hubbard secured him a patent and set up the Bell Telephone Company. It made Bell wealthy. The Hubbards reconsidered Bell's proposal of marriage to Mabel and gave their permission. She married him on July 11, 1877.

Their daughter Elsie May Bell would ultimately meet her husband, Gilbert H. Grosvenor—my grandfather—through the National Geographic Society, which Hubbard had helped found and shepherd through its early years. They married in October 1900 in London, after Elsie, having run through nearly a dozen ministers, finally found one willing to omit the "wilt thou obey him and serve him" clause in the prayer book.

Their son—my father, Melville Bell Grosvenor—was born in 1901, followed by Gertrude, Mabel, Lilian, Elsie (known as Carol), and, in 1918, Gloria. One child, a son, died at the age of six. Yet my grandfather described the Society as "our eighth child" and used the expression "our two families, one personal and one professional."

The "professional" family came into being 11 years after Bell's marriage to Mabel, on the evening of January 13, 1888, when Bell's father-in-law, Gardiner Greene Hubbard, and 32 other men sat around a table in Washington, D.C.'s Cosmos Club. Among them were sunburned geologists, topographers, hydrographers, naturalists, and survivors of disastrous Arctic expeditions. Though many represented government scientific bureaus locked in competition for scarce funding, they were united by a shared passion for geography.

Hubbard was elected its first president; Bell succeeded him as the second. In addition to founding the Society itself, these men would create a journal devoted to the study of and appreciation for geography: *National Geographic,* with my grandfather Gilbert Hovey Grosvenor as its first full-time editor.

And there we have it. Two intertwined families: one the Hubbard-Bell-Grosvenors; the other, the National Geographic Society. To understand the latter, and its impact on American culture and popular geography, you have to know something about the former.

One photograph captures it all. My grandfather, still in his early 30s, working away at *National Geographic* manuscripts and layouts in the shade of a tent beneath the spruce and fir of Beinn Bhreagh. He is surrounded by his children, including my father—joined by Alexander Graham Bell, standing there like an old, particularly large kid waiting for Dad to finish so that everyone can go out and play. In that picture, Gramp was remaking the old dry journal of a geographical society into the *National Geographic* we know and love today. That magazine is a trove of some 1,500 issues with more than 7,000 articles on subjects from anthropology to zoology. To disparage its older content as racist, as some have recently done, is to use a hammer where an archaeologist's probe would suffice. The early magazine was a product of a culture that has, thankfully, evolved.

Unseen in the background of that single photograph is a saga of scientific and technical achievement. During those years Bell was experimenting with gigantic tetrahedral kites, which he believed to be more stable than planar surfaces. That endeavor was followed by the Aerial Experimental Association—Bell, Frederick Walker "Casey" Baldwin, John Alexander Douglas McCurdy, and Glenn Hammond Curtiss—that gave Canada the *Silver Dart,* which on February 23, 1909, made the first manned flight in Canada when it glided over the frozen surface of Baddeck Bay. The AEA also invented the hinged-surface wing-tipped aileron and the tricycle landing gear found on practically every fixed-wing aircraft today.

Research on aerodromes financed by Mabel Bell led to work on hydrodromes, Bell's name for what we call hydrofoils. To the Bell Laboratory on Beinn Bhreagh was added a boatyard—the Bell Boatyard or Beinn Bhreagh Boatyard—on Baddeck Bay. Work on the hydrofoils culminated on September 9, 1919, when HD-4 rose up over the water and achieved a speed of more than 70 miles per hour, a world record that would stand nearly a decade.

Meanwhile, my grandfather had met a botanist who had just returned to the capital after many years in the East Indies. David Fairchild had established the U.S. government's Office of Foreign Seed and Plant Introduction. He would marry Elsie Bell's younger sister, Marian "Daisy" Hubbard Bell. The arrival of a botanist and plant hunter credited with introducing over 80,000 varieties of mangoes, nectarines, and more to American shores would not only be a boon to The Point's 22 landscaped acres; it would also benefit the National Geographic Society, when Fairchild became a member of the board of trustees and the Committee for Research and Exploration. Because Elsie and Daisy were so close, my grandfather and Fairchild became close too.

I close the guest register and walk into the dining room, engulfed by memories. I recall the stories my aunt Mabel told me about the days when Bell sat at that table's head, children sitting around it in pinafores and sailor suits, gleeful with laughter as the great inventor mimicked barnyard noises, performed magic tricks, or discussed interesting things he had noted that day.

As Wiley and I leave The Point for our log house, we pause to scan the lake. Watching sunset from The Point as it gilds the water, I can't imagine how anybody fortunate enough to be here couldn't love the place. But some of the spouses found the big, close-knit family—let's say—a tad overbearing. Some even came to dislike Beinn Bhreagh. One of them was my mother.

It was my father's sister Gertrude who introduced Melville in 1922 to Helen North Rowland, her best friend at Washington's Mount Vernon Seminary. Helen, a fun-loving, sociable girl with brown hair and shining eyes, proved irresistible to a young man who had seldom dated. She was from Waterbury, Connecticut, where her father, Herbert Rowland, was a pillar of the Republican Party and the Country Club of Waterbury. It must have been on that golf course that my mother learned to wield clubs so skillfully that by the time she met my father she was already one of the best woman golfers in the state. She had wit, charm, and a tongue like a lash if provoked.

What she saw in turn was a handsome young midshipman at the U.S. Naval Academy who hailed from a famous family and possessed a personality so enthusiastic and generous that his yearbook declared that even his mess dish "is yours if he can force it upon you."

They fell in love and married in January 1924. Dad was lucky. Because the Washington Naval Treaty had been signed two years earlier, the U.S. Navy had to downsize. After completing an obligatory battleship cruise and freed from his commitment, he resigned his commission and joined the National Geographic staff. That became a problem; his eagerness to defer to my grandfather increasingly annoyed my mother.

My sister, Helen Rowland Grosvenor, born on December 24, 1925, was always called Teeny by a world that adored her unfailing kindness and generosity. Two years later, on December 7, 1927, Mother delivered my brother, Alexander Graham Bell Grosvenor. Burly, muscular, Alec was spirited, competitive, and a born warrior. Three and a half years later I was washed onto the shore of life.

Every child's mental map begins with home, and so does mine. I opened my eyes and beheld this world on May 5, 1931, in Washington, D.C. The first geographical setting to leave its impress on me were the rolling ridges of upper Northwest Washington, with views of the Washington Cathedral, then being built.

Our house was on Woodland Drive in a lovely neighborhood tucked into a curve of Rock Creek. I thought our house cozy, perhaps because the family's polar bear rug with the head still attached was now mine. I could lie down on that rug and prop up against the head and read.

Dad and Gramp moved in social, scientific, military, naval, and diplomatic circles and worked in the Italianate building at the corner of 16th and M Streets that was the National Geographic Society headquarters. The year I was born, Andrew Mellon, then secretary of the treasury, still walked to work every day down 16th Street. You could set your watch by the moment he passed the Society's heavy brass doors.

Inside those doors Dad's and Gramp's paneled offices were similarly lined with bookcases, maps, and pictures of wildlife, sequoias, and ships. It was more fun to peek into John Oliver La Gorce's office. He had been my grandfather's right-hand man since 1905; his walls recalled big-game hunting clubs and military museums lined with kudzu horns, swords, and spears from the far corners of the world. Or I could ride the elevator to the fourth-floor photo lab, where its chief, Edwin L. "Bud" Wisherd—not much taller than I was—loved to tease me.

If we kids had to wait for Dad to finish work, we could hang out in the small museum downstairs, where flags that had flown over the poles could be seen near a scale model of the *Explorer II* gondola, the Society-sponsored stratosphere balloon that carried aeronauts 14 miles above the planet's surface. I was particularly attracted to the chronometer used by Ernest Shackleton, one of my heroes, in his 1908-09 attempt to reach the South Pole.

The White House was only four blocks from headquarters. President Franklin Delano Roosevelt seemed to live there my entire life. After he died in early 1945, I shimmied up a tree to watch the funeral cortege move down Pennsylvania Avenue, and from an arching limb I looked straight down at the flag-draped coffin on its caisson pulled by six white horses.

Those places were insignificant compared with old Griffith Stadium, where my idol, Slingin' Sammy Baugh, played quarterback for the then Washington Redskins. My own career as a halfback began and ended at Sidwell Friends School. When Baugh attended our football banquet, I got to sharpen the pencils he used to sign autographs.

No one in Washington could escape the impact of World War II. Temporary wooden structures blanketed the Mall. Night and day the streets overflowed with men and women in uniform.

Gas rationing crimped everyone's movements. But Mom found some so that I could continue my golf lessons. I improved enough to play with Gramp, which delighted us both. One day after playing at the Chevy Chase Club, we got in his car to go to Wild Acres, his home 15 miles north of the city, where I would spend the night. We exited the club and turned left on Wisconsin Avenue, a heavily traveled road even in the early 1940s. Gramp hit the gas pedal quickly to avoid oncoming traffic but swung too wide, scraping the right fender and headlamp on a tree. "Damn!" he yelled. "I hit that same tree last month."

I was flabbergasted. I didn't care that he had hit the same tree twice. I was astonished that he of all people had uttered a curse word! All his life he exerted a remarkable degree of self-control.

"Control in the extreme," my mother might have said. One of the reasons my parents' marriage never got off on the right foot was her belief that Gramp was overcontrolling, especially when it came to my father. "Dictatorial," she might have called it in a flash of temper. That was the main reason she didn't like going to Beinn Bhreagh. I've often wondered how she felt whenever she drove me north on Wisconsin Avenue and turned up the curving driveway at, well, 5400 Grosvenor Lane.

That was Wild Acres, as my grandparents called the old farm they bought in 1913. With its old-field pine, wild grapes, and blackberries, it was good bird habitat. My grandfather, who could identify perhaps five birds when he first moved there, quickly got to know more than 50, thanks to Frank Chapman's pioneering field guide. His success at putting out nesting boxes even converted his skeptical neighbors; he now set out to convert the National Geographic Society membership. Although color illustrations were expensive to print, so many bird portraits were issued in the *Geographic* that it became an inside joke. Similar series on mammals, fish, and insects amounted to the first widely disseminated field guides put into Americans' hands. What started as a family obsession turned out to have an enormous cultural impact.

By 1928, the old farmhouse that had been primarily a summer retreat had been replaced by a gray stone mansion. Bird iconography was every-where—owls on plaques, songbirds on wall friezes. When Teeny laid the cornerstone, it was filled only with pamphlets on birds. Gramp even removed the bulb from a porch lantern so a Carolina wren could nest comfortably there.

That mansion soon became my grandparents' principal residence from Easter until after Christmas, except for July and August, when they were usually at Beinn Bhreagh—or off globe-trotting.

During Christmas every aunt, uncle, and cousin in town crowded around the big dining room table like a family in a Norman Rockwell painting. The tree was cut from the fields of the estate and set up in front of the drawing room window near the library entrance. Guests at the annual eggnog parties included many National Geographic staff; some pocketed flasks in case the chief's temperance policies extended to the festive eggnog bowl. (They need not have worried; my grandmother oversaw the parties.) Now that many of its 120 acres lie buried beneath asphalt, high-rise offices, condominiums, and superhighways, I remember the Wild Acres of my youth as the very picture of gracious country living.

It was just the right kind of home for the distinguished couple the press had dubbed "Mr. and Mrs. Geography," by then well embarked on their lifetime program of viewing every corner of the globe. Before I turned 10, they were logging some 10,000 miles a year: astounding in an age before jet travel. They knew Europe best, but many summers were spent motoring all over the American West. They crossed Canada by rail. They took steamers to South America. In 1937 Elsie and Bert became the first paying passengers to board a commercial flight across the Pacific.

My grandparents lived up to that Mr. and Mrs. Geography moniker, not only thanks to their extensive travels, but also because the Grosvenor name was pinned to places all over the globe. The Grosvenor Mountains still point the way to the South Pole. Lake Grosvenor winds through Katmai National Park in Alaska, and Mount Grosvenor looms over the Great Gorge of the Ruth Glacier near Denali. Assorted birds, a fish, a Brazilian orchid, and even a fossil shell bear some version of *grosvenori* in their Latinate designations.

That strewing of names was the work of explorers grateful for National Geographic Society sponsorship and coverage in the magazine. Many were welcomed at Wild Acres, including Senator Hiram Bingham of Machu Picchu fame, Admiral Richard E. Byrd, and the great Arctic explorer Commander Donald MacMillan. I suspect Charles and Anne Morrow Lindbergh crossed that threshold too. Also soldier-statesmen George Catlett Marshall and Dwight D. Eisenhower—not to mention most of Washington's society matrons, who were drawn to Elsie's Sunday luncheons.

Welcoming the accomplished and notable fell square into the grand tradition pioneered by Gardiner Greene Hubbard and Alexander Graham Bell. My grandfather did so even in their more modest "winter" home back on 18th Street, where Dad remembered sitting in the dining room, eating ice cream with Robert E. Peary and Roald Amundsen at the age of 12.

There is one more place from my childhood that bears mention.

In 1928, when my uncle David Fairchild retired, he and Daisy left Washington and moved to his beloved tropics—at least as close as he could get and still remain on the U.S. mainland.

The southern tip of Florida, when the Fairchilds first saw it, was not the overdeveloped concrete jungle of today. "Biscayne Bay Country" was then a place of great natural beauty. Tall, twisted mangroves, interspersed with coconut plantations, covered the outlying keys. South of Miami—then a village—Daisy and David bought property facing Biscayne Bay that was already incorporated as Coconut Grove, just as Miami Beach was rising across the water. They began transforming the site into the tropical garden of their dreams, naming it the Kampong. Within a decade, my grandparents bought an adjoining property and built Hissar, their own winter retreat, where they stayed from January to March.

That living room of the Kampong was where the idea of making the Everglades into a national park was initiated in 1928. Uncle David was the first to articulate an important shift in conservation thinking: What is defined as park-worthy is not necessarily spectacular scenery but rare ecosystems too. Established by law in 1934 and dedicated in 1947, Everglades National Park saved one of the rarest ecosystems not only in all South Florida but arguably in the United States as well.

The Kampong was—and still is—that neighborhood's main attraction. Step beneath its entrance arch and you found yourself in Java or Japan; it changed every few feet you walked. The compound had so many structures hidden in the greenery that it resembled a Malay kampong, or village. The white coralline walkways wound among swaying palms, mahogany, tamarind, and even a baobab from Africa.

The warm breath of the nearby tropics and the Gulf Stream only 15 miles away had Uncle David dreaming of establishing a marine biological station in southern Florida. He wasn't the only one; in 1943 a transplanted Englishman, Dr. F. G. Walton Smith, moved into an abandoned boathouse on Belle Isle in Miami Beach and grandly called the ramshackle place the Marine Laboratory at the University of Miami.

Soon, several National Geographic grants were steered to the expanding facilities in Coral Gables and on Virginia Key. Today it is the Rosenstiel School of Marine and Atmospheric Science. But its main building on Virginia Key was named for Gilbert Hovey Grosvenor to honor his early support—another tradition launched by those intertwined families of the National Geographic Society.

CHAPTER TWO

PASSAGES

When I was a boy, I was a happy Robinson Crusoe on an island all my own. On charts it is called Gibson Island. But in memory it is my island, because while I roamed its seven miles of shoreline as a child, those components so necessary to exploration—curiosity and self-reliance—began to emerge.

My island lay in the mouth of one of the lesser rivers of the Chesapeake's western shore, the Magothy. Once it was pine woods and farmland, but in the 1920s the Symingtons of Baltimore purchased it, built a causeway connecting it to the mainland, and turned it into a gated community catering to Baltimore and Washington families interested in spending their summers sailing, playing tennis, or golfing. Within 10 short years its harbor sported the tall, serried white sails of a Star Class fleet, the Gibson Island Yacht Squadron.

That is what attracted my father, the Star boats being the first one-design class for racing. Each had the exact same configuration—23 feet long with identical masts and sets of sail—and each had room for only two: skipper and crew. This meant that a race would not go to the man with the most expensive boat but to the best sailor. That appealed to Dad.

My mother wanted a summer getaway for our own family, a place closer than faraway Beinn Bhreagh and unburdened by all the cousins. Since she had taken to sailing too, they chose a two-story cottage on the wooded slopes of Gibson Island with an expansive view of the bay. My father christened it Skipper's Retreat.

I learned to sail at Gibson Island on an 11-foot, flat-bottomed, practically indestructible craft, a proud member of the Junior Fleet. Its day-to-day operations were managed by its sailing instructor: my sister, Teeny.

Dad worked in Washington during the week; mother and us kids would stay down at Skipper's Retreat and welcome him back every Friday afternoon. Since my sister was busy with the Junior Fleet and my brother was cutting lawns to make money, I was left on my own. While my mother kept a careful eye on me, it was with a very long leash, since there was no way to leave an island gated community except by boat. The only rules were to avoid marshy areas where water moccasins might lurk, to be home by dinnertime, and to go to bed when the nightly ferry from Baltimore to Norfolk passed Baltimore Light, which marked the Chesapeake Bay ship channel. About eight o'clock we'd be sitting on the porch when the ferry would appear in a blaze of lights. At the very second it passed the Light, I would dutifully go to bed.

I went barefoot and shirtless from June through August, climbing on my bike every day and pedaling to every corner of the island reachable by road. The island was big enough that I could cover a lot of territory, and small enough that I could never get lost.

Most residents went to the club, the beach, or the sailing harbor. But I often frequented lonely places in the woods or along the shore, searching among the sea wrack for shells, bits of colored glass—anything to take home to Mom for show-and-tell.

My father built me a pram, a small, flat-bottomed rowboat that I named *Popeye*. The only parental restriction was not to row into the bay, where the Chesapeake's short, choppy seas, amplified by the wakes of ships, could easily swamp a small boat—as could its ferocious summer squalls.

The spacious harbor was permissible if no storm threatened. Its outer reaches were a different world, with quieter, less frequented waters—the domain of herons, muskrats, and the few ducks that remained for summer breeding. I felt like an explorer quietly rowing to isolated coves. I drifted over immense beds of underwater grasses, which were then so abundant, hiding grass shrimp, razor clams, and the occasional diamondback terrapin. Above all, they were the realm of that arch scavenger, the blue crab.

The summer of 1942 was my last idyllic one on Gibson Island. The war was raging. The Yacht Squadron was mothballed. Gasoline rationing was imposed. At Norfolk and Hampton Roads, convoys were assembling, and U-boats lurking off the mouth of the Chesapeake had already damaged or sunk at least five ships.

My summers on Gibson Island rank among my happiest recollections. I lived, played, and explored in a microcosm of the great Chesapeake, which I grew to love as few other ecosystems south of Cape Breton Island. Those were my first lessons in habitat and ecology—lessons that led me, many decades later, to fight shoulder to shoulder with some of this nation's finest conservationists to preserve the bay.

IN THE SUMMER OF 1943, when the world was on fire, I returned to the serenity of Cape Breton Island.

My parents were tied to Washington. My siblings were too, either in summer school or preparing for boarding school. With Gibson Island practically shuttered, the question became what to do with Gibby, as I was called. In the end, it was decided that I would accompany my aunt Mabel to Baddeck, where I could spend a carefree summer.

Fine by me. I hadn't been to Beinn Bhreagh since the summer of 1939, when I was eight; now I was 12.

Between naps on our two-day train trip, I was taught the geography of the passing scene by my surrogate mother for the coming season. At a time when few women worked in the professions, my aunt Dr. Mabel Grosvenor, still shy of 40 years old, was a practicing pediatrician trained at Johns Hopkins. With her hair pulled back into a bun, her wire-framed glasses, and her habitually grave expression, she resembled my grandfather. Born at The Point, she had been very close to her grandfather Bell, even serving as his secretary during experiments and trips abroad. She was unmarried, highly intelligent, keenly observant, and well read, with a sly sense of humor. I loved her more than I did any other aunt, thanks in part to our shared summer in 1943.

Baddeck seemed eerily deserted. The boats slept high and dry on beaches or in fields overgrown with tall grass. Only old men, children, and women were visible in the streets and doorways. Lonely women waited forlornly for their men to return home. When we turned onto the Beinn Bhreagh Road, everything was too quiet as well; the bustle and energy had vanished. After arriving at The Point, we found out why. Canada as part of the British Empire had been at war since 1939, and the strain was telling.

Beinn Bhreagh reflected the anxiety. My grandmother, with great sensitivity, had pruned back all superfluities at the main house. *Elsie,* the family yacht, slouched on blocks at Pinaud's boatyard.

I was thrilled to be given the first-floor guestroom, with its own fireplace and bathroom. Adults might come and go over the next few months, but I would be the only child in the house, since my cousins were tethered stateside. What's more, I soon found the ideal companion.

We had arrived with Aunt Mabel's dog, Tacky. But it wasn't long before another canine friend attached herself to me. One day a gregarious collie mix with a large bushy tail trotted up and adopted me—appointed me, really—as her master.

She was one of the farm dogs; why this one chose me I'll never know, but within a day we were inseparable. I called her Topsy. Most mornings she'd be at the door of The Point to greet me. Evenings she trotted back home.

That summer she became my very first dog. With her at my side, I began to explore an estate that encompassed some 2,000 acres of woods, meadows, and lakefront shoreline. The ground rules were similar to those at Gibson Island: I could go where I pleased as long as I didn't venture beyond the Beinn Bhreagh gate. Topsy and I would hike to the top of the mountain to visit Alec and Mabel Bell's grave. We'd ramble across fields and ease down the steep trail leading to Melville Tarn, the pond where Bell once moored his houseboat. In the forest, a pack of grouse might explode in a heart-stopping whir and glide off into the gloom.

Life at Beinn Bhreagh in those early summer weeks was a throwback to a bygone era. Except where the telephone was hooked up, The Point still had no electricity—the place was too big and rambling to wire. The kitchen had iceboxes, cooled by ice blocks harvested from the lake's frozen surface.

At that latitude the June twilight stretched deep into the night. Every evening only the adults were permitted to turn on the wall sconces to light the gas lamps. These were acetylene lamps that burned brightly and, if lit correctly, released only a whiff of acrid odor. (Years ago Grampy Bell had replaced kerosene lighting—an irreplaceable fossil fuel—with acetylene gas, easily generated from water and calcium carbide tablets.)

At The Point they would light only the lamps needed for that evening. Then we'd all sit around, bathed in gaslight, reading books, flipping through magazines, or listening to war news on a tabletop radio powered by a battery pack. When it was time for bed, every knob on every sconce was turned counterclockwise to turn off the gas. That was the drill: Take no chances with gas leaks that might lead to fire—or, worse, an explosion. Many nights, only moonlight guided my steps to bed.

July was filled with the earthy scent of freshly mown hay. John MacDermid, the farm manager, had an elderly crew haying a meadow near Baddeck Bay. Topsy and I joined them, by way of an overloaded horse-drawn wagon. Inevitably a wheel found a ditch; the wagon would overturn, burying me in the hay. Although I was quickly rescued, the men turned ashen. They thought "little Gibby" was injured. I laughed; they did not. Jobs were scarce.

If not picking hayseed from my hair or Topsy's tail, I might be back at The Point playing golf. Years earlier Gramp had laid out a nine-hole course that stretched from Bell's former sheep pasture to a spot where it tucked around the house.

One night at dinner, Gramp groused he was out of golf balls. Too many had been lost to errant swings, and no more would be manufactured until war's end. He announced he was closing the course. I suggested that Topsy could find and retrieve the lost balls. Though everyone laughed, she proved them wrong. Topsy loved it, I made a quarter for each ball found, and Gramp could play golf. Topsy became the hero of Beinn Bhreagh.

Two of Gramp's friends often came to play: Dr. Carleton MacMillan, a local doctor, and Douglas McCurdy, aviator and future lieutenant governor of the province. A third, Casey Baldwin, might have joined us had he not been so busy down the hill building hydrofoils for the Royal Canadian Navy.

Casey was Bell's associate who had helped design, build, and pilot the HD-4 hydrofoil. The Bells thought so highly of him that they gave him and his wife, Kathleen, a cottage on Beinn Bhreagh.

Topsy and I often drifted down there to watch the workmen. Casey and his team built about six of these craft that summer, so every stage of the process was visible. First, they framed the hulls, planked them, caulked them with oakum, and added the fittings. I didn't get to the engine-building side as much because Topsy couldn't stand the sound of an engine revving and would charge after it.

In evening, back at The Point, my grandfather would emerge from long hours reviewing layouts, planning maps, or making the decisions he could not entrust to subordinates. Later I would understand how stressful the war years were for the Society, with paper shortages and reduced staff. He needed those hours of relaxation. Someone might play the piano; we all might play cards; mostly we read. Among the magazines, I particularly remember the *Saturday Evening Post,* then at the height of its influence.

It was during those evenings that I came to admire my grandfather. He was 67 and accurately described in a *New Yorker* profile—written that year—as incarnating that "mixture of business sagacity, intellectual curiosity, regard for tradition, and tolerance of temperate innovation that is sometimes found in the president of a fairly wealthy college." He looked the part, with his wire-framed glasses, carefully trimmed mustache, and trademark bow tie, worn every day, even at The Point. I remember his kindly smile and attentiveness whenever I described my day's adventures.

I also admired my grandparents' marriage—doubtless the result of decades of minor adjustments and readjustments. He was exacting; she, perhaps, a little more careless. He could be puritanical; she, more relaxed. Yet they had arrived at a mutually supportive understanding.

June, July, now it was August. The nights had stealthily grown shorter. One night, at lamp-lighting time, Gramp, accompanied by Aunt Mabel, took me into my bedroom and handed me a box of matches. Carefully he explained the "sniff test": I must sniff each sconce to make sure no residual gas was escaping a poorly shut fixture. Then he showed me how to turn the knob that opened the valve, strike the match, and light the mantle. To neglect one step could be catastrophic. I knew I had been handed a solemn trust. From then on, I lit every lamp at The Point.

The day of departure arrived too swiftly. Twenty-four hours before Aunt Mabel and I would board the mail boat to commence our return journey, I excused myself from the luncheon table and trotted down the road with Topsy to say goodbye to the Baldwins. The workmen had taken one of the hydrofoils out of the water to tinker with the engine. All I remember now is the sound of the engine being revved. Topsy must have charged—because I've never forgotten the sight of that great happy tail caught in the shaft, then savagely ripped from her body.

I don't recall the men shutting down the engine; I don't recall the furious activity; I don't recall being hustled out. I remember only that awful image. Someone took my hand and started me up the road to The Point. I must have jerked away, because I was later told I wouldn't let anyone get near me. I never saw the truck sneaking around to the animal hospital. I didn't need to because I already knew she was dead or dying and no amount of "she's doing just fine" would persuade me differently.

The next thing I remember is Aunt Mabel's arm around my shoulders. I don't think I cried then, but tears would come the next day. And I had a duty to perform.

The hour to light the lamps had arrived. I found the matches, marched up to the first sconce, performed the sniff test, turned the filigreed knob to the right, and lit the mantle. I progressed from lamp to lamp. That was my responsibility, and I fulfilled it the next night too, my last one at The Point that summer. Three-quarters of a century later, the metaphorical meaning of that passing of the torch is all too clear: Like my father before me, I would light that lamp and hold it high.

IN JUNE 1947, with the war over, my parents decided it was time I went abroad. The three of us boarded a propeller-driven Lockheed Constellation for a 14-hour flight from New York to London.

The trip was timed in part to see my midshipman brother, Alec, who had just finished his plebe year at the U.S. Naval Academy and had already embarked on his "Youngster Cruise," the warships making port calls in the British Isles.

It was a holiday for Mother and part working trip for Dad, busy on a story on Cotswold villages. For me, then 16, it was an education, starting with London.

War-damaged London. Crater-pitted London. Rubble-heaped London. Just walking from Piccadilly Circus to Fleet Street, I was overwhelmed by the sheer scale of destruction and aftereffects of a war that I had only read about.

I had little time to explore that great city because I was to rendezvous with Irving Johnson aboard his brigantine *Yankee* in the Devon port of Brixham. With my first seaman's duffel bag slung over my shoulder, I walked down the cobblestoned streets to the snug home port of ketch-rigged, red-sailed fishing trawlers. There we saw, set into the limestone cliffs on the harbor's eastern face, the sheds of the J. W. and A. Upham Shipyard. A long gray ship's hull was sitting in a stone-lined dry dock.

I had flown across the ocean but would return under canvas. Standing near that dry dock was one of the great sailors of the 20th century, Captain Irving Johnson. Skipper, as everyone called him, was short of stature but long on chiseled muscle. He would thrust out an oaklike arm and grasp your hand with his firm, calloused paw. He had followed a life of adventure at sea for nearly three decades and had rounded Cape Horn on a four-masted bark with 32 great sails. He met Electa "Exy" Search aboard a yacht he was crewing on and married her soon thereafter.

It was his idea to sail around the world, hers to carry crews of young men and women to defray expenses while teaching them something about life and how to set a sail. In the 1930s they made three circumnavigations in a gaff-rigged schooner called *Yankee*. He made motion pictures. She wrote books and articles, including one published in the January 1942 *National Geographic* under their shared byline.

My father admired them both and had just seen their second *Geographic* article through to publication. Irving had told Dad about the new

Yankee; the old one had been sold. That long gray hull—a 96-foot-long German North Sea pilot brigantine—had been a war prize. Once she was refitted, the Johnsons would need a skeleton crew to sail her across the Atlantic to Gloucester, Massachusetts, her new home port. I'd be part of that crew.

My father would have loved to hang around the shipyard, but mother was firm about letting me become a member of the crew on my own. As they took their leave, Dad instructed me to stay close to *Geographic* photographer B. Anthony Stewart, on hand to document the refitting operations for a potential article.

"Do whatever Tony does," he said. "Take the same pictures he does. Do whatever Tony says; follow him wherever he goes." At which point my mother put her foot down: "Not after six o'clock do you follow Tony Stewart!" (Tony had a well-known predilection for heading to the local pub at that hour and staying until last call.) My parents thought, each in a different way, that I was still more boy than man.

And so I was left to Tony's uncertain attentions and Irving Johnson's exacting ones. Skipper had small eyes with a piercing, no-nonsense gaze and was reticent in the extreme unless he needed to bawl out an order. Exy was petite, with dark curly hair, an engaging smile, and an outgoing, comforting manner. They balanced each other well.

We were three weeks in Brixham outfitting *Yankee.* Watching the shipwrights, spar makers, riggers, and painters at work was fascinating. They did everything by hand.

Mostly I was learning the ropes—technically braces, stays, sheets, shrouds, and halyards needed to hoist the sails. I spliced wires and strung ratlines, the 14-inch-square rope steps for climbing into the rigging. I loved weaving strands of old Manila rope around marline to make bushy buffers called baggywrinkles; they prevented the ever moving spars and rigging from chafing the sails.

The engine was dropped in place, the hull painted white, and provisions stowed. One moonlit night we slipped from our mooring and put out to sea, easing into the English Channel.

Our first port of call was St. Malo in Brittany. If I thought the destruction in London was devastating, what we saw in this old medieval fortress was truly staggering. In June 1947 the city stood a perfect wreck; only 182 of its 865 buildings remained habitable.

Once ashore, I clambered all over the multistory German bunkers that honeycombed the nearby granite cliffs. Immense siege guns, which could lob shells 11 miles, had been the target of repeated Allied naval and air attacks. They were destroyed and lay about with their titanic barrels grotesquely twisted. Unknown to us, clambering around had been dangerous. Unexploded ordnance was strewn everywhere.

The next port of call lay 1,200 miles away in the Azores, rising green and lovely out of a cobalt sea. We also stopped at São Miguel and Ponta Delgada, where we took aboard scores of pineapples for our next long leg.

Bermuda-bound, we ran before the light northeast trades around the southeastern arc of the Bermuda high, which dominates the weather patterns of the North Atlantic summer. When we reached latitude 32° north, Skipper set a new course following that parallel all the way to Bermuda, which lies athwart it. (If you can run down a latitude to a given destination, you didn't need time-consuming longitude readings.)

Once, when the wind dropped and the sea was glass-smooth, some of us boarded the dinghy and rowed out to make pictures. *Yankee* was a beautiful sight, slightly skimming over the surface with all eight sails full and drawing. My photograph was chosen to accompany the January 1949 *Geographic* article "*Yankee*'s Wander-World"—my first published picture.

My favorite spot on *Yankee* was a perch high up in the rigging, where I swayed with the swells. I loved the changing moods of sea and sky and wondering about the world beneath the keel.

Because the sailor comes upon Bermuda suddenly, and it is rimmed by dangerous coral reefs, Skipper enlisted everyone to be vigilant. I think we all saw her at once and shouted, "Land ho!" By the time we were threading the Old Town Cut into St. George's Harbor, the mayor and practically everyone else was out on the quay at the uncommon sight of a full-rigged sailing ship.

In Bermuda we picked up another seaman: my brother, Alec, who was on leave and anxious to join *Yankee* on the final leg. We had three days together in Bermuda and explored the islands. Alec told me how he had been invited to a Buckingham Palace garden party with a group of midshipmen and chatted up then princess Elizabeth. If anyone could talk his way into that prime position, it was Alec.

We were fortunate not to encounter any of the hurricanes swirling in the North Atlantic that summer. But as we fetched up in the entrance to the Cape Cod Canal on the final day of our passage, a gusty storm was brewing in the north. Suddenly, while I was far out on the end of the foreyard taking in sail, a tremendous gust heeled *Yankee* almost to her gunwale. For a dizzying second I seemed within touching distance of the towpath! But the gust passed, the brigantine stabilized, and we were under way.

The only real cloud over me was the nagging realization that soon this cruise would be over. We'd disembark and go our separate ways. *Yankee* would remain in Gloucester for six weeks, preparing to sail with a different crew of young people—while the school bell tolled for me. I was due to enroll at Deerfield Academy in Massachusetts in two short weeks.

Fortunately, two fellow crew members, Edmund Hopkinson Kendrick and Mayotta Kendrick, had taken a shine to me. Ed had about the same amount of time before returning to graduate school. The couple planned to spend those last precious days sailing New England waters on their own boat. They invited me to come along, and I leaped at the opportunity. But as *Yankee* headed north for Gloucester Harbor, where my mother would meet me, I worried about her reaction. I knew she was looking forward to spending time with me in Connecticut while helping me prepare for Deerfield. I hoped I wouldn't hurt her feelings by choosing to go sailing instead.

When we passed Ten Pound Island Lighthouse, I climbed back up the rigging for a final time.

I SPOTTED MOTHER IMMEDIATELY, hopped on the wharf, and gave her a long hug. She was smiling. I'm sure she saw a more muscular, more sun-bronzed, more windburned version of her boy, with the light of the sea still in his eyes.

Had I divined what would soon befall our family, I would have quit the proposed venture then and there. Instead I lobbied to sail just a little longer. Mother kept smiling and nodding her approval. She understood, though in retrospect, I realize, I was the one who didn't.

Grabbing my sea bag, I hurried after my friends, then turned back for one final look. She was still smiling and waving.

CHAPTER THREE

THE ROAD
NOT TAKEN

When I recall that first year at Deerfield Academy, my first semester had all the bright expectancy of new beginnings in a new place, where the nearby hills were ablaze with the promise of fall foliage. There were new friendships, a new soccer team, and trips to athletic rivals like Choate and Andover. When I think of the second semester, I see the snowbound landscape, the gloomy sheen of ice at twilight, and the painful memory of the night I heard the shattering news from home.

My parents' marriage had imploded.

The details don't matter so much now. Suffice it to say that while each was a wonderful person, together they just chafed each other in all the wrong places. That mutually supportive understanding that was the hallmark of my grandparent's marriage had eluded them. Mother never felt part of the close, self-contained clan that was my father's family; being at Baddeck only heightened her feelings of emotional estrangement. Clearly their happiest days had been at Gibson Island—neutral territory, racing Star boats together, even wearing matching clothing.

Because both parents hid their pain from us, we didn't know how raw those wounds had become and couldn't foresee how they would fester when charges such as abandonment were hurled back and forth and reported in the press. The divorce was finalized in January 1950. The house on Woodland Drive was sold, and I never set foot on Gibson Island again.

The interim was turbulent. With Teeny married and Alec embarked on his naval career, I was the one still at home and, perhaps, most severely impacted. That boiled down to my grades tumbling as I poured all my energy and sorrow into sports: soccer in fall, squash in winter, and baseball in spring, all under the watchful eye of Deerfield headmaster Frank Boyden.

Boyden is a legend in U.S. education, chronicled by my Deerfield schoolmate John McPhee. His book, *The Headmaster,* is the affectionate portrait of a man who left a deep impression on many. Boyden's interest in me had two sources: One was his alma mater, Amherst College in Massachusetts, where his favorite professor was Dr. Edwin A. Grosvenor, my great-grandfather. The other was my passion for sports—especially baseball, which he coached.

Boyden was of the old breed, convinced that athletics helped shape character. He nurtured my dedication to sports on the theory, I assume, that such disciplined ardor might backflow into academics, lifting the entire boat. As I played wing on the soccer team and advanced from outfielder to pitcher on the baseball team, my grades did rise, although we—parents, headmaster, and me—decided I should stay an extra year to enhance my prospects of getting into the college of my choice.

That final year I was made proctor of the freshman dorm and often conferred with Mr. Boyden. He kept a desk in the main hall so that, behind his wire-framed glasses, he could make eye contact with each student every day. If he sensed anything amiss among the freshmen, he would have his secretary pull me out of class. "Young Reed seems to be hanging his head today. Is he all right?" he'd ask.

"Not so well, sir," I'd respond. "The boys are picking on him again."

"Well," he'd say, adjusting his glasses. "Do something about it." Never a man to wield the switch, our headmaster thought boys could be trusted to police themselves. I'd round up the malefactors and tell them to knock it off. Years later, Nathaniel Reed became one of America's most effective conservationists and a member of the National Geographic Society's board of trustees. In effect, my boss.

I couldn't see a clear path to the college of my choice, but Mr. Boyden did and pitched the sports angle offered by Amherst. He said I could play both intercollegiate soccer and baseball there; that might not be the case elsewhere. Tantalizing, but I resisted. I had fallen in love—not with a girl (oh, there were plenty of them, even if not always reciprocated)—but with a place.

CONNECTICUT—EVEN THE SOUND of the name suggests the ripple of the untrammeled Naugatuck River in the days when it was filled with migrating salmon. But layered on top of that image is a series of complex emotions: nostalgia, even regret.

That's where I spent school vacations with my mother. Waterbury was her childhood home, but after my parents separated, she lived with her brother, Alfred "Sol" Rowland, in a hamlet with an all-American sound: Middlebury. There wasn't much there but the Westover School for girls, Arthur Blick's garage, and a scattering of country estates. Among them was a fine old place with a lovely name, Tranquility Farm, near Lake Quassapaug and the western Connecticut hills.

The main house was a shingle-clad manor. The nearby carriage house, its upper story refurbished into an apartment, was where my uncle Sol lived. It was spacious, with windows opening to a breathtaking view of the hills near the lake, where I could sail my 16-foot Comet. Because I needed someplace to scuttle my sorrows, those environs became my refuge. I grew to like, then love, the quiet rhythms of Middlebury.

I don't remember seeing my father but once during those years. The distance effectively separated us, but an invisible barrier loomed when I learned, in early August 1950, that he was engaged to be remarried. It was distressing—not so much the marriage itself but the way he announced it: He sent a telegram.

Uncle Sol typified the ideal Connecticut Yankee—unpretentious, thrifty, and industrious. Where else would you find, in the state capital, a statue honoring the "workman inventor"? Connecticut was not just the Nutmeg State but the State of Steady Habits. All Connecticut Yankees, it seemed, led well-managed lives.

Geography tugged at me too. I loved driving up the Connecticut River valley and watching the woods modulate from oak and elm to birch and maple. The sparkling surface of the waters of my idealized New England was a cloud of sails on summer weekends. In winter there'd be snow and skiing. There was room for both society and solitude. New York City was close—but not too close. I didn't want to return to Washington, full of painful memories of happier times in my family. Connecticut whispered, "Live here."

Frank Boyden urged me to give Amherst a closer look, but Connecticut offered a tantalizing alternative—Yale University, provided I could get in. Massachusetts might prefer its sons go to Harvard or Amherst; Connecticut Yankees usually chose Yale. I had deep roots in both. At this juncture I preferred the road leading to the State of Steady Habits.

The day college acceptances arrived, I was playing an away baseball game at Choate. Coach Boyden invited me to return to school in his car. He never broached the subject of college, and I began to worry. Perhaps I didn't get admitted anywhere. After we arrived back at Deerfield, I raced down Albany Road to retrieve my mail. The letter was thick, a good sign. I opened it with trembling fingers. Yale said yes.

My decision was made. I would move to New Haven.

ON THAT SEPTEMBER DAY IN 1950 when I first stepped through Phelps Gate, my ambitions were limited. The Korean War had just erupted, and I tried to sign up for Naval ROTC, preferring that to being drafted into the Army. I also wanted a professional degree so that I could afford to live in Connecticut, raise a family, and spend weekends sailing in regattas.

Despite several tries, I failed the Navy's vision test, sealing my fate: It was the U.S. Army for me.

Another disappointment was the demise of my early ambition to become a well-paid surgeon, wrecked by a demanding class in semimicro qualitative analysis. My roommate, Charlie Neave, would go on to achieve this profession. But I was at loose ends and shrugged when asked my goals.

I was restless. Deerfield's motto, "Be Worthy of Your Heritage," was exceedingly difficult for me to live up to, considering the towering achievements of my forebears. What motivated me more was the simpler adage inculcated since birth: Great advantages entail great responsibilities. *That* I could follow—if only I could find the path.

"Why not go work for your grandfather at the Geographic?" was the frequent follow-up. "I just don't see a future there" was my ready response.

It was true. While the Geographic had been a family heritage, it was not an entitlement. Yes, my great-great grandfather and great-grandfather had helmed it during its modest beginnings. Family had donated its headquarters building. My grandfather had built it into an American institution.

But as I approached 21, my grandfather was still in charge, and it wasn't clear that my father, hampered by his recent divorce, would succeed him. Dad, in turn, had failed to persuade my brother to follow in his footsteps. Truth was, Alec was not to the National Geographic manner born; he was a jet jockey who evolved into a successful naval officer. When I was wrapping up at Deerfield, he graduated and soon was off the coast of embattled

Korea aboard the carriers *Yorktown* and *Essex*. He would wear Navy blue the rest of his life.

I saw no real role at the National Geographic Society. I had never shown any interest in joining the editorial staff of any school paper or yearbook. I had never shown much interest in photography. Then there was the matter of Geography 101.

In 1948 Harvard eliminated its geography department because it doubted the subject's value as a college-level study. Yale, to its credit, seized an opportunity to best its rival and, noting the evolving geopolitics of the Cold War, supported a department dedicated to the discipline. I signed up for a course offered by the department . . . and promptly dropped it. The tonnage of bananas shipped annually from Brazil didn't interest me.

At a time when the Korean War and the Mau Mau Uprising were grabbing headlines, I couldn't help noticing that whenever I visited the library, Yale's best and brightest were devouring *Time* and *Life* to understand what was happening. A poll on students' reading habits confirmed that Yale's own Henry Luce was trouncing Amherst's Gilbert H. Grosvenor: *Life* came in first, *Time* second, the *New Yorker* a distant third. On the library shelves the *National Geographic* magazines appeared untouched.

Even so, I was amazed how often the name Gilbert Grosvenor on my license or personal check brought a swift glance from merchants, bankers—anyone, really. I could not even go down to Arthur Blick's garage during vacations without him mentioning the most recent issue, even when showing me how to grind the valves in my Chevrolet engine.

After taking an extraordinary class from Professor Leonard Doob, I decided to major in statistical psychology. I liked statistics and loved devising experiments that might produce reliable results. I didn't know what I would do with that degree, but I wasn't sure of my future anyway: The war in Korea had become a bloody stalemate, and my draft lottery number was unfavorable. Uncertainty fogged my future.

Maybe I was in the Psychology Department when it happened. Or playing cards or sipping a beer at the Fence Club. Wherever I was, a tremendous storm was whipping the faraway North Sea into a foam-flecked fury that flooded Europe's Low Countries—particularly the Netherlands.

CHAPTER FOUR

A CHANGE
OF COURSE

D reary midwinter New Haven, and the only news I remember
following was the increasing possibility that the Korean War
would end before I was drafted and became cannon fodder.
Somewhere between the inauguration of President Eisenhower in January 1953 and the death of Joseph Stalin a month later, a
two-day North Sea storm had flooded the Netherlands, destroying 10,000
buildings, damaging another 47,000, and killing 1,836 people.

I might have missed the news altogether had it not been for a bulletin
board in Yale Station, where our mailboxes were located. There, Charlie
Neave and I saw a notice, posted in colleges nationwide, calling for volunteers to spend the upcoming summer vacation helping rebuild the
Netherlands. The sponsoring organization, the Netherlands Office for
Foreign Student Relations (or NBBS, for its Dutch acronym), would
provide free housing and defray most of the passage costs in exchange for
three weeks of work. The Dutch government was rebooting a successful
1945 program that cleaned up the devastation left when dikes were deliberately breached during the war to thwart the Nazis. The appeal was aimed
at students who wanted to see Europe after their labors ended. I was one,
having not set foot on the continent since visiting St. Malo in 1947.

I looked at Charlie. If he'd call NBBS, I would look into securing photographic equipment. We could slip off into New York and buy cheap used gear in good condition. I called crotchety Bud Wisherd, head of the photo lab at the *Geographic,* for advice. "Get your ass down here," he barked.

I got more than I bargained for. Why be a tourist when I could do a story for the magazine, as my sainted brother, Alec, had once done in 1948? "The upshot, as I knew, was that Wisherd would set us up if we drove down there on a slow weekend.

Actually, the Geographic was already onto this program. The Dutch Embassy in Washington had contacted a few editors before making the offer known publicly. They wanted the publicity a *Geographic* article could bring to boost tourism after the cleanup.

In early March, before we could meet Wisherd, my father called. Sure enough, he mentioned Alec's popular article on his Youngster Cruise. Wouldn't it be great if Charlie and I went to the Netherlands and documented our experiences for the *Geographic*?

Why not? I thought.

YEARS HAD PASSED since I had been in the old Geographic headquarters on 16th Street. Both my father and my grandfather were delighted to see me. But the chief thing I remember is our long afternoon with Bud Wisherd.

After a warm, profanity-laced greeting, he took us to the fourth floor, where he laid out on a suggested kit: Leica cameras and three lenses, flashbulbs, color film, a tripod, and a light meter.

Bud's most important advice was to shoot, shoot, shoot. "Don't worry about wasting film. That's the cheapest part of the business." Shoot more than you think necessary. Bracket your exposure: Fire one on the correct setting; overexpose a click, then underexpose a click.

We headed back to school, hoping to find enough time to practice.

OUR THREE-WEEK WORK SESSION took up most of August. Charlie went over on the ocean liner; the NBBS had chartered an entire ship to carry the student volunteers across the Atlantic. I flew to Amsterdam and met him at our worksite nearby, close to the town of Brielle.

Without that camera gear, we might have been disappointed; the only part of Europe we seemed to see was the sand we shoveled all day, filling one rail wagon after another. Weekends were free. Most guys took off to explore Amsterdam or Paris. For us, weekends were work. We rented a car and drove around Holland taking pictures.

Had we been tourists, we would never have gathered the requisite material for a *Geographic* article, and my life would have taken a different trajectory. But serendipity arrived in the form of a bunker mate, Ernest Kuhinka. Born in Hungary, he was about 10 years older than we were. He had spent years in the Netherlands and was fluent in Dutch, English, and undoubtedly several other languages. When he discovered what Charlie and I were doing, he volunteered to be our guide and translator.

Ernest made us into journalists because he got us behind the scenes— the only way to understand any place, as opposed to the superficial view afforded tourists. That first weekend I wanted to look for an inn for the night. Ernest shook his head and said to knock on a farmer's door, explain why we were in Holland, and ask to spend the night in the hayloft. We did, it worked, and so we did that every weekend: a different farmer and a different hayloft each time. Because Ernest could talk to the locals, I could make portraits that didn't look posed. On the isolated island of Marken, I visited an old lady living in a one-room cottage with an interior straight out of the 18th century. I captured it all in one frame, making the best picture of the feature.

Those weekends changed my life. Traveling with a mission—traveling with purpose. The camera became a tool and not the play toy it had been. In addition to being fun, photography was valuable and important.

BACK AT YALE, Charlie and I pecked out an amateurish manuscript. I still pity the wordsmith tasked with cleaning it up, Nat Kenney, a former newspaperman with Baltimore's *Evening Sun,* now a *Geographic* staffer and a friend of Dad's from Gibson Island. His father, Captain Nat Kenney, ran the Junior Fleet when Teeny was chief instructor. That was my first inkling that the Geographic was about family—not just mine, but a wider family.

After Holland, I couldn't see the point of my major. I still enjoyed designing statistical psychology projects, but it didn't match the satisfaction I experienced that summer. I lived for that walk down to Yale Station to find manuscript drafts, page and map proofs, and illustrations of dikes in cross section in my mailbox.

We had worked where a calamity had occurred and documented the recovery. I reveled in knowing that millions of people who may have missed the news altogether could share in the joy of the resulting resurgence.

I was hooked, a convert to journalism. I read *National Geographic* anew and practiced photography like a man possessed. By graduation in May 1954, I had accepted a job at the Society in the Illustrations Division.

MY FIRST DAY ON THE JOB was to be Monday, June 14, 1954. This would give me two weeks to pack and leave Tranquility Farm for a small apartment mother still kept in Washington. I would stay there during my apprenticeship until summoned by the draft board.

But my start date at headquarters was postponed a week, as I was recruited to help staff photographer Bob Sisson cover the annual Harvard-Yale Boat Race on the Thames River in nearby New London, Connecticut. I drove over, met Bob, and for two days scouted vantage points and secured permissions to use them.

Bob positioned himself on the riverbank, where he could photograph the shells streaking downriver for the finish line by the railroad bridge crossing the river. I would be on the bridge on a platform beneath the tracks used by work crews.

On Saturday, crowds and boats lined both banks of the river. As the shells surged into view, the chartered train full of partying Harvard and Yale alumni pulled into place on the tracks directly above me, as it did every year.

I had picked my place carefully, set up my camera, and raised the viewfinder to my eye, confident I could squeeze off a few good shots. Unwittingly, I was kneeling directly beneath the train's drop-chute toilet, and hadn't even snapped the first frame before I was doused by a soaking discharge of sewage.

The race ended, Yale won, crowds cheered—and I screamed in rage and humiliation. Nauseated, I ran back to my hotel room and dove into the shower so quickly that I neglected to close the door to the room. As a result, my camera was stolen, along with the exposed film.

Sisson found me, wondering what had happened. Telling him was even more mortifying. I thought I detected a stifled smirk. It was a long drive back to Tranquility Farm.

The next day I finished packing my old Chevrolet and prepared to leave my uncle's house forever. I didn't think that might be the case; I knew it. This was the beautiful place that had sheltered my mother and me during the difficult years following the divorce—and for that alone I would have loved it. As I took my last walk around, down to the lake, up past the house and its gardens, I tried unsuccessfully to stifle tears.

I gave my mother a long, long hug. She never said a word, but I knew my decision to work at the Geographic had saddened her. I pulled back and gazed into her eyes. I have been trying to parse what I read there for nearly 70 years. My return to my father's tribe clearly disappointed her. Affection? Always there. Pride in me? Always there too. A hint of the old defiance? Absolutely.

Somewhere along the road south I made a solemn vow to never let that bond with my mother lapse. I kept that vow until the day she died. I keep it still, until it's my turn to cross the bar.

IT WAS WELL-MEANING but totally baffling advice. On my first full morning at work, John Oliver La Gorce ushered me in his office.

After 54 years, my grandfather Gilbert Hovey Grosvenor had finally retired as president and editor and had been succeeded by his long-serving lieutenant, Dr. La Gorce, who, nearing retirement, would hold that title for only three years. He was stocky and pugilistic; he also stuttered.

As I sat there in front of the desk, the walls around me still lined with those daggers and spears, he concluded with one piece of counsel.

"Don't d-d-dip your pen in the c-c-company inkwell!"

Did he really think I would embezzle money? That troubled me all day. Only when I was eating crab au gratin that evening at the Yenching Palace did it hit me: He wasn't talking about money! I was still very naive.

I ate crab au gratin every night at the Yenching Palace because I was alone, and it was near my mother's apartment. The finest Chinese restaurant in a premier diplomatic capital, and I chose comfort food reminiscent of that on Gibson Island. I had a lot to learn about cuisine too.

I was seconded to the Illustrations Division on the third floor of the 16th Street Building, but I couldn't take on any major projects because the Army was going to scoop me up for the draft in six weeks. I listened and watched. My father wisely wanted me to be enlisted as an employee before my Army service began so that I could accrue benefits while I was in the military.

I was seeing him every day now.

Although noticeably grayer, Melville Bell Grosvenor was as generous and gregarious as he had been before the divorce. How he had come back from the depths of despair and a nervous breakdown associated with the rupture of his marriage was nothing short of remarkable. He had wed Anne

Elizabeth Revis, a former researcher and sometime writer for the magazine, in a small ceremony near Charlottesville, Virginia, in August 1950; they would remain happily married until his death 30 years later. He had built his own house on the Wild Acres estate, and I already had a young stepbrother, Edwin, soon to be followed by a stepsister, Sara.

For my father, coming back to work took courage. Courage to maintain his dignity, despite the swirl of whispers behind his back. And there was something else. His enthusiasm had always been able to sweep anyone along with him. Now it was slightly different: He wore it unselfconsciously, bore it so lightly it was invisible. But it was there all the same, along with an air of authority, a habit of command. Perhaps most important, he was ecstatically happy with his new marriage and family. I began to look at Dad with newly appreciative eyes.

Only it wasn't Dad anymore, at least not in the office. Should someone come up to me and say, "Your father wants this . . . ," I'd stop him and reply, "My father? You must mean MBG." MBG, Melville Bell Grosvenor, and GHG, Gilbert Hovey Grosvenor, were now the only way I would ever refer to my immediate forebears in a National Geographic context.

Three-letter acronyms were a fixture there then, and a thicket of them would bewilder outsiders. Another that was tossed around the Society that summer belonged to a man fast becoming famous: Though he didn't work at the Geographic, the Geographic's flag—striped blue, brown, and green, for sky, land, and sea—flew from the mast of his research vessel, *Calypso*. JYC was Jacques-Yves Cousteau, the oceangoing explorer and filmmaker. Few people had heard of him four years earlier, when MBG discovered him and brought him into our fold.

Two decades earlier my grandfather GHG had adopted his own Jules Verne–like character: Dr. William Beebe of the New York Zoological Society. Suspecting that the slimy harvests winched aboard oceanographic vessels by trawls were about as representative of marine life as those of an alien spaceship dragging a dredge through the Manhattan streets would be of human life, Beebe decided to explore the depths for himself in a deep-sea observation chamber called a bathysphere.

That famous series of dives culminated in 1934, when Beebe and his engineering companion, Otis Barton, plunged one half mile beneath the surface, dangling in the dark at the end of their tether among vast shoals of luminous creatures. No one had ever been that deep and survived, nor would do so again for another 15 years.

It was a proud moment for GHG; the Society's flag fluttered from the bathysphere's cable. Beebe was probably the first oceangoing scientist to become a household name. Because deep-sea photography was nonexistent then, National Geographic articles describing the creatures down there had to be illustrated by paintings.

When Dad discovered Cousteau, he realized that this slim, 42-year-old French naval officer might become another Beebe. Cousteau had co-invented the automatic regulator, the breathing device that made scuba diving possible. *Calypso*—a former British Royal Navy minesweeper that he had converted into a state-of-the-art research vessel, complete with laboratories, diving well, and photographic facilities—was the ideal platform for putting cameras into the sea. The two struck an agreement. Our Committee for Research and Exploration would provide much of the funding for Cousteau's projects in return for North American rights to his pictures and articles.

MBG had a genius for finding charismatic individuals and signing them on just before they became household names. By the summer of 1954 Cousteau was pioneering underwater archaeology; his scuba divers were the first to excavate a Roman-era shipwreck in the Mediterranean. Only a few weeks before my arrival he had been feted in the executive dining room with lunch served on 2,000-year-old plates recovered from that wreck. You could do that in those days.

We were still trying to get a National Geographic photographer aboard *Calypso* to capture, perhaps for the first time in color, the sunlit shallows around then pristine coral reefs. Harold "Doc" Edgerton, inventor of the high-speed strobe, was already onboard devising camera housings and side-scan sonar that could withstand the incredible water pressures of the dark abyss, practically creating deep-sea photography along the way.

Other exciting projects had been funded by our Research Committee. A photomapping of the night sky as seen from the Northern Hemisphere was nearing completion. The eminent archaeologist Dr. Matthew Stirling was in Panama seeking clues to its pre-Columbian past. An expedition was exploring Central Africa. Maps were in the works for all these projects.

Whenever I had a spare minute, I'd walk down the third-floor hall into the new wing, off the 16th Street Building. There, in a room full of enormous filing cabinets and huge drafting tables, was the Cartographic Division. Whatever my earlier reservations about the Geographic, I was never indifferent to its maps; they spoke to the heart of our mission.

With the draft still in effect and Uncle Sam knocking at the door, I slipped up to Beinn Bhreagh for my first visit in nearly a decade. Gramp and Grandma, Dad and Anne, my siblings and cousins, clambered onto *Elsie* and sailed every day. It felt like old times.

I returned to Middlebury and said goodbye to friends and to Mother, who dropped me off at dawn at the Army depot for the long bus ride to Fort Dix, New Jersey.

AFTER BASIC TRAINING and several months at the U.S. Army Psychological Warfare Center in Fort Bragg, North Carolina, I shipped out to a psychological warfare unit at Fort Shafter, Honolulu: Army headquarters for the Asia-Pacific theater. (Though large-scale involvement in the Vietnam War wouldn't begin until the 1960s, U.S. military advisers were present in South Vietnam in modest numbers.)

I volunteered for the Southeast Asian desk and drew old French Indochina, which, after a bloody war, had been broken up in 1954 into the new countries of Cambodia, Laos, and North and South Vietnam. I thought I would spend the rest of my enlistment living near Diamond Head. But Colonel Edward Lansdale summoned a few of us to South Vietnam for three months.

Lansdale, a former advertising executive who had one foot in the U.S. Air Force and the other in the CIA, knew the art of propaganda—not just its civilian version but also its darker disinformation-heavy military version: psychological warfare. His first order was to assist the new ministry of defense in building an Army of the Republic of Vietnam to counter both the Viet Minh and the formidable army of the north. He wanted our psychological warfare unit to teach the new South Vietnamese officers "civic action" in a land where soldiers had always trampled the peasantry.

The last French troops had left only a few weeks earlier, and I was going to be one of the first American military advisers to step, so to speak, into their abandoned boots.

We were four privates; three spoke French and one—me—did not. I was told to photograph and record everything germane to psych war. We were first sent to the Philippines, where we were trained in Lansdale's approach to "civic action."

Psychological warfare uses various techniques to influence people's thoughts; I was relieved to learn that we weren't expected to employ any of its darker arts. We were taught that to triumph in a war without boundaries, you must win the hearts and minds of villagers. You find the pulse of that culture in its values, beliefs, even superstitions. We would teach South Vietnamese officers not to steal food and supplies from villagers but instead to help them tend fields, mend fences, and care for the wounded—a tall order in Vietnam in 1955.

When I submitted my observations to my commanding officer on my return back to headquarters in Honolulu, he took one look at my typed-up thoughts about cultivating better relations with the Vietnamese and tossed them in the safe to never be seen again, except when he removed his sandwich for lunch. "They don't want to hear that," he said dismissively, meaning the high brass in Washington. "Body counts win wars," I was told.

That high-handed dismissal of the factors that make friends and foes tick lost us the war in Vietnam. Reaching the "hearts and minds" of people works because their convictions grow out of where and how they live and their traditions and beliefs—cultural geography, in short.

My Army experience left me with an enmity to propaganda that spurred my subsequent efforts to keep *National Geographic* strictly objective, accurate, and nonpartisan, along with the conviction that "hearts and minds" is always the best strategy—in war, business, and life.

It also extended my geographic horizons. I spent three weeks in Japan, seeing cities like Hiroshima still rising from the ashes, spent a memorable weekend climbing around Angkor Wat in Cambodia, and visited Hong Kong, where I and two yachting friends engaged the Cheoy Lee Shipyard to build us a yawl as its first overseas commission. We named her *Mah Jong* and planned to sail her home via the Suez Canal, thereby circling much of the globe.

Dad scuttled that plan. Upon my discharge in June 1956, I was accepted into the graduate program at the University of Missouri School of Journalism. The best thing the Army ever did for me was to delay by one day my scheduled separation in Oakland, California. I canceled my reservation on TWA Flight 2, Los Angeles to Kansas City, which took off on June 30—and collided with another plane over the Grand Canyon, killing all 128 people in what was then the deadliest airline disaster in history.

Instead of that degree, I received the finest photojournalism training in the world in that glorious decade when MBG, my father, was the National Geographic Society's president and editor.

PART TWO

UNDER A LUCKY STAR

CHAPTER FIVE

THE GEOGRAPHIC EYE

Nearly two years had passed since I had walked out those 16th Street doors for my military service. In the summer of 1956, when I stepped back in, nothing had changed.

The bronze seal of the Society was set in the same marbled foyer floor. The same receptionists sat at the same desks next to the small museum exhibiting the displays that had entertained visitors for a generation.

GHG's office in the corner of the second floor hadn't changed either. Looking in, I saw the same paneling adorned with photographs and maps, and the same bookshelves housing my grandfather's leather-bound volumes of *National Geographic*. If I opened one emblazoned "1954," the photographs and layouts looked distressingly like those in "1934."

That was worrisome. The Society was its magazine: the principal bond with members whose annual dues funded everything.

Despite our News Service, which provided media with geographical background to current events, a lecture series at Constitution Hall, and a division that produced a school bulletin, such activities were subsidiary compared with the importance of the monthly *National Geographic*. Even the occasional books we published were compendiums of magazine articles on natural history. GHG kept up with all the technical advances in color photography, but the style and content needed updating. Otherwise our two million members might start drifting away.

I didn't have to knock on the adjoining door to know that nothing had changed in Dr. La Gorce's office either. As president and editor, he was staying the course GHG had set. But he was retiring at the end of the year, and everyone knew the heir apparent was waiting in the wings, in the office adjoining GHG's. If I poked my head in and my father, MBG, was not there, I knew he'd be wandering the building, striding down a hall, listening to younger people feed him ideas, and responding, "Hey, that's great! Think we can do it?"

If MBG gained 60 pounds and grew a long beard, he would have been the spitting image of Alexander Graham Bell. He had the Bell nose and profile, and his grandfather's questing curiosity. But Dad was not technically oriented; he would never have succeeded as an inventor, unless revitalizing a geographical magazine could be considered an "invention."

He edited for the average member—"the little old lady in Dubuque"—dismissed "intellectuals," and teased me for using "Yale words." "Forget fancy adjectives," he would preach. "Use strong active verbs." He was an intuitive genius with an eye for possibilities and saw them everywhere—something he had inherited from Bell and GHG.

Now MBG wanted to teach those principles to me, since I had slipped back into my previous role as a picture editor. That meant learning about pictorial storytelling and huddling over light tables in darkened offices, scrutinizing thousands of 35mm slides, teasing out the story the pictures must tell. The picture editor had to cultivate what we called the "*Geographic* eye," selecting, from thousands of frames, the 80 or so that he or she deemed the most telling, out of which perhaps 30 were published.

And nobody was better at picture editing than Bill Garrett.

ONLY DAYS AFTER I LEFT FOR the Army, Garrett arrived as a new hire. My grandfather had discovered him. Feted at retirement by practically every photographic group in the country, GHG had gone to receive an award from the University of Missouri School of Journalism. His escort was the school's star graduate, Wilbur E. Garrett—Bill, as he was known. GHG came back with such a glowing report that MBG hired him before anyone else could.

Hardly had I returned in the summer of 1956 than MBG advised me to befriend Bill Garrett: "You could learn a lot from him."

The man I shook hands with was a brash, headlong guy from Kansas City with a gap-toothed grin. Garrett had won his spurs as a U.S. Navy cameraman during the Korean War before he even attended university. Charismatic and a magician at juggling picture layout, he quickly charmed three generations of the *Geographic's* Grosvenors.

MBG wanted Garrett to bring up-to-date photojournalism into our pages. Bill quickly lured two fellow Missouri graduates to the Illustrations Division. One was Tom Smith, an acolyte of Clifton Edom, Missouri's dean of photojournalism. The other was the more quiet, self-effacing Bob Breeden. This was the nucleus of the "Missouri mafia" at the magazine, which MBG hoped would reinvigorate the picture division.

I became good friends not only with Garrett and Breeden but also with two talented young women in adjacent offices, Charlene Murphy and Mary Griswold. Mary was the younger daughter of MBG's friend General Francis "Butch" Griswold, vice commander in chief of the Strategic Air Command. She had skipped college to travel the world with a camera and would become one of the best picture editors we ever had.

Since Charlene and Mary—roommates as well as colleagues—lived not far from my rented quarters in Georgetown, we socialized on weekends but not at lunchtime. In the Geographic's cafeteria, women had to peel off to the ladies' dining room, men to the gentlemen's dining room.

MBG was assembling a team of fresh, young talent. Everyone awaited the changing of the guard, anticipating a burst of creative evolution like the one generated by my grandfather during the first decade of the century, when he single-handedly transformed the magazine, laboring deep into the night with Elsie at his side or under a canvas tent at Beinn Bhreagh.

IN AUGUST 1956 I went on vacation to Beinn Bhreagh, staying with Dad and Anne in Burns Cottage on the shore of Baddeck Bay. Gramp and Grandma were up the road in The Point. GHG was past 80, and Elsie was increasingly frail, but they still enjoyed traveling the road of life together. I admired how they infused a tincture of adventure even into everyday routines. Instead of having Hamilton, their driver, take them into Baddeck, they climbed aboard a dinghy and sailed themselves across the bay.

Gramp was my role model: brilliant editor, shrewd business mind, ingenious promoter, sensitive manager—everything I yearned to be. He also chafed at incompetence. Dad, on the other hand, was a "go with the gut" decision-maker, but difficult for me to emulate. Since I was temperamentally more like GHG, I'd follow in his footsteps.

August was the social season on Cape Breton Island, when most of the summer people came to escape the heat of the lower 48. Among our neighbors on the peninsula were Dabney and Margaret Jarman, who lived over the hill at the place called Poker Dan's. He was a Washington physician; by chance, an Army friend and I had rented the house two doors away from his in Georgetown. Anytime we entertained in the backyard— lighting a grill, perhaps—one of their little girls, the freckle-faced one, would spy on us from behind the fence. She was as curious as a cat and shy as a deer; if we spotted her, she'd be gone.

One August evening everyone at Beinn Bhreagh went over to Poker Dan's for a party. The light was still in the sky, so the view over the Bras d'Or Channel could still be enjoyed. I stood there talking when I saw the little freckle-faced girl walking across the lawn, fishing pole in hand. "Dabney, what's your daughter's name?" I asked. "We see her over the fence from time to time."

"Oh, that's Wiley," he said, waving her over. "She's our tomboy." When she came up, he introduced us.

"Hello, Wiley," I said. "I'm your neighbor."

She gave me a candid once-over and seemed unimpressed.

"I know," she said, turning to walk away.

What neither of us could have known then was the part she would play in my life two decades later.

AUTUMN MEANT A RETURN TO the office. Dr. La Gorce had schooled Dad in every aspect of Society operations—illustrations, lectures, legends (as we called picture captions), advertising, membership, and fulfillment, or distribution. MBG wanted the same for me, with more emphasis on the business side. Thomas W. McKnew, secretary and executive vice president, was particularly adamant about the emphasis on business as well.

Though I occasionally spent a few days in the business offices, much of it was postponed because work on illustrations took precedence. That was fine with me; editorial life was far more interesting.

Over the next few years I would get to know those on staff who represented that intangible quality of the old *Geographic*: its cosmopolitan, urbane appeal. That first summer it was Franc Shor, an assistant editor. Although Franc claimed to know every royal family in the world, he more likely knew every renowned restaurateur. He really was larger than life: He gained and lost weight so often that he kept three separate wardrobes, one for the heavy phase, one for the slender phase, and one for the in-between zone.

Once past his often charming but sometimes abrasive personality and issues with women and liquor, I discovered a worldly-wise old China hand from World War II who could speak Turkish, Persian, and Mandarin. Franc, raised in Dodge City, Kansas, adroitly spun a web of half truths about his past, which no one ever managed to disentangle.

After the war he remained in China, where he met a Texas girl, Jean Bowie, working for the United Nations in Shanghai. They married and, as the Communist Party surged to victory in 1949, spent their honeymoon retracing Marco Polo's journey to Cathay across the Gobi. The resulting book, *After You, Marco Polo,* secured Franc a place on our foreign editorial staff, an elite corps of writer-photographers who could take on exotic assignments. Franc and Jean rode with Qashqai herdsmen in Persia, traversed the remote Wakhan Corridor in Afghanistan, and covered Greece, where they became friends with the royal family.

GHG appreciated these talents, though averted his gaze from the less seemly aspects of Franc's character. That autumn of 1956, Gramp was coming into the office more frequently—in part to revise his short history, *The National Geographic Society and Its Magazine.* I'd often spend my lunch hour visiting him in his office, lounging in a Windsor chair while he put in "Little Sister," his hearing aid. Inevitably, in the company of those bound volumes, I began learning Society history. He especially enjoyed talking about maps and the Cartographic Division he had created.

Maps had been issued as folded supplements from the earliest days of the magazine. The federal government supplied some, but many were commissioned from outside firms. GHG wanted to bring mapmaking in-house, and World War I gave him the opportunity. He tapped a former U.S. Geological Survey man, Albert Bumstead—who had mapped Machu Picchu for Hiram Bingham—and put him on the hunt for more talent. GHG foresaw that in the wake of the empire-demolishing conflict at hand, the world would need remapping, and he wanted to do it the National Geographic way. Despite the challenges of building a department from scratch, he succeeded, and we were soon producing timely, handsome, informative, and distinctive maps compiled and drawn in our Cartographic Division.

GHG loved telling stories about how some of the Geographic maps produced during World War II had become national military assets. One of them probably saved the life of Admiral Chester Nimitz, commander in chief of the U.S. Pacific Fleet. In September 1942, his plane became lost in a severe squall above the Solomon Islands. Fortunately, an aide aboard figured out where they were by checking the NGS map of the Pacific that he'd carried aboard.

I vowed that if ever I had a say, I would ensure that our rich mapmaking legacy continued and expanded in scope.

Since MBG wanted me, as part of my general tutorial, to occasionally sit in on meetings of the board of trustees and Committee for Research and Exploration, I sometimes had to quit my light table for the boardroom and be another "backbencher": seen, not heard. The boardroom, located in Hubbard Memorial Hall, with walls adorned in photographs of Society-sponsored expeditions, was on the first floor, adjacent to a great marble staircase decorated with murals painted by N. C. Wyeth depicting discovery and exploration.

It was in the boardroom where retiring Geographic leadership handed off the reins of power. On January 8, 1957, John Oliver La Gorce tendered his resignation and recommended his replacement be Bell's silver-haired grandson: my father, Melville Bell Grosvenor. The vote was unanimous. "With God's help," the new president and editor declared, "I will do my best to carry on the traditions of the National Geographic Society."

The MBG era had begun.

MBG, AGE 55, was off to an auspicious start. Almost immediately he announced a plan to publish a world atlas, declaring that nothing outside the magazine "would better help to carry out our Society's aims."

Such a grandiose plan worried GHG. He thought our map supplements already constituted a valuable world atlas when housed in binders, which we offered to members. He felt that an atlas would divert attention away from our flagship magazine and be ruinously expensive. Who could compete with the five-volume *The Times Atlas of the World*?

I think something else troubled him as well. Only four days before MBG was elected president and editor, *Collier's* magazine ceased publication. *Collier's* had rivaled the *Saturday Evening Post* as one of America's favorite illustrated weeklies, its circulation peaking at some 2.8 million—a little more than ours then. It, too, had been around since 1888. But its circulation had been ebbing at the same time as its owner, the Crowell Company, branched out into encyclopedias and radio stations. If GHG, conservative to his core, saw a parallel between Crowell's diversification and my father's plans to establish a National Geographic Book Service and publish an atlas, he never shared it with me. But I could tell he was leery of overextending the mission.

That was driven home at the board meeting at which the atlas committee's report was presented and officially authorized. I was Gramp's minder that day, and just before the vote, he stood up to excuse himself. I followed him out of the room, noticing that he looked a little pale.

"Are you okay?" I asked.

"Oh, yes," he answered, managing a twinkle in his eye. "I couldn't vote for an atlas, and I certainly wasn't going to vote against my son!"

In the end, both were right: The atlas did become the most expensive project then undertaken. MBG financed it by publishing atlas plates as magazine supplements for years. I worried that members might resent subsidizing a project they would pay for again should they buy the finished product. I should never have worried. Sales reached an astonishing 280,000.

As that five-year crash program played out, I watched the unfolding drama of producing a first-class reference book. Franc Shor was in charge, but the entire staff pitched in. Along with maps, an atlas needs text. MBG loved explanatory notes everywhere. Example: the Antarctica plate. He took one look at that proof and saw an icy white blank: a few scientific stations huddling on its shores and one at the pole. He soon filled in the desolation with 90 explanatory notes.

During the International Geophysical Year—a comprehensive scientific study of Earth's environment with global participation, which took place from July 1957 through the end of 1958—Antarctica was crawling with scientific expeditions. MBG got so tired of getting on his hands and knees to study the White Continent on the underside of his big, immovable floor globe that he summoned Jim Darley, our chief cartographer. "Fix it, Jim," he told him. Darley fetched a cradle globe—one that rests in a cradle and can be rolled in any direction. That caught MBG's eye and lit Jim's imagination; soon we had a more viable globe. I can still hear him now: "Hey, Jim, that's great!" Then a nanosecond later: "Say, our members would love this! When can we produce one?"

We were in the globe business. Our globe would have a new spin. Although intended for household use, it would also be a "globe for the space age," featuring tracings of ocean currents, trade winds, bathymetric data, and a transparent plastic "geometer" that enabled a user to compute longitude, latitude, and satellite orbits.

Meanwhile, the magazine was showing signs of change. "Freedom Flight From Hungary" in the March 1957 issue looked like something found in *Life,* which MBG had studied for years; he'd sent Bob Sisson to cover the Hungarian Revolution in late 1956. Though Budapest was closed to him, Bob documented one group of refugees from the moment they crossed the Austrian border to their arrival in the United States.

Back then the new photojournalism was largely black and white. Monochrome film was faster than color and better for capturing the "moment of truth." It was mostly the province of newspapers or news magazines.

The *Geographic* was focused on color photography. But that didn't mean that we "young Turks," as we called my generation at the magazine, couldn't apply the principles of photojournalism to our color images.

It took teamwork. Sometimes photographer and picture editor researched every aspect of a given place, soliciting permissions needed to shoot in palaces, in museums, or from an airplane. Ultimately there were the nerve-wracking projection sessions—slide shows—where MBG might tear up the entire layout.

One late winter day in 1957, I knocked on the door of a cottage in Pinehurst, North Carolina, owned by a retired general. This particular five-star had been the architect of the American military victory in World War II and the author of the eponymous Marshall Plan that rebuilt Europe after that conflict: General George Catlett Marshall. He was also on the Society's board of trustees. When he agreed to write a story for us as chairman of the American Battle Monuments Commission, responsible for military cemeteries on foreign fields, I was assigned as picture editor.

I was in Pinehurst to show him the layout. He welcomed me at the front door in a suit and tie, as befits a solemn occasion. I'll never forget the tears in his eyes, this man who had sent so many men to battle—and sometimes, to death—as he gazed at the photographs of newly dedicated World War II memorials.

There was the chapel and graveyard at Cambridge, England, where 3,811 men are buried. There was the U.S. military cemetery on the bluff overlooking Omaha Beach, where 9,385 men lie, killed in the Battle of Normandy. Page after page, one solemn picture after another. Photography has the power to move us to joy, laughter, or—in the case of a general recalling the tragedy of war—tears.

Now it was my turn to step out of my role as picture editor and into the role of a photographer on assignment.

WHEN MY FRIENDS ABOARD *MAH JONG* approached the Suez Canal, MBG released me to join them. I gathered my gear—cameras, lenses, Polaroid, flashbulbs, film, notebooks—and in the summer of 1957 embarked for "the Archipelago," as the Byzantines once called the Aegean.

Franc Shor, of course, knew King Paul and Queen Frederica of Greece, as well as all the top people in the Greek national tourist bureau. The blessing of the royal family was practically useless when it came to getting behind the scenes for a story. The guide provided by the bureau was indispensable.

Denis Tateos was not only smart, well informed, and well connected; he was also a good companion, important when living on a boat—whenever that boat showed up, that is. Denis and I spent days scanning the horizon from the ramparts of the Crusaders castle in Rhodes for *Mah Jong's* distinctive mainsail.

I had promised MBG that my coverage would focus on the islands and not on the boat. But it was quite a boat. The 52-foot yawl had a teak deck, cabinetry fashioned from exotic woods, and a carved dragon above the cabin way. Its crew was tired, having battled headwinds most of the way from Hong Kong. The two friends, Mike Merle-Smith and Hovey Freeman, were *Mah Jong's* principal owners; mine was a minority stake. Hovey's wife, Joan, accompanied them, as did my friend Mary Warner.

Rhodes is a picturesque island—with its castle of the Knights of St. John, Valley of the Butterflies, and ancient port of Lindos, where St. Paul landed—and, I thought, comparatively easy to cover. Each island was a new world, and entering them ranked among my most cherished moments in Greece.

It was smooth sailing until I read the waiting telegrams from Mary Griswold, my picture editor, who was raking me over the coals. She had received my initial shipment of film. Most of my pictures were too dark. Had I forgotten to use those "seemingly unfamiliar objects called flashbulbs?" Too much "potshotting, not enough planning." And "quit using Super Anscochrome!"

The most painful news was that my pictures of a festival I'd shot, taken on Super Anscochrome at dusk, were unusable. I didn't go the extra step and use some flash.

Two important lessons were engraved in my soul. One became my motto: The picture that I miss today I can never replicate tomorrow. The other: Fear of failure is the best motivator for me.

Knowing that my photographs would be viewed—and judged—by millions of people around the world was intimidating. I became so driven by fear of failure that I pushed myself from well before dawn to long after dark to create the best photographs in my power. That fear shadowed my every move on every assignment. I learned to control it, but it never vanished.

I left *Mah Jong* in Corinth, and my friends steered for the Mediterranean and home. Dressed in my best clothes, I went to the Athens airport with a large shipment of unprocessed film. I distrusted the Greek mail—as did the Greeks—so I marched straight into the first-class waiting room and asked if anyone flying to the United States happened to be a member of the National Geographic Society? Several hands went up. Eventually one gentleman, after scanning my passport and assignment letter, took my film and said he'd be glad to see it delivered to headquarters. He refused any payment and fulfilled his promise to the letter. The film arrived, and "The Aegean Isles: Poseidon's Playground" was published in December 1958.

IN THE EARLY DAYS, filling magazine pages wasn't so easy. A young GHG, facing deadlines and trying to build membership, sometimes had to scrounge material from government agencies, embassies, friends . . . or even publish his own photographs. So when a former congressman named George Shiras walked in with a box of photographs, he was eager to look at them.

Shiras had exchanged hunting with a gun for "hunting with a camera"—
one of the first to do so. In the woods and waters around his family cabin
on Michigan's Upper Peninsula, he pioneered the first flashlight photos
and the first trip-wire photography of animals at night. The mesmerizing
images won gold medals at exhibitions in Paris and St. Louis. GHG published all 74 plates in the July 1906 issue as "Hunting Wild Game With
Flashlight and Camera."

That issue generated a tremendous response. President Theodore
Roosevelt, outdoorsman and naturalist, heaped praise on both Shiras and
the Society. GHG described it as "one of the pioneering achievements of
the National Geographic . . . Nobody had ever seen pictures like that of
wild animals."

Not everyone was swayed. Alfred Brooks, a famous explorer of Alaska
and a member of the board, grumbled that GHG was turning our official
journal into "a picture gallery." He didn't feel that natural history had a
place in the magazine. "Wandering off into nature is not geography," he
sniped, and resigned from the board.

How shortsighted. Wandering off into nature marked the emergence
of the conservation stream that would flow strongly through the magazine
pages, as well as the birth of wildlife photography in the *Geographic*. Shiras
was a pioneering photographer and ardent environmentalist who laid the
groundwork for the 1916 Migratory Bird Treaty that arguably saved the
ducks and geese of North America from overhunting. Where he led, GHG
followed, putting his older friend on the board and getting to know his
circle of conservation-minded friends (including ornithologist Frank
Chapman, who turned Gramp into a lifelong bird-watcher).

Yet one more stream nourished the growth of conservation in our
Society—and it flowed straight out of a grove of trees in a national park.
It was symbolized by a photograph hanging in Gramp's office that depicted
20 men linking their arms around the mammoth trunk of the General

Sherman—"king of all trees," the caption noted—in the heart of Sequoia National Park. The men looked as though they were protecting it. One of the men in the picture was Stephen Mather, the "20 Mule Team Borax" tycoon who showed "Tenderfoot" Grosvenor the western wilderness.

In 1915 Mather was the most prominent advocate for a government agency that might protect America's nine major national parks—at that time only spottily patrolled. To publicize his crusade, Mather invited a group of prominent citizens, including GHG, to California and led them on a pack trip through the mountains into spectacular Sequoia National Park. There, beneath those towering forms, my grandfather's conversion was instant, complete, and lasting.

Thus began that "special relationship" with the national parks that has characterized National Geographic Society history. My grandfather became Mather's most effective publicist. He helped draft the legislation that eventually established the National Park Service in 1916, with Mather as its first director. He used *National Geographic* to show members the nation's "scenic wonderlands."

And there was more. Learning that private inholdings within Sequoia National Park threatened the Giant Forest, GHG stepped in to protect them from logging. Using a fraction of each member's dues, he amassed nearly $100,000—about $1.3 million today—and bought up nearly 2,000 of those endangered acres as a gift from the National Geographic Society to the Department of Interior.

Did I learn all this history from a few sessions sprawled in a Windsor chair in my grandfather's office? Of course not. Only the foundations were laid during those lunch hours. But on those foundations, another great Society tradition would be established that both MBG and I would vigorously support: the tradition of family, a special esprit de corps, that incorporated and embraced the Grosvenors, the Geographic staff, and the membership.

CHAPTER SIX

OF FRIENDS AND FOES

One evening in early October 1957, I climbed to the top of the hill on Beinn Bhreagh and lay in a blueberry patch to watch the dying sunset. I was squeezing in a few days at Baddeck before returning to Washington. As the sky grew darker and twilight burned out, I picked up my binoculars, scanned low on the eastern horizon, and found the tiny reflective disk that was Sputnik, history's first man-made satellite. The Soviets had beaten us into space—a frightening thought to most Americans.

Whenever I visited GHG in the office, all we had to do to catch a glimpse of the Soviets was look out the window. The beaux arts mansion across the street was their embassy.

In 1913, GHG, Alexander Graham Bell, and their wives had toured Russia. My grandfather loved his glimpse of that great sprawling empire. He devoted an entire issue of the *Geographic*—November 1914—to this "land of unlimited possibilities." Most of the pictures were his own.

That was before the Russian Revolution overthrew the old order and replaced it with the world's first communist regime. Afterward he turned his back on that embassy across the street, scarcely publishing anything on the Soviet Union in *National Geographic* for nearly 30 years.

If 1957—Dad's first year as president and editor—had begun with a bang, it would end with one as well. In the weeks leading up to Christmas, our members received an announcement of a new Society book, *The World in Your Garden,* a popular geography of food. It was the first publication issued by our brand-new National Geographic Book Service. MBG was stretching his wings. But the real fireworks came with the December issue and its lead story: "I Found the Bones of the *Bounty.*"

It was a classic quest: a National Geographic writer-photographer determined, in the early days of scuba, to recover remnants of His Majesty's Armed Vessel *Bounty,* which had been scuttled off Pitcairn Island in the South Pacific. The 18th-century ship harbored a mutiny made famous by the historical novel *Mutiny on the Bounty,* as well as a Hollywood version featuring Clark Gable as Fletcher Christian.

In Pitcairn's pounding surf and dangerous undertow, Luis Marden retrieved copper spikes, sheathing, and nails that attached that sheathing to wood long consumed by flame or worms. The discovery surfaced in the press and on national television, introducing Marden to the world.

I FIRST MET LUIS MARDEN when I was too inexperienced to appreciate his talent and achievements.

As a teenager, he had mastered a basic knowledge of Egyptian hieroglyphics and taken up color photography as a hobby. He spoke five languages and was a man of theatrical flair who flew a fabric-covered biplane from Boston to Washington for his interview with the magazine.

In 1936 Marden introduced Kodak's new Kodachrome film to the *Geographic.* It was a tough sell. Nobody believed a tiny piece of 35mm film could be enlarged to produce *Geographic*-quality printing.

Marden (along with Bud Wisherd, who figured out the engraving part) proved it could. The film, coupled with the 35mm camera, became the standard at the magazine. After Cousteau appeared in the mid-1950s, Luis shipped aboard *Calypso* and shaped the course of modern underwater photography. When *Omnibus*, a television show hosted by Alastair Cooke, broadcast the 16mm film Luis made of his *Bounty* adventure, the high ratings convinced MBG that television was a promising medium for us.

In 1958 I got to know Luis and his wife, Ethel, a mathematical genius with the National Bureau of Standards and one of the few women who, during and after World War II, helped bring about the computer revolution. The two hired Frank Lloyd Wright to design a house they built on the Virginia side of the Potomac above roaring Little Falls. It was small and stylish, all plate-glass windows and ample shelves, to house Marden's 20,000 books.

They treated me like a son. Once the house was finished, I went there for an evening of contract bridge. Ethel was my partner, and such a virtuoso that when the telephone rang, she answered it and, while standing 15 feet away and conversing, played her cards perfectly from memory, winning the contract without missing a beat.

Almost immediately after taking command, MBG recruited a new cadre of photographers to join Luis and Tony Stewart on staff. They were around my age and came mostly from newspapers. Dean Conger came from the *Denver Post*, Tom Nebbia from South Carolina's *Columbia State Record*, and Winfield Parks from the *Providence Journal-Bulletin*.

Of that generation, the most remarkable of all to me was the man who joined our ranks in 1956. The connection came through Bill Garrett. When GHG had met Bill at the University of Missouri, he had escorted my grandfather around a photo exhibition. At the show, GHG stopped abruptly at a picture of a bird. Not just any bird, but a baby robin ferociously tugging a worm out of the ground—the camera only two feet away.

The photographer was Thomas J. Abercrombie—a friend of Garrett's who had joined the staff of the *Milwaukee Journal*. A few weeks later that picture appeared in *Life*. About a year later Abercrombie joined our staff.

Abercrombie helped pioneer modern photography in our magazine. I should know; I was often his picture editor. For a nuclear energy story, he didn't just photograph scientists posing before a cyclotron at Argonne National Laboratory; he photographed energy itself—the blue glow of speeding particles rushing through ionized air—from the cyclotron's emission. He ruined a camera when the magnetic force sucked it into the cyclotron, but that picture made the story.

He was fortunate to arrive during the best of times, when the *Geographic* and *Life* created the two most successful photo staffs in magazine history; when television was not yet a threat; and when expense accounts were generous and leashes were long.

Tom photographed ice fishermen on Lake Superior—from beneath the ice. Although his primitive wet suit leaked, he made his pictures—"the act of a madman," he observed wryly. The coverage won him the 1959 Magazine Photographer of the Year award from the Pictures of the Year competition.

I had nothing but admiration for this short, compact man who puffed on a pipe and wisecracked his way through the day. As he would exclaim, through stem-clenching teeth, "Jesus! You wonder sometimes!"

Dispatched to Antarctica in 1958 during the International Geophysical Year, he decided he'd rather not hang out on the fringes of the continent with scientists and reporters. He wanted to see the South Pole. It was almost easier to get to the moon, but there was a research station at the pole where men endured the plunging temperatures at the bottom of the world.

Lucky again: Abercrombie drew one of two winning lottery slots to ride a supply plane headed there. Two reporters went, but Tom is widely credited with being the first reporter to set foot on the South Pole. He was scheduled to stay only a half hour, but the plane's engine blew a gasket—so he stayed three weeks documenting station life and the surrounding frozen universe. Back at the office, MBG tore up the magazine, which had been almost ready for printing, to include this unprecedented material.

Tom Abercrombie would become one of my best friends at the *Geographic;* we'd also own a sailboat together. But all of us—writers, photographers, and picture editors—would be the nucleus of the Geographic family.

A REMARKABLE DECADE at the National Geographic Society closed in 1959. The space program had launched with Project Mercury. Dr. Hugh C. Dryden, who would become deputy director for NASA, was on our board; this relationship would pave the way for us to document nearly all the American launches of earth-orbiting satellites and space probes in the wake of Sputnik.

Despite the Dryden connection, we were outmaneuvered by *Life* magazine, which snared exclusive rights to the personal stories of the first U.S. astronauts: the famed Mercury Seven, which included John Glenn. That infuriated the rest of the media—especially MBG.

Labeling *Life*'s deal "darned unfair," he leveraged the *Geographic*'s preeminence in color photography and offered Dryden full-time use of Luis Marden to document these events in color. For the next decade and beyond, this gave us the inside track to NASA operations.

It was an exciting time for everyone at the Society, but especially me. As chairman of our Lecture Committee, I found the lecturers, managed logistics, helped shape their talks, and introduced them when they spoke. Fortunately, I had a secretary smarter than me: a Bryn Mawr graduate named Joanne Hess, who would eventually run the entire audiovisual division.

I had hardly taken this program on before I learned an important lesson. Fairfield Osborn, Jr., president of the New York Zoological Society, was to give a lecture on the Bronx Zoo. I nervously awaited his arrival at

Constitution Hall, where thousands of people gathered to hear him (severe flooding had delayed the train). When he finally arrived—in the nick of time—I let my youthful exasperation show. "Young man," he replied, "I've been alive a lot longer than you have. Do you want me to go back to New York right now?"

I must have placated him. Fairfield appointed me to the board of the New York Zoological Society. But I learned my lesson: Never let exasperation show, especially to friends of my father, grandfather, and the National Geographic Society!

OF ALL THE POINTS on the globe that the Society explored with our members, few gripped my imagination as much as the polar regions. In my early years as a picture editor, I was fortunate to work with U.S. Navy commander James F. Calvert.

Admiral Hyman Rickover, father of the nuclear navy, had studied maps of the Arctic Ocean during the Cold War; the Soviet Union lay on its Siberian side. Nuclear submarines could lurk undetected beneath the Arctic pack ice for months. If they could break through to the surface, they could, in the event of war, fire Polaris missiles at very close range.

Calvert, commander of the nuclear submarine U.S.S. *Skate,* was tasked with breaking through the ice. Since he would attempt that at the North Pole—then a significant feat of navigation—*National Geographic* wanted to document it.

It was dangerous; a submarine's conning tower, which housed radio, sonar, and navigational equipment, would act as a ram, risking damage. A submarine stranded in the Arctic waste would probably be doomed. In August 1958 the *Skate* began the attempt. Calvert chose small openings in the ice cap called "leads." Skate easily pushed through such lightly frozen openings several times during that voyage, once scaring off a polar bear. But the ice beneath the pole itself was too thick to penetrate.

When Calvert returned in March 1959, he found ice thin enough to break through—helming the first submarine to surface at the North Pole.

Tom Abercrombie's images of the South Pole and Jim Calvert's photographs of the Arctic Ocean ice fields, published almost within a year of each other, were among the first extensive photographic records of those desolate places.

MORE MUNDANE, PERHAPS, but pivotal to the Society were meetings of the Committee for Research and Exploration—CRE, as we called it, our grantmaking arm.

Backbenchers, like me, Franc Shor, and Mary Griswold attended to see how the magazine could support and publish the work of research grantees. Some—like Cousteau and the archaeologists Matthew and Marion Stirling, who discovered gigantic stone heads in the Mexican jungle made by the long-vanished Olmec culture—practically became National Geographic franchises. So did twin brothers Frank and John Craighead, whom I met in the late 1950s. Our association with the Craigheads—three generations of them—would span 50 years.

In 1930, the 14-year-old twins discovered an old *National Geographic* article on falconry and were hooked, becoming among the first Americans to take up the "sport of kings." Born into a Washington, D.C., family of naturalists—their father, Frank Craighead, Sr., was an entomologist with the Agriculture Department—the boys were active outdoorsmen who climbed trees, scaled cliffs, and established a traveling menagerie of hawks, owls, and even a peregrine falcon. At the age of 19, on leave from Penn State, the twins walked into the Society's headquarters with a manuscript and box of pictures.

They were excellent and "Adventures With Birds of Prey," published in the July 1937 *National Geographic,* introduced the Craigheads to the world. Eight more articles followed over the next two decades. Readers followed them out West, where they studied prairie falcons, burrowing owls, goshawks, and golden eagles.

When I first met them, John worked with the U.S. Fish and Wildlife Service's Montana Cooperative Wildlife Research Unit in Missoula. Frank had been a wildlife biologist with the U.S. Forest Service and would establish his own wildlife research institute.

They had climbed every peak in the Tetons (not to mention trees and gorges) in quest of raptors, with claw marks and lacerations to show for it—helpful for the challenging project they pitched to the Research Committee in late 1958.

The Craigheads approached authorities at Yellowstone National Park about the precipitous drop in the park's grizzly bear population. Only 500 to 1,000 grizzlies remained in the lower 48, most of them in Yellowstone. Although they were still plentiful north of the Canadian border, it seemed likely that they might soon disappear in the south. All anyone really had was anecdotal stories dating back to Lewis and Clark; a meticulous study of grizzly bear biology that could lead to better management was desperately needed. The twins would track the largely nocturnal grizzlies to their dens in thick timber, monitor them, and measure vital statistics.

We signed on. The Craigheads spent that first season—the summer of 1959—setting up fieldwork, devising baiting and trapping methods, and experimenting with dart guns, dosages, and syringes to render the bears temporarily unconscious—a tricky proposition.

IN EARLY NOVEMBER 1959, a 56-year-old paleontologist and curator of the Coryndon Museum of Natural History in Nairobi turned up at Society headquarters.

I'm not sure MBG had ever heard of paleoanthropology. He did know the name Louis Leakey and that of his archaeologist wife, Mary, through a mutual friend in Nairobi. After decades of hunting, they had found fragments of a humanlike skull dating back some 600,000 years in Oldu-vai Gorge. That made it older than either Java man or Peking man, the previously earliest-known hominid fossils. The discovery might vindicate Darwin's contention that Africa, and not Asia, was the cradle of humanity. Dr. Leakey was in Washington seeking funding to continue the search.

MBG quickly intuited the importance of paleoanthropology—the study of human origins—to our members. And he realized that Louis Leakey, who could captivate children with elaborate string tricks and adults by knapping flakes off flint cores to craft cutting tools, was the messenger who could make the field come alive. At a meeting of our Research Com-mittee, Dad steered a handsome stipend Leakey's way, stating, "I can think of no more worthwhile project than this."

MBG had tapped the richest vein of ore the National Geographic Society would ever mine.

Dad's quicksilver mind was never at rest. One day in early 1959 he called some of us into his office and tossed a few *Geographics* onto the carpet. "Boys," he said, "pick out the issue featuring the article on Japan."

Puzzled, we dropped down on our hands and knees to sort through them until we found it. MBG then picked up another stack of issues and tossed them to the carpet. "Now show me the one with the article on Japan."

That was easy. He had scotch-taped illustrations on each cover. You could see from a distance the cover with the geisha. The message was obvious. "Pictures on the cover will help our members find particular issues more quickly," he said.

True, except that meant altering the cover design—a table of contents bordered by oak leaves and acorns, surmounted by a garland of laurels that had been in place since February 1910 and was practically sacred to mem-bers. I was initially dubious, wondering how GHG would feel about that. Our cover was our trademark.

MBG persisted, and the first photograph to appear on our cover was an image of the U.S. flag on the July 1959 issue. The second, in the September 1959 issue, was a U.S. Navy F3H Demon jet fighter racing at supersonic speed. I was not surprised that my ex-Navy father picked his favorite branch of the service for the cover; the pilot of that jet was my brother Alec. Bill Garrett had taken the picture from an accompanying jet during his coverage of the Pacific Fleet.

A cover picture was now a permanent fixture. We drew a lot of critical mail—typified by "If God had intended a picture on the cover of *National Geographic* magazine, He would have put one there in the first place"—but it was affirming to know how strongly members felt about their publication. Garrett and our young designer Howard Paine were ready to trim all the oak leaf foliage off, and I eventually sided with them. But "gradual" was the word describing the *National Geographic* evolution.

MY OWN EVOLUTION AS A STAFFER was proceeding as well. Though I viewed my years in the Army with scant enthusiasm, one positive outcome was my friendship with Mate Meštrović, who also served in our psyops unit and was a Yugoslav émigré whose father was Ivan Meštrović, the beloved Croatian sculptor.

Mate was born in Zagreb and educated in Switzerland, where the family lived in exile during World War II. His new U.S. citizenship entailed two years' service in the Army. After our discharge, I invited him and his wife, Jane, to join me on the Dalmatian coast as an interpreter and adviser for an assignment I would write and photograph. The setting was picturesque and worthy of serious photojournalism: Yugoslavia, still communist, had repudiated the Soviet Union. Its strongman, Marshal Josip Broz Tito, was courting the U.S.S.R., Europe, and the United States for aid.

We drove along Yugoslavia's coast to Split in May 1959, covering what is now the Croatian coast. This was Yugoslavia's window on the West; Tito, the ex-Partisan of World War II fame, was playing the Western world against the Soviets and keeping both where he wanted them—out.

Most of our time was spent in either Split, the city built in and around Emperor Diocletian's 1,600-year-old palace, or Dubrovnik, the former Republic of Ragusa.

We drove awful roads documenting agriculture, still rooted in picturesque 19th-century terraced slopes, or visiting cement plants, can factories, and shipyards to document the country's feverish efforts to industrialize. We were never hassled by the secret police, although we knew we were being tracked. What I remember most, though, is how we handled two difficult and intertwined problems.

As early as April, before I even left the office, we were in touch with the Yugoslav Embassy in Washington, hoping to clear two requests: One was help arranging an interview and photo session with Marshal Tito on the isle of Brioni, where his presidential retreat was located. The other was permission to make aerial photographs along the spectacular Dalmatian coast. Without aerials, the story would collapse.

I thought the former would be harder to arrange than the latter. I was wrong.

The young ambassador, Marko Nikezić, promised to help, knowing that National Geographic was the best means of promoting American tourism in Yugoslavia, especially along the coast. I felt confident that it would just be a matter of jumping through the usual bureaucratic hoops. Wrong again. Belgrade bureaucracy proved impenetrable; only the request to interview Tito had been approved.

We ran the aerials-permission maze until it led back to Split, headquarters of the man responsible for security along the Adriatic coast: an old ex-Partisan colonel deeply loyal to Tito. He listened, unmoved; the answer was no. His responsibility was to protect the coast. He would not permit foreigners with cameras to fly up and down its length.

Of all the roadblocks leading to hard-to-get permissions, his was the most formidable. Mate explained why. "Gil, you must understand that in communist countries, it is always safer to say no than yes," he said. We must make 'no' more dangerous to his well-being than 'yes.'"

I had to find a way. Maybe convince him that Tito himself endorsed the request. That was tricky. What if he checked?

Then we got word that our interview with Tito was eminent. We moved close to Pula, jumping-off point for nearby Brioni, and decided to wait it out in Opatija, a beautiful seaside resort tucked into the Istrian Peninsula. We waited. And waited. At night I'd lie in bed, watching the ceiling fan spin, haunted by the concept of "making 'no' more dangerous than 'yes.'" Watching moonlight fall on my equipment, my old fear of failure reemerged. The lens of the Polaroid stared at me accusingly. The Polaroid! That's the answer, I thought and drifted off to sleep.

The next morning I instructed Mate how to take a Polaroid picture of me with Tito. When I explained my plan, he thought for a moment.

"Might work," he said and shrugged.

A few days later, word came. Be at the Pula dock the next morning. Dressed in our finest attire, we drove down the Istrian coast to Pula. We were hustled aboard a fancy government powerboat for a short, speedy run across the Adriatic to Brioni, home to the plush state summer residence, but really its presidential palace.

Arriving early, we climbed into a horse-drawn buggy for a tour of scenic Brioni. I was asked to leave my aluminum Halliburton camera cases behind. The landscape, thickly planted with oak and laurel, was cool and shady, unlike any other place I saw that summer in the Adriatic.

Tito was then apparently ready to receive us, because the carriage abruptly returned to the dock. I retrieved my cases and we boarded the speedboat for the trip to another island: Vanga, his personal retreat.

A small dock came into view. Disembarking, we followed a path until we emerged onto a small, beautifully appointed flagstone patio.

Suddenly, Marshal Tito stepped out of the shrubbery. Although short and thickset, he cut an impressive figure in an immaculate white silk suit, white shoes, light blue striped shirt, and blue-and-white tie secured by his trademark diamond stick pin. His cigarette was fixed in an ivory holder.

Greeting us in English, he shook our hands and motioned for us to sit at the table. I opened with a gambit about photography, having heard it was his hobby. That might open the door to more substantive questions. While Jane translated, I fumbled with the latch to the Halliburton case holding my long lenses—causing my gunstock tripod to tumble out.

In a flash I was flung onto the flagstones. Men emerged from the shrubbery and pinned my arms. Once they were waved off by Tito, they released me and vanished back into the hedge. Tito laughed uproariously. "In your country you might have ended up badly," a pale-looking Jane translated. Sheepishly brushing myself off, I realized that security had checked out the cameras while we were on that carriage ride but hadn't replaced the gunstock component properly.

"It steadies a camera while it is on a tripod," I explained. "I made it myself." I showed him how it worked, then unpacked my Leica and Nikon range finders and lenses. Squinting through a viewfinder, he marveled at the optics.

Next I unpacked the Polaroid camera. He appeared interested. To demonstrate, I asked whether Mate could take a picture of us. Tito dismissed a glance from his aide. Security already knew it contained no gun or bomb. Mate took the picture. I handed the print to Tito, who gasped in amazement, studied it carefully, fingered the surface, then laid it on the table.

Show-and-tell over, Tito turned to Mate and asked about his father. I retrieved my gear and packed it carefully, casually slipping the Polaroid print into my pocket.

As expected, Tito brushed off any questions on social or economic policy. Finally, I said as diplomatically as possible: "Because of your strong partisan leadership during World War II, you afterward successfully forged Slovenia, Serbia, Croatia, Bosnia, Herzegovina, and Montenegro into one strong country. Do you believe your successors can hold these traditionally independent peoples together?"

Working through an interpreter gave him time to frame his thoughts. "If they all work hard to keep the country together, yes. Otherwise Yugoslavia will be split apart," he replied, intimating he believed the latter.

His hunch, history tells us, was correct.

Several days later we again sat in the office of coastal security in Split. The colonel looked annoyed when I again asked permission for aerial photography, then skeptical when we casually mentioned our recent visit to interview Tito. He waved his hand in outright dismissal. He wasn't about to fall for that ruse.

Reaching into my coat pocket I carefully pulled out the Polaroid print and spun it across his desk.

"I now must leave Yugoslavia for home," I said. "When I write Marshal Tito to thank him for his hospitality, I will tell him you prevented my story from being published. To be certain he receives my note, I will hand deliver it to my friend Ambassador Nikezić in Washington."

"You know Ambassador Nikezić?" His eyes narrowed.

"Of course I know Marko," I replied casually. "Washington is a small city."

He picked up the Polaroid print, studied it again, looked up at me, glanced at the print again, and noticed I was wearing the same suit, shirt, and tie as in the picture. He asked us to step out for a moment.

Soon we were called back. With a strained attempt to be pleasant, he instructed me to "be at the civil aviation sporting club tomorrow afternoon."

I had made it safer for him to say yes than no.

When we flew down the coast toward Dubrovnik, I photographed everything but naval installations, my only concession. The pilot of the small aircraft allowed me to remove the side windows so that I could make sharper images. By the time we approached Dubrovnik, I placed fresh film in each camera.

The real success of the assignment hinged on the next 15 to 30 minutes. Conditions were perfect: late afternoon sun, clear skies, excellent visibility. We circled Dubrovnik three times before we got the height and angle right. The motor drive whirled, and I had my pictures.

Then it hit me: I hadn't changed film in the last 10 minutes. Clearly, I had shot more than 36 images. I turned the film advance lever, but the rewind knob spun freely. The film had not advanced a single frame. I must have improperly loaded it.

A string of unprintable four-letter words ensued.

Quickly reloading, making sure the film engaged the sprocket, I signaled the pilot to go around again. He pointed to the gas gauge: Time to head home! I held up one finger and frantically gestured to go around once more. With a frown, he banked around the city one last time while I snapped off two rolls, being careful to place my finger against the film rewind knob to be certain the film had advanced. Then we flew straight back to the airport in Split.

Five pages of aerials were published from that one flight. Thanks to the *Geographic*'s cachet, I was the first foreigner permitted to make aerials of the coast and the first to use color film.

Shortly after arriving home, I was seconded to the business department, to be idled for 18 months among adding machines and spreadsheets.

Then another opportunity materialized.

CHAPTER SEVEN

ABOARD THE EISENHOWER EXPRESS

t first it was a low whine that gradually increased to a high-pitched scream. The accelerated tempo caused the plane to vibrate, but we were going nowhere because the aircraft's brakes anchored us to the runway. Then came a noticeable tug, and the plane bolted forward.

My back and neck were jammed deep into the seat cushion; the runway began peeling past my window so fast it made me dizzy. Liftoff, and something sank in the pit of my stomach as the plane seemingly went straight up into the sky; I was certain the tail would drag on the concrete runway. I wasn't alone in my anxiety. Conversation, even among seasoned correspondents, ceased.

Quickly, we leveled out. Below, Washington, D.C., vanished from view. Once we reached a high-enough altitude, the pilot throttled back the engine and the whine subsided. We seemed to float in space. It was exhilarating.

Evening, December 3, 1959, and I was on the trip of a lifetime, accompanying President Dwight D. Eisenhower, a man with the most winning grin in human history, on his historic three-week "Friendship Flight" tour of Europe, Asia, and North Africa. We would travel 22,000 miles in those three weeks, twice cross the Atlantic, transit the Mediterranean, visit 11 countries, and meet (among other dignitaries) Pope John XXIII, President Charles de Gaulle of France, Generalissimo Francisco Franco of Spain, Prime Minister Jawaharlal Nehru of India, and Reza Pahlavi, the shah of Iran.

No one yet had spanned so much geography in three short weeks; this pivotal trip marked the first sustained use of jets in international relations. In 1959 the first Boeing 707s were just coming off assembly lines to start revolutionizing passenger service. By traveling twice as fast as any of their winged forebears, they effectively shrank the globe by half. Ike had launched the age of shuttle diplomacy.

PRESIDENT EISENHOWER'S INITIAL airborne fleet consisted of propeller-driven Lockheed Constellations: reliable and comfortable but limited to 350 miles an hour. He took delivery of his 707s—including the first aircraft to be dubbed Air Force One—in time to travel to Europe in August 1959 for NATO meetings. Massive turnouts in Paris, Bonn, and London welcomed him, and he fell in love with flying by jet.

That's when he decided to really travel, accompanied by his son and aide-de-camp, Major John Eisenhower. John's wife, Barbara Eisenhower, would play the role of first lady, since Mamie had opted out. I was one of 97 in the accompanying press plane—and at 28, possibly the youngest representative of a major magazine on board. Others included Jim Hagerty, Eisenhower's press secretary; Russell Baker of the *New York Times;* and the future queen of television interviewers, Barbara Walters.

I had just returned from my assignment in Yugoslavia in October and was editing pictures from that story when MBG—dipping a tentative toe in the waters of spot-news journalism—decided I was the only culprit around he could apprehend on short notice.

I resisted at first. This wasn't our cup of tea. But MBG and Franc Shor persuaded me that I would have a different perspective. Forget the grip-and-grin pictures. Focus on "the geography," the memo said, ". . . show Eisenhower in various geographical surroundings."

The president was winding down his second term and nearing retirement from public life; this was his farewell to the world. I should seek images portraying Eisenhower reassuring the people of Europe, the Middle East, Asia, and North Africa that the United States of America would continue to protect them if the Cold War heated up, supporting them in their quest for peace and prosperity.

Okay . . . but I barely had time to research each country, assemble a photographic kit, and take care of the necessary paperwork and inoculations. Setting off half prepared was not the *National Geographic* way; three weeks to glimpse 11 countries when we often took three months to cover one felt wrong. Shooting from roped-off pens would be tedious. I would have to be creative and make the most of whatever opportunities arose to find that single photograph—the "lead picture"—to tell the story. Geography on the fly, I thought dismally.

I worried most about the expectations heaped upon me. I had been assigned when more talented staff photographers might have been chosen; I had to pull it off. Fail, and I'd end up in the business department: a number cruncher for life.

AFTER AN ATLANTIC CROSSING that took only seven hours, we landed in Rome. Ike's August trips to Britain, France, and West Germany had generated a lot of press coverage; now he needed to show that Italy had put its fascist past behind it and was now a valuable member of NATO. President Giovanni Gronchi was rumored to be a closet communist, so Ike may have wanted to intimidate him too.

Our press plane always landed first so that correspondents could disembark and be positioned to cover the president's arrival. Inevitably, we would clamber aboard a flatbed truck and precede the open presidential limousine on the motorcade into town. That way we could photograph Ike waving at the crowds lining the route. The motorcade, I soon realized, might be my best opportunity to picture the president interacting with the local people and local geography.

When we arrived, Rome was rainy and dreary, which didn't stop a huge delegation from *Life* from assembling around Don Wilson, the magazine's Washington bureau chief, on the rain-slick tarmac. I had only my colleague Tom Nebbia to back me up in Rome and Athens and an illustrations editor on vacation in India to help there. Otherwise, I was a one-man band.

Our first motorcade was disappointing. The Appian Way was a muddy track, and I couldn't portray the Italians reacting to President Eisenhower's presence when only a few huddled knots of people stood here and there. Even a glimpse of Gina Lollobrigida's house couldn't dispel the gloom.

I awoke in my room at the Grand Hotel the next morning to find that my shoes, which I left outside my door to be shined, had been stolen. I rushed out to buy an inexpensive pair of Italian shoes—only to discover that there was no such thing, and then worried about how to justify the purchase. I could just hear them in the business department saying, "Young Grosvenor hardly arrives in Rome before he's buying fancy shoes on the Geographic dime." I would write a long memo explaining the situation.

Most of my Kodachrome would stay in its Halliburton case. President Eisenhower climbing the steps of the Victor Emmanuel II Memorial to lay a wreath at the Tomb of the Unknown Soldier in a driving rain had to be shot in Ektachrome—the only alternative in poor light.

On December 6, a Sunday, President Eisenhower had an audience with Pope John XXIII in Vatican City. In 1959 that was almost unprecedented.

Woodrow Wilson had been the only chief executive to ever meet a pope, because diplomatic relations between the United States and the Holy See had never existed. The overwhelmingly Protestant establishment in America had always been too suspicious of Catholicism.

In only 20 minutes in the Vatican's Apostolic Library, Eisenhower and the pope overturned those animosities. After Ike's visit that morning, every subsequent U.S. president has met with the bishop of Rome, although another quarter century would elapse before full diplomatic relations were instituted.

That pivotal meeting had been off-limits to press. We were restricted to posed pictures outside the Apostolic Library, then ushered into the Vatican's consistorial chamber, where the pope welcomed us; no photographs were allowed.

That didn't stop Tom Nebbia, one of the most instinctive and gifted photographers I ever met. Nudging me aside, he put range finder to eye and snapped a shot. In the hushed room, the shutter sounded like a cannon. I was appalled. No *Geographic* man should do that! After the picture was published five months later, the Vatican was reportedly delighted. I learned a valuable lesson: Pack audacity in that camera bag.

I gave Nebbia my exposed rolls to carry back to the States, not expecting much; I thought Rome was a bust. Naturally, the sun emerged just as we left for our next destination: Ankara, Turkey.

Ankara was no Istanbul, but a city as eternal as Rome. We wouldn't have time to visit the old town, with its Roman baths and mosques. Instead, we saw the new one: an industrialized, modern, prosperous small city—the creation of Mustafa Kemal Atatürk, leader of the Turkish War of Independence and founder and first president of the Turkish Republic. Our motorcade rolled down Atatürk Boulevard, and in twilight I photographed Ike standing bareheaded in Atatürk's own 1934 Lincoln touring car, waving at the cheering crowds along the flag-lined way.

WE ARRIVED IN KARACHI, PAKISTAN, on a hot afternoon on December 7 and stripped off our overcoats.

As usual, a massive crowd awaited our motorcade from the airport. We photographers were packed so tightly into the back of a truck that I had to hang on to the tailgate for dear life. The driver's incompetence with the clutch made it worse; the vehicle frequently lurched forward. Suddenly, 30 photographers crashed backward into me, causing me to fly off the truck and into the street.

Fortunately, I rolled with the fall, scrambled to my feet, and frenziedly gathered cameras, lenses, and film—barely avoiding the team of black horses pulling a gilded carriage where Ike sat side by side with President Mohammad Ayub Khan, Pakistan's military dictator.

From the gutter, I managed to get a shot of the presidential carriage against the background of the Khyber Hotel, each window crowded with men in baggy pants, women in bright saris, and women in dark, enveloping burqas, all watching the passing show. It was a picture none of the other correspondents got because, well, none were in the gutter.

I was enveloped in a surging sea of Pakistanis. I had no passport, no map, no money, and no knowledge of Urdu, nor had I memorized the name of our hotel. The undertow of people threatened to sweep me away. I ran to catch up to the motorcade.

The horses paced at an even gait. I was young and reasonably fit, and could slow to a jog and take pictures as I went along. Fortunately, I had loaded three cameras, so I had plenty of film and could keep up.

Eisenhower loved to interact with any crowd, and this one was almost frenzied in response. The security guards strained to keep the Pakistanis at bay. They must have recognized my press badge, because they simply ignored me as I hung close to the carriage, hoping we all ended up at the hotel together.

At times, the crowd surged into the street, a tide that might carry me away. Then panic turned to elation: This was why I came to Karachi, to photograph Eisenhower from a point of view no other correspondent could.

As it turned out, that attitude got me in trouble. After an hour of running, the press corps' lorry peeled off for the Hotel Metropole. When I caught up, my colleagues angrily claimed I had jumped off the truck deliberately. Jim Hagerty was on me in an instant. I must have looked so embarrassed as I explained and pointed out my skin burns and torn trousers that he relaxed. His eyes even twinkled when he asked, "Did you get a decent picture?"

"Oh, no!" I replied, not entirely forthcoming.

Was I injured?

"Oh, no!" I repeated, although I had aggravated an old back injury. He never mentioned the incident again.

WE WERE IN PAKISTAN FOR three days. The president rarely stepped into a dirty street. Carpets cushioned his feet; fringed canopies shaded his head. He laid a wreath at the tomb of Pakistan's founder, Mohammed Ali Jinnah. He ate curry and spiced rice. He grinned at snake charmers.

Every head of state we visited had reasons for putting on a spectacular welcome, and President Ayub Khan was no exception. Pakistan's real worry was not the Soviet Union but its larger neighbor, India, which had sought U.S. protection. Ike was ready to provide it, in the belief that India was not as threatening as the Soviet Union.

While Ike discussed security matters with Ayub Khan, or promised him arms, or planned top-secret U-2 spy plane missions (the U-2 base from which Francis Gary Powers would soon fly was hidden in Pakistan), I roamed nearby streets. I'd never seen such poverty as in Karachi. People spent their lives in improvised outdoor shelters. They were born on the street, grew up, had babies, and died on the street. A million people, perhaps, were living in squalor; most were refugees from the bloody

Partition of India 12 years earlier. Meanwhile, the government was buying expensive arms.

It was a subdued young photographer who went to bed at the Hotel Metropole each night.

THE PREDAWN AIR WAS sultry when I left the Hotel Metropole and climbed into the car to the airport. At that hour the streets weren't thronged with bikes, pedicabs, cars, buses, or even cart-drawing camels. But the back alleys we passed, lined by endless cardboard shelters, were already bustling, and the smoke from hundreds of thousands of dung-fueled fires hovered oppressively over the city.

I concentrated on the task ahead. Rome, Ankara, and Karachi were behind us; Kabul, New Delhi, Tehran, Athens, Tunis, Paris, Madrid, and Casablanca lay ahead. I wasn't happy with my progress thus far. I had to nail this next opportunity.

At the airport my driver drove past the press plane and threaded the maze of security to Air Force One itself. I was pool photographer for this early dawn flight to Kabul because no one else had wanted it. It would take less than two hours and involve only a few posed pictures of the president at work. But I wanted it for a photograph I'd envisioned.

I approached the pilot and asked a question about the flight plan. He barely deigned to notice me. But I heard what I'd hoped. I was ushered to a little room designated for reporters. There I sat for several hours, waiting for the president to board the plane.

Finally, Air Force One was wheels up. I set my exposure to capture detail outside the window. Then, wrapping the flashbulb with a handker-chief, I tilted it so that the flash would bounce off the cabin's ceiling, suffusing the light that would bathe the president.

I was ready, hoping for the unbroken clouds to dissipate. Finally came that telltale bank to starboard indicating a course change; I felt a tug of excitement. The sun brightened, and I grew ever more hopeful. Another turn of the plane, and a functionary led me forward through a warren of hallways, ushering me into the presidential suite.

Ike sat at a little folding table, talking to his son and aide-de-camp, John Eisenhower. I heard my name and affiliation announced. The president turned toward me with a nod and a twinkle in his eye. He knew my grandfather.

I explained what I wanted. With camera B I took the perfunctory black-and-white pool pictures of the two Eisenhowers. Soon, word came from the cockpit to look out the window. I swung camera A, loaded with color film, into my hands. Ike moved to the window. Air Force One banked sharply for a better view.

"Khyber Pass visible portside," the pilot announced. Ike gazed intently below at a green cleft carved in the mountains by the small Jhelum River, absorbed by the sight of this historic piece of geography.

Few names in geography resonated more with me than that of this main gateway between the arid plains of Central Asia and the fertile ones of India. The tide of history has endlessly ebbed and flowed through the Khyber Pass. Alexander the Great, Genghis Khan, Tamerlane, Babur the Mughal, the imperious British, thousands of nomads— all marched or fled through the pass. Rumor had it there were two things on the trip Eisenhower particularly wanted to see: the Taj Mahal and the Khyber Pass.

That's why I had sought out this pool position nobody else wanted. With my father's words echoing in my head—"show Eisenhower in the various geographical surroundings"—I was hoping for a picture of the president looking down from Air Force One at the storied Khyber Pass.

Pakistan had never let anyone fly over its portion of the pass and had notably refused permission for Soviet premier Nikita Khrushchev to do so only a few weeks earlier. But Eisenhower was special. The day before this flight, Jim Hagerty, the press secretary, released a bulletin stating that the president might fly over the pass today.

There it lay, touched by the rising sun.

I took as many pictures of Ike looking out the window as I could, given time constraints and the challenges of 1950s film photography. I made some final shots of the pass itself, then took a few seconds to relish the moment.

Even the sight of Soviet-made MiGs didn't dampen my elation. Piloted by Afghans, they were our official escort once we left Pakistani airspace. In Afghanistan, Ike hoped to assess the degree to which King Mohammed Zahir Shah had been pulled into the Soviet sphere.

Afghanistan, created by the British to be a buffer state between their empire in India and Russia, was always pulled in two directions. North of the Hindu Kush, the tribesmen felt more affinity for Central Asia; south of that range, the affinity switched to Pakistan. Only a line on a map, the infamous Durand Line, separated clans and families who did not recognize its existence, much less its binding force.

Franc Shor had whetted my appetite for this once forbidden land. He showed me a picture of him with Zahir Shah, a copy of the *Geographic* prominently displayed on the royal desk. "I know of no better way to learn about the other peoples of the world," the king supposedly said (perhaps with Shor's prompting).

The king, looking like a Soviet marshal, greeted us at Bagram airport. Perhaps his handlers thought I was in the presidential party; when I stepped off Air Force One, I was not herded over to rejoin the correspondents. I slipped off to grab a few shots of Afghan soldiers, their tall banners set against the dramatic backdrop of the towering Hindu Kush. For a few moments I had the unique vantage point. Then someone realized a photographer was on the loose, and I was collared.

In an age when photography was entirely manual you didn't have much time to think about anything but the mechanics of getting the picture. Yet

Depicted in a 1963 painting commissioned for our 75th anniversary are the 33 men who met at Washington, D.C.'s Cosmos Club on the evening of January 13, 1888, to establish the National Geographic Society. Seated and wearing a long white beard is my great-great-grandfather Gardiner Greene Hubbard, the Society's first president. (Stanley Meltzoff)

▲ My grandfather Gilbert Hovey Grosvenor (far left) and my grandmother Elsie Bell Grosvenor (at top) relax with their children at the early Bell home on Nova Scotia's Cape Breton Island in 1907. Elsie's parents, Alexander Graham Bell and Mabel Hubbard Bell, are in the middle; at right is my great-uncle, the botanist David Fairchild, and my great-aunt, Marian "Daisy" Bell Fairchild. (Dr. Gilbert H. Grosvenor)

◀ Alexander Graham Bell and his grandson Melville Bell Grosvenor—my father—stroll through the meadows of the Bells' Cape Breton Island estate, Beinn Bhreagh—Gaelic for "beautiful mountain"—in 1908. The man—inventor of the telephone and the National Geographic Society's second president—and the boy were mirrors of each other, each overflowing with exuberance. Dad never lost that look of infectious enthusiasm. (Bell Collection)

◀ In a celebrated 1909 portrait, Robert E. Peary faces the camera with a steely gaze. To my family and to the National Geographic Society, he was a hero for being the first explorer to reach the North Pole. After his claim was widely debunked, I would lead the battle to redeem his name and honor—a battle we won, in my opinion. (Robert E. Peary Collection)

▼ My grandfather Gilbert Hovey Grosvenor prepares his camera to photograph hydrofoil experiments in Baddeck Bay, off Beinn Bhreagh, 1919. In his 66 years of service to the National Geographic Society, he rose from being the only employee to directing a staff of hundreds. In turning a scholarly journal into the popular *National Geographic*, "GHG" became, in my view, the father of magazine photojournalism. (Wallace W. Nutting)

▲ During a 1929 birthday party for former first lady Helen "Nellie" Taft, guests pose for a group portrait against the backdrop of my grandparents' fine new house, Wild Acres. They include (from left center) my great-grandparents Edwin Augustus Grosvenor and Lilian Waters Grosvenor; Mrs. Taft (in hat); and William Howard Taft, the former U.S. president, who was then Chief Justice of the United States. (Dr. Gilbert H. Grosvenor)

▲ This 1930 Christmas portrait of my grandparents' extended family was made in front of the entrance to Wild Acres, their house near Bethesda, Maryland. From back, left to right, are my uncles Cabot Coville and Paxton Blair and my aunts Carol, Gloria, and Mabel Grosvenor. In front, left to right, are my aunts Lilian Coville and Gertrude Blair, my grandmother Elsie, and my grandfather GHG, who holds my sister, Helen "Teeny" Grosvenor. Seated on the far right and holding my brother, Alexander Graham Bell Grosvenor, is my mother, Helen Rowland Grosvenor. My father, Melville Bell Grosvenor, stands next to her, his arm on her shoulder. The three children in the front row (from left to right) are Gilbert Coville, Joan Blair, and sitting on Elsie's lap, Grosvenor Blair. (Dr. Gilbert H. Grosvenor)

My first appearance in *National Geographic* magazine was in this image, which appeared in the July 1939 issue. To help illustrate an article on the Smithsonian Institution, my father, Melville Bell Grosvenor—known to all in the office as "MBG"—asked a staff photographer to take me down to the Mall, where I posed on this meteorite. (Volkmar Wentzel)

▲ Jacques-Yves Cousteau (left) and *National Geographic*'s dazzlingly talented Luis Marden stand on the deck of the research vessel *Calypso,* 1955. MBG discovered Cousteau, and the Society helped make him famous. Marden was a scholar, linguist, photographer, writer, and raconteur with an unfailing instinct for adventure. His most famous discovery was the remains of the Royal Navy's celebrated H.M.S. *Bounty.* (Pierre Goupil)

▶Thomas J. Abercrombie sports an ice mustache one fine day in 1957 at the South Pole, where temperatures might warm to minus 60°F. Tom, one of the first journalists to reach the pole, was perhaps the most talented, versatile, and accomplished member of *National Geographic*'s foreign editorial staff. He was my best friend at the Society. (Robert F. Benson)

▲ With ballots in hand, three generations of Grosvenors—from left, GHG, MBG, and me, inevitably to be known as "GMG"—vote in a National Press Club election in Washington, D.C., 1958. (Willard R. Culver)

▶ This portrait of an unnamed woman, photographed in New Delhi, India, in 1959, became the opening image of my 1960 article on President Dwight D. Eisenhower's 11-nation tour of Europe, Asia, and North Africa the previous year. Her reaction to the American president's speech embodies India's response to Eisenhower's message of hope. (Gilbert M. Grosvenor)

▲ Accompanied by translators Jane and Mate Meštrović (second and third from left), I interview Yugoslavia's president Marshal Josip Broz Tito in 1959. My slightly rumpled hair betrays a not-so-slight mishap that occurred shortly before this picture was taken: Tito's bodyguards had slammed me to the pavement when they mistook a piece of camera equipment for a weapon. (Gilbert M. Grosvenor)

▼ Interviewing Marshal Tito was not the only feat we accomplished in Yugoslavia. Through persistence and guile, I finally obtained permission to make aerial photographs along the Dalmatian coast—the first in color that Yugoslav authorities had ever permitted. This image from that flight, taken in 1959, ran in the magazine in February 1962. (Gilbert M. Grosvenor)

▲ One shimmering afternoon in 1961, the *Elsie,* my grandfather's 54-foot yawl, eases into Boulaceet, one of the many secluded anchorages in the Bras d'Or Lakes of Cape Breton Island. The Cruising Club of America was founded in *Elsie*'s cabin while she was anchored here in 1922. (Winfield Parks)

▼ Members of the Cruising Club of America gather outside The Point, the multi-turreted, many-gabled summer house the Bells had built in 1893. The entertainment offered that day in 1961 reflected Cape Breton Island's Scottish heritage. (Winfield Parks)

▲ MBG (far left) looks on as President John F. Kennedy and First Lady Jacqueline Kennedy examine *The White House: An Historic Guide,* 1962. At the first lady's request, the Society created the book for the new White House Historical Association. Its success would boost the Geographic's book-publishing efforts. (Winfield Parks)

▶The camera does not lie: Princess Grace of Monaco—the former movie star Grace Kelly—was the picture of elegance on that sparkling day in 1962 when I took her portrait in the palace garden. (Gilbert M. Grosvenor)

MBG always had a flair for the dramatic. On this day in 1964, he landed on Sable Island, a fogbound sandbar southeast of Nova Scotia surrounded by 500 shipwrecks, in his 46-foot yawl *White Mist*. Rowing through the breakers to the beach, he waited for just the right moment to hop into the surf and stride victoriously ashore, imitating General Douglas MacArthur's 1944 return to the beach at Leyte in the Philippines. (Gilbert M. Grosvenor)

This 11-foot globe—the largest freestanding example in the world—spun serenely for decades in Explorers Hall, which housed National Geographic's museum. Shown here in 1964, it was the chief attraction among a number of exhibits designed to inspire a lifelong love of geography. (Emory Kristof)

My first wife, Donna Kerkam Grosvenor, climbs the Great Pyramid of Khufu at Giza, 1964. ("I didn't know how worried I should have been!" her father said upon seeing this image.) Donna and I shared credits for three *National Geographic* stories in the 1960s and contributed to countless others during the time we were together. (Gilbert M. Grosvenor)

◀ On assignment in Ceylon (now known as Sri Lanka) in 1965, I document the making of palm wine—which involved a precarious perch on a rope walkway in order to capture a "toddy tapper" gathering sap high in the treetops. (Gilbert M. Grosvenor)

▼ Three National Geographic Research Committee members are the first Society representatives to visit Jane Goodall at her camp in Tanzania's Gombe Stream Game Reserve, 1965. They are (from left) committee chairman Dr. Leonard Carmichael; future Society president Melvin Payne; and Dr. T. Dale Stewart, an anthropologist at the Smithsonian Institution. None would have believed that Goodall's pioneering study of chimpanzees would still be running nearly 60 years later. (Hugo van Lawick)

An exceptionally funny comment breaks up an editorial meeting in the magazine's Control Center, 1967. White-haired MBG sits in the front row, with Ted Vosburgh to his left; Carolyn Bennett Patterson wears a lime green dress and Mary Griswold Smith wears a red one. In the back, Bud Wisherd lights a cigarette and mustachioed John Scofield is seen across my outstretched arm. (James L. Stanfield)

Tiller in one hand, mainsail boom in the other, Robin Lee Graham epitomizes the solitary sailor pitting himself against the sea aboard the *Dove,* 1968. He would soon complete his solo voyage around the world—the youngest person to do so at that time. (Patricia Graham)

something in the back of my mind found the experience surreal. That's the Hindu Kush! it was saying. That's the famous Hindu Kush!

I was herded back to the photo corral. Not to worry, I felt I had nailed Afghanistan—at least as much as you could in less than 10 minutes. I climbed aboard the Soviet-built buses. The road was lined with men who looked as if they had just stepped out of 19th-century photographs. Hard-eyed, hawk-nosed, turbaned men. Armed men. Warriors.

Ike was conferring with the king, who told him that Russia was not the enemy; Pakistan was! Ike was hoping to play Afghanistan the way Khrushchev was playing Cuba, recently lost to Castro: as a new base on the doorstep of the enemy. If that never played out, American aid, over the next few years, did allow Afghans to enjoy the only spell of happiness they would experience for many sad decades to come.

BACK ON THAT CATTLE CAR, the correspondents' plane, I marveled that in one day we had gone from Karachi to Kabul and would soon land at the next stop of our jagged itinerary, New Delhi.

The four-hour flight gave me time to think about how my coverage was progressing. Rainy Rome may have bombed. But Turkey and Pakistan had gone well. I still lacked a lead picture. Surely, I'd find one in India, as my father had predicted.

By the time we crossed the Himalaya, it was twilight, and we touched down on the plain of the Ganges in darkness. We would follow the president into town in a bus, because there were no picture opportunities in the dark—or so we thought.

On hand to greet Eisenhower was India's prime minister, Jawaharlal Nehru, perhaps the cagiest leader we met on that journey. He was a Cambridge-educated Brahmin, handsome, with dark, intelligent eyes, who had been imprisoned by the British during the twilight of the Raj. He, too, had courted the Soviet Union for arms and economic aid, criticizing the

British for their aggression in the 1956 Suez Crisis while saying little about the Soviet crackdown in Hungary that same year. Yet he craved the opportunity to be seen with Eisenhower, wasn't that obsessed with archfoe Pakistan, and worried more about Red China chipping away at his nation's mountainous frontier.

I watched the two leaders climb into the presidential limousine and depart for New Delhi. Suddenly, we were engulfed by the sounds and smell of India—spices and bullock sweat—and the deep roar of hundreds of thousands of humans lining the 13-mile-long route into the capital.

The clamor of hands pounding our metal bus became deafening; a blizzard of marigold blossoms, a traditional sign of welcome, pelted the vehicle and flew through the windows, falling into our laps. By the time we entered New Delhi, we were ankle-deep in marigolds.

Though it was late at night, the crowds grew larger and surged closer, straining against the arms-locked police. In Connaught Place, the heart of New Delhi, they pressed so close that they rocked the buses. Nehru jumped out of the presidential limousine, strode in front of the vehicle, and stretched out his arms. He was Moses parting the Red Sea, and did so until we reached our hotels.

Good news: In the hotel I was handed a cable from Bob Gilka, my picture editor, soon to become one of the most famous directors of photography in American photojournalism. "EDITOR REMINDS YOU TO EMPHASIZE GEOGRAPHY STOP ROME COVERAGE SURPRISINGLY GOOD STOP."

The next day, Thursday, December 10, Eisenhower planted a magnolia tree at Gandhi's grave and spoke to the Indian Parliament about India's role in world affairs. The day was capped by the official state banquet at Rashtrapati Bhavan, the presidential mansion—an event filed away under the category "life's more embarrassing moments."

The press corps showed little interest because everyone knew that nothing of significance would come of a ceremony dominated by endless toasts. But I grabbed the pool slot; I hoped the pomp and glitter rolled out for Eisenhower would symbolize India's welcome to the American president.

The banquet, in a long, formal dining room, was lit by massive chandeliers and carpeted with an exquisite Indian rug. Crystal goblets sparkled. I was permitted to photograph—no flash, please—the moment when, with great flourish, Presidents Eisenhower and Rajendra Prasad, the Indian head of state, Prime Minister Nehru, and the John Eisenhowers and their retinues entered into the room. Once the army of red-jacketed, white-turbaned waiters began serving, no further photography was allowed until the banquet was over. I was to sit quietly in a corner for two or three hours.

My day had been long and fatiguing. The banquet, tedious. I must have dozed off during the dessert service, because the next thing I registered was the loud clang of a lens that had rolled off my lap and hit the marble floor. To my horror it rolled relentlessly toward the head table. Shaking off my stupor, I struggled to my feet and in front of some 40 turbaned waiters, not to mention some of the free world's leaders, staggered over to retrieve it. I prayed Jim Hagerty hadn't witnessed that mortifying moment.

The next day, my best opportunity came when Ike was awarded an honorary doctor of laws at Delhi University. I was hoping instead to capture an image of him with Prime Minister Nehru in an offhand but telling moment.

Faculty members and guests paraded past in their academic regalia. Nehru in a gown of red and yellow silk, Eisenhower in red and blue. A mortarboard capped the president's head. Because I was stationed too far away from where they sat beneath a pavilion, it was a "long lens" day for me. I glumly put the 135mm on the Leica.

Because the dais was crowded, Nehru and Eisenhower were sitting so close together that I could fit both of them into the viewfinder. If I could capture them in the same frame wearing meaningful expressions, I'd have a dynamite photograph.

Studying the situation through the viewfinder, I decided to produce an image that symbolized the two leaders' personalities: Nehru, the shrewd and enigmatic politician, would play opposite classic Eisenhower, grinning from ear to ear. My two unwitting actors did not disappoint me—except for one problem. The tassel hanging off Ike's mortarboard kept obscuring his eyes. Patience. Patience. The tassel remained defiant. The upside: Ike was all grin. That spoke volumes.

I still needed my lead picture. Our remaining stops—Tehran, Athens, Tunis, Paris, Madrid, and Casablanca—would be too brief to offer much hope.

That Saturday morning we drove to Agra to fulfill the rumored inspiration for this journey: Ike's desire to see the Taj Mahal, the fabled "mausoleum of love" constructed by Shah Jahan for a favorite wife whom death had claimed so early in life. It was my first sight of it too. I remember how it seemed to float in space, how immaculate it looked, despite the brown dust of Agra, and how it dazzled, offset by the blue waters of the Yamuna River.

This most photogenic of palaces was a photographic bust. The press corps was roped into one corral, forced to take the same trite picture of Eisenhower, Nehru, Barbara, and John in front of that shining marble backdrop. No lead picture there.

Leaving the Taj Mahal's main gate, our motorcade entered the sprawling outskirts of Agra, where blocks of mud hovels teeming with destitute people. Those indelible images of poverty remain with me today, and I suspect affected Eisenhower as well.

Back in New Delhi, we had one final event. Over a million people waited in the scorching sun on the sprawling Ramlila Maidan to hear the American president. Werner Wolff of the Black Star photo agency had drawn the pool position, so the rest of us enviously watched him set up his tripod on the back of the stage in just the right spot, where a wide-angle lens could silhouette Eisenhower speaking to a throng of humanity—the perfect image of the United States reassuring India.

I was confined to a roped-off bullpen below the podium. It was colorful enough, but that sea of humanity huddled on ground level was terrible for a crowd picture. In desperation, I abandoned the crowd scene, concentrating on long-lens portraits. But nothing satisfactory materialized. "Another long-lens day," I sighed.

Then I saw her.

I'm not sure what attracted my notice, but as I focused on her face, the viewfinder images converged to reveal an ordinary-looking Indian woman, middle-age, bespectacled, a shawl drawn around her head, and a tiny U.S. flag in her hand. Nothing more. I scanned the crowd again. And snapped back. Something was there, but I couldn't put my finger on it. Watching through the viewfinder, I saw her gaze grow more intent as she cupped a hand to her ear.

That cupping of hand to ear embodied the act of listening. I could hardly breathe. Don't focus on Eisenhower; focus on the people reacting to his presence. Here she was, listening as Ike promised that her nation's starving masses would be fed, that the United States would provide India with aid, and that "as you prosper, the whole free world will prosper." Hers was the telling image; it was not about the president addressing a vast crowd but rather about how a single Indian woman, her American flag in hand a token of trust, was receiving Eisenhower's message.

If she would only stop waving it! The flag obscured her face every time I pressed the shutter release. But whenever she stopped waving the flag, she wasn't cupping her ear. I needed all three elements—flag, face, cupped hand on ear—for the picture to work.

I rechecked my light meter and camera settings, refocused, bracketed my exposures, moved a little closer, slid a bit to my right. Occasionally I scanned the crowd in order not to betray my intentions. "Dear Lord," I thought, "don't let me mess this up." Then—just as I brought her back into focus, I saw her quit waving the flag but still cupping her ear. Perfect! I pressed the shutter.

Nearly 60 years later that image still glows in my memory. The next thing I remember is her gaze meeting mine through the viewfinder. She had spotted me—and broken the spell.

Did I capture the "moment of truth"? In the days before digital, you could never be sure, sometimes for months, until you saw the transparency from film that had been processed thousands of miles away. I hoped that I had not only the lead picture for the story but also the single best photograph of my assignment. I didn't anticipate it would become the most pivotal photograph of my career.

We left New Delhi before dawn on December 14 and raced the rising sun northwestward to Tehran.

BEFORE HIS OVERTHROW IN 1979, Shah Mohammed Reza Pahlavi ruled Iran as one of America's closest allies, a magnet pulling in thousands of American diplomats, oilmen, and military personnel. Yet throughout our four-hour flight, discussion on the press plane was not focused on geopolitics but on the beautiful Farah Diba, who would soon marry the shah. I had a 10-rupee bet with my friend Paul Schutzer, a photographer for *Life*, that I would gaze on her face and bring back a Polaroid to prove it—for I had snagged the pool spot to photograph Ike's visit to the royal palace.

Before leaving Washington, Franc Shor, friend to Eastern potentates, suggested I try for the pool position, should Ike be formally welcomed in the Golestan Palace, the shah's official palace in Tehran. Being from the *Geographic* might confer special access. "Mention my name," Shor had said. "I think he'll remember me." That probably meant that they had gone carousing together during the shah's freewheeling bachelorhood.

Although I was still worried about dropping that lens at the New Delhi banquet, Hagerty hadn't noticed or didn't care, because he penciled me in for the palace slot.

The shah met us at the airport surrounded by phalanxes of soldiers and saluted us with flying formations of military aircraft. Some 750,000 people lined the motorcade route, standing beneath U.S. and Iranian banners waving in the cool, stiff breeze. The road into the city was practically paved with Persian carpets laid end to end, backdropped by the Elburz Mountains against a cloudless blue sky.

I stepped across the threshold of—not the Golestan—but the smaller, more intimate Marble Palace, recalling the famous, if slightly disorienting, reception room called the Hall of Mirrors. When the shah stepped forward to make the official welcome and present a Persian carpet and mosaic table to the U.S. president, I had my only look at the king of kings. Despite an aquiline profile that might have adorned an ancient Persian coin, he was surprisingly short and undistinguished-looking. Perhaps his countenance would have improved with Farah Diba on his arm, but on that day she was nowhere to be seen.

The heads of state sat down to partridge, steak, and Caspian caviar, and I was herded out of the palace.

That night I paid Paul my 10 rupees. President Eisenhower had been the only American to lay eyes on the ravishing Farah Diba.

IT HAD BEEN ONE LONG DAY. Up before dawn, we had seen the lights of Delhi fall away beneath us. Long after dark we glimpsed the floodlit Parthenon as we descended into Athens—3,100 miles altogether, spanning in little more than a dozen hours the entire empire of Alexander the Great.

I was exhausted, and the fall in Karachi had aggravated an old back injury. While Eisenhower was greeted by King Paul and Crown Prince

Constantine and whisked off to the Royal Palace to meet Queen Frederica, I retired to the nearby King's Palace Hotel and a hot soak.

As I relaxed in that scalding but soothing water, I did what I did every night: dictate my notes into my portable tape recorder, an expensive toy in those days and not nearly as portable as those now. Nearly submerged, with only enough space to balance the recorder on my chest, I did more than catch up on my notes. I caught up on my sleep, because the next thing I heard was *ker-plop* as the machine slid off my chest into the bathwater.

Damn! I jumped up, hurriedly extracted the reel of tape and, stark naked, dried it with the hotel hairdryer before unwinding it and draping it around my room. But the machine was ruined. Something else to explain back at the office.

The following morning President Eisenhower met with King Paul and Prime Minister Konstantinos Karamanlis, then addressed Parliament. Greece had joined NATO in 1952. Then we left—but not by jet. Ike and John and Barbara boarded the cruiser U.S.S. *Des Moines.* He would have two days' rest away from us while he steamed for Tunis. We followed on the aircraft carrier U.S.S. *Essex.* I was asleep by the time we left the Aegean and would sleep most of those two days.

We headed for Tunisia, then Morocco, because both had been independent from France for only three years and no one wanted them to follow the path of Algeria—then in a bloody war with France—or emulate Nasser's Egypt and embrace the Soviet Union.

In Tunis I heard for the first time the haunting ululating wail of welcome of North African women. I swallowed my disappointment at being so near the ruins of ancient Carthage with no chance to see them. Instead I photographed our president speaking with Tunisian president Habib Bourguiba, who presented him with a Persian Arabian gelding and gold-trimmed Moroccan saddle.

In Paris I received another cable from Bob Gilka. He now had the film through Tehran. "YOU ARE MAKING MY TASK TOUGH BY SHOOTING SO MANY EXCELLENT PICTURES DON'T STOP . . ." I eased into my bath that night with a sense of relief.

Madrid remains a rain-swept blur. I recall the huge arches, festooned with gigantic portraits of President Eisenhower and Generalissimo Franco. Supersize flags and more portraits were draped over the facades of all the main buildings. The dictator had all the Madrileños turning out. He had posted thousands of tough-looking soldiers; when they told us to stay in the trucks, we stayed in the trucks.

On December 22 we visited Casablanca for a few hours. Ike met with King Mohammed V, discussed the Algerian situation, and agreed on a date for withdrawing the Strategic Air Command bases still there.

Then we climbed aboard the jets for the final leg home.

TODAY NO CROWDS WOULD GREET a president returning to the White House from a tour abroad like those that welcomed President Eisenhower that night at Lafayette Park. The national Christmas tree flickered while the president reiterated that the purpose of his trip was to spread the gospel of "peace with justice" for all mankind.

Back home, my first call went to a neurosurgeon, then my dentist. I was barely convalescing when I plunged into the hectic process of preparing a picture layout for the editor's approval. Text would follow later.

Scheduled for May 1960, the 64-page package was already late to the engraver. My portrait of Ike and Nehru at Delhi University made the cover. When Nehru came to Washington on a state visit, I presented him with an enlarged print. In turn, he and President Eisenhower autographed one for me. The flag-waving Indian woman was the article's lead picture, providing the unspoken conclusion to the title, "When the President Goes Abroad"—the world listens! My picture of Ike and the

Khyber Pass didn't make the cut. No one could make out what he was looking at.

No other article of mine generated the torrent of mail that this one did. Although it won first place in the Pictures of the Year competition for, ironically, Best News Coverage, the recognition I prize most was a brief note.

"I am of course gratified by the coverage given to my good-will trip to Europe, Asia, and Africa, and I congratulate you on the excellence of the photographs," the president wrote. "I hope you enjoyed the trip as much as your comments indicate!"

CHAPTER EIGHT

YOUNG MAN IN A HURRY

The Eisenhower feature was rushed into production while I was healing from back surgery. I'd published three other stories—beginning with my first, on Holland—but Yugoslavia, my most ambitious effort, was hanging fire and might die an ignominious death if I neglected it.

I thought about my colleagues on the third floor. I'd become close to Bill Garrett and his wife, Lucy. We worked side by side during the weekday and socialized on weekends. We built prams—small boats like I had at Gibson Island—during the weeknights. When Tom Abercrombie wasn't on assignment, I'd hang out with him and his wife, Lynn, as well.

I'd met another man around this time who would also become a lifelong friend: Barry Bishop, an Air Force aide to Admiral Byrd in Antarctica and a capable young photographer with a mountaineering background who was invited on staff after his discharge. Sir Edmund Hillary, conqueror of Everest, had asked Barry to join him in a high-altitude study in the Himalaya. By the time my Eisenhower story was being sent to members, MBG had given him a leave of absence to do so.

Dad made changes at the Geographic almost daily. Along with the pictures adorning the cover, there were modern layouts, more white space, and improved photography. MBG had successfully diversified: In addition to the atlas and new globe near completion, his Book Service was thriving. Within a year he'd hire a former producer of NBC's *Huntley-Brinkley Report*. Robert C. Doyle would set up a television department with one employee—himself.

So why, surrounded by all this excitement, was I being seconded to the business department for 18 months?

Thomas McKnew, its chief, explained. "While your father has done a fantastic job with the magazine," he told me point-blank, "he never had business experience, and I believe that was unfortunate."

McKnew had a hawklike gaze that could pin you to the chair. He was all polish, from gleaming eyeglasses to shoes buffed to a high sheen. Nothing was out of place on his desk, in his office, or anywhere in his life. He had served in the Navy during World War I and was deeply embedded in the nation's naval and aviation establishment. He had been the whiz kid for the George A. Fuller Company, one of the country's leading contractors, and had supervised construction of Washington's National Cathedral. After he did the same for the Society's 16th Street headquarters, GHG lured him away from Fuller.

McKnew had probably made enough money by the time he was 36 that he could afford to come to the Geographic. His first project was working with construction firms, as well as scientific and governmental agencies, to coordinate the National Geographic Society–U.S. Army Air Corps Stratosphere Balloon Project of 1934–35. He pulled it off without a hitch, and on November 11, 1935, the *Explorer II* balloon ascended nearly 14 miles above Earth's surface, paving the way to the space age.

As executive vice president and secretary, McKnew was in charge of the Society's business affairs; his judgment was unimpeachable. He had mapped out the equivalent of a master's degree program in the economics of magazine publishing for a class of one: me.

"Your name and heritage might attract people's notice and lift you up the management ladder," he said candidly. "But you'll be watched very closely, and you'll have to be better at what you do than anyone else. You'll have to make very good decisions, and that's what I intend to teach you."

Although stern, he was indulgent with me because he was a family friend; he and his wife, Virginia, never had children of their own. He was always a force to be reckoned with: If you left out the "Doctor" when addressing him, though it was an honorary degree, that basilisk eye would nail you on the spot.

"As you well know, I enjoy working with MBG, but clearly we have different styles and different leadership philosophies," he observed. "What I say to you here stays within this office and won't be repeated in his. Agreed?"

I nodded solemnly. My apprenticeship in the business side of publishing began.

FOR THE NEXT 18 MONTHS my desk was situated just outside Dr. McKnew's office. The business department was very different from editorial. Business was more tightly controlled—not only by Dr. McKnew but also by his chief lieutenant, Melvin M. Payne.

Mel Payne was about 50. The son of a railroad conductor who had died young, Mel was raised by his aunt and uncle. He was a self-made man who worked by day, attended law school by night, and came to the Society as Dr. McKnew's assistant a few years before the stratosphere balloon launch. A conservative in-house legal counsel, he was one of the most effective leaders the Society ever had. He also bore a sizable chip on his shoulder. Of all the metaphorical silver spoons hurled at me over the years for my name and lineage, he lobbed the vast majority.

Payne and Dr. McKnew shared an antipathy toward editorial's freewheeling ways. They particularly targeted Franc Shor, caring nothing for his editorial brilliance. They despised his boozing and womanizing, which increased after Jean finally divorced him in 1959.

I wasn't at that desk outside Dr. McKnew's office much. Because my apprenticeship included shifting from one division to another, I was often elsewhere: in accounting, printing, purchasing, promotion—even the cafeteria and the carpenter's shop. But those months I sat at the master's feet were invaluable.

The first principle of business is obvious but often ignored: Total income must exceed total expenses. Back then, the Geographic income came overwhelmingly from membership dues; some (but less so) from advertising. Expenditures flowed into the "Six Ps" of publishing: printing, paper, postage, promotion, payroll, and plant operation.

Sustainable circulation is the heartbeat of a magazine, Dr. McKnew stressed, emphasizing the word "sustainable." Properly managed, it provides financial stability and the funding to create a superior editorial product. Every magazine had its own peculiar heartbeat, or circulation—its own "sweet spot"—above which or below which it might run into trouble. The formula was simple: Revenue generated from a unit of circulation must exceed the cost of obtaining it, the cost of servicing it, and the cost of producing the magazine, including all editorial expenses. "Never, ever, allow your ego to drive circulation," he warned.

At the Geographic, the sweet spot had long hovered around two million members—a figure constrained by the capacity of our Washington printer, Judd and Detwiler. I spent four weeks in that plant; the sheet-fed presses devoted to printing the Geographic couldn't handle more than two and a half million copies a month. They were already clattering away 24 hours a day. It was high-quality printing, but MBG wanted to increase membership and product diversity, particularly with atlases and books.

That led to the daring decision in 1957 to migrate printing from Judd and Detwiler to the R. R. Donnelley Company in Chicago, the largest commercial printer in the country and printer of *Time, Life,* and the *Encyclopedia Britannica.* Donnelley's new high-speed letterpresses offered a quantum leap in capacity, allowing for an almost limitless circulation and substantial savings while maintaining quality. McKnew and MBG took a tremendous risk making the switch.

So many subtleties like ink quality, paper weight, and thickness are vital to a magazine's appearance, yet frequently they are the first place publishers choose to economize. When we switched to Donnelley, we rid ourselves of a paper mill that couldn't produce the coated roll paper we required and that we never should have bought. Dr. McKnew unloaded it on the Oxford Paper Company and struck a deal for roll paper in return. During negotiations, he told MBG to "keep quiet." Dad would invariably get squirmy and jump at the first offer. Predictably, he started shifting around and fooling with his hair. McKnew gave him a covert glare. Soon MBG excused himself and left, allowing Dr. McKnew to negotiate a much more favorable deal.

MBG did win one victory. Late one afternoon I poked my head in his office. He looked at his calendar and saw he was to meet Dr. McKnew the next day. "What's this about?" he asked.

"Something about the budget," I mumbled, having been filled in by my business tutor. The next day when McKnew entered MBG's office, MBG looked up and boomed, "So what's this about the budget?" McKnew turned toward me with an icy stare. I almost crawled under the Persian carpet—I seemed to have forgotten my pledge not to mention business with Dad.

"We have a little shortfall this year," McKnew said. "We'll have to cut expenses and staff."

MBG sat there, blinked, and suggested, "Why not increase revenue instead?" Then after a moment, he continued: "We could rush into print a U.S. atlas for Christmas." He already had the atlas plates for the United States—the first part of the big world atlas project—in hand.

MBG called the atlas staff to his office. "We have a revenue shortfall this year," he began solemnly. "We must publish a U.S. atlas to raise revenue. I apologize for lost vacations and postponed assignments, but I refuse to cut staff or services. Division chiefs will be sensitive to family issues. I have instructed Personnel to be generous about any family problems this causes. Lastly, I thank each and every one of you for your sacrifice and understanding. I'll make it up to everyone—some way."

He had laid it out honestly and with profound emotion. It was the perfect example of the Geographic family spirit, and I was proud of him.

The atlas was finished and delivered by Christmas. Members gobbled up 242,000 copies. Problem solved. Lesson learned? Whenever possible, increase revenue rather than cut staff or services.

I quickly learned that the renewal rate was the key to the *National Geographic* sweet spot. Content and editorial again: If a member liked the magazine, they renewed; if not, they were gone. Each month's issue and each year's run should exhibit an appealing, balanced mix of articles. Paper, printing, and reproduction in each issue should be second to none.

I didn't need a business apprenticeship to learn that. For years I had been flipping through GHG's bound volumes in his office. I couldn't help noticing that the quality of the printing and paper in the 1920s looked as fresh and bright as last month's issue. I remarked on that to him once. He gave me that knowing smile, then changed the topic.

"Gibby?" he asked, using my old family nickname. "You're pushing 30 now, aren't you?"

I admitted as much.

That little smile again. "It's about time a man of your age settled down with a wife. I tell you what, the day you get married, I'll give you my personal bound volumes as a wedding gift."

Believing that milestone was still a few years into the future, we both shared a little laugh.

My tutorial had revealed that success boiled down to attracting and keeping each member. That meant that one of the most important stops in my business apprenticeship was the fulfillment and membership relations offices near Union Station, where magazines were mailed out, remittances processed, and member queries addressed. Every employee stressed mission and the importance of membership; there were no "subscribers" or "eyeballs." We treated members with dignity; they responded with renewals. Loyalty to the institution was paramount to our success.

One day near the end of 1960, I was sent to the section of member correspondence that dealt with our foreign membership. Older ladies, its usual tenants, quietly typed answers to queries. An attractive young woman sat at one desk; I maneuvered my way over to a seat near her. She and her counterparts had each been assigned 10,000 foreign members to take care of. This woman—friendly, vivacious, outgoing—seemingly knew each of her coterie on a personal basis. She was even helping one Spanish couple with their daughter's wedding plans.

Donna Kerkam, a recent graduate of Sweet Briar College, had been working here for six months, her first job out of school. I smiled at her. She smiled back. Dr. La Gorce's long-ago warning about dipping my pen in the company inkwell? Filed away and forgotten. We started dating—on the sly, of course.

FEBRUARY 24, 1961, was a de facto Louis Leakey Day at headquarters, and marked my first meeting with the charismatic paleoanthropologist. In the morning he was the star of a press conference in our auditorium. He showcased his newest fossil from Olduvai Gorge, a juvenile even older than *Zinjanthropus*, the July 1959 find that had launched him into the headlines. The fractured skull had apparently resulted from a heavy blow—a case of "murder most foul," Louis, always the showman, told the audience. That afternoon and evening he delivered two sold-out lectures in Constitution Hall. As chairman of the Lecture Committee, I was his minder.

After the morning press conference, the committee granted Leakey an immense sum of money and also agreed to cover his salary for three years. This generosity was prompted by the redating of "Dear Boy," as *Zinjanthropus,* their July 1959 find was affectionately known, from a mere 600,000 years to 1.75 million years ago. Its discovery had blown the field of paleo-anthropology wide open. Louis's first *Geographic* story, "Finding the World's Earliest Man," published in September 1960, was a smash hit.

That day, another event occurred that would change the course of Geographic history. Leakey pulled aside Dr. Leonard Carmichael, secretary of the Smithsonian Institution and chairman of our Research Committee, to mention a small side project of his. He explained that his research assistant was doing a study on chimpanzee behavior at the Gombe Stream Game Reserve on Lake Tanganyika. Because of open parkland in the forest, the chimpanzees could be studied from a safe distance. Leakey thought that knowledge of chimpanzee habits might shed light on the behavior of early Miocene-era primates whose fossils he had recovered.

That, as far as I know, was the first mention of Jane Goodall in our headquarters.

I suspect Leakey had already dropped a hint to MBG that a photogenic young woman surrounded by wild chimpanzees might make promising material for *National Geographic.* Scarcely had the board approved Leakey's enormous grant—$28,000 with $1,400 thrown in for the Chimpanzee Research Project—than MBG began arranging photographic coverage. Ultimately, he met resistance from Goodall herself, who had worked hard to habituate the chimpanzees to her presence and knew they were not ready to accept a male *Homo sapiens.* MBG had to be content with Goodall's sister, an amateur photographer.

Then there was another bump in the road. At its December meeting, the Research Committee balked at a request: Louis wanted a mere £400 to cover Goodall's living expenses while she wrote up her first year's observations of wild chimpanzees during her residence at Cambridge University.

Skeptics on the committee were concerned that Goodall was an unknown factor—a former Coryndon Museum employee possibly not trained for potentially dangerous field observation. Since Leakey was the first grantee they had ever reimbursed for living expenses, they were worried about the financial consequences of establishing it as a precedent.

Today I'm glad none of us knew that Jane Goodall didn't have so much as an undergraduate degree, or that it was Leakey's hunch that women might prove more empathetic observers of animals than men were. And we certainly didn't know that Louis had in his back pocket, along with the string tricks and bits of fossils for charming children and donors, a bit of secret knowledge.

MBG sat on the other side of the table. His enthusiasm usually swept the field; it was notably checked. I knew he was waiting for pictures of Goodall surrounded by chimps to arrive. He threw up his hands and said, "Then I'll pay for [her expenses] out of the magazine budget!"

Dr. Carmichael, sensing discord, suggested that we table this one until Dr. Leakey submitted a detailed report on the chimpanzee project. Meeting adjourned.

A few days later, the rolls of film from Gombe arrived. After one look at the underexposed images, MBG declared them "not suitable for reproduction," and the coverage was killed.

Then Dr. Leakey reached into his back pocket and retrieved that bit of secret knowledge. He submitted a report—"highly confidential"—laying out a series of unprecedented observations.

Herbivorous chimpanzees had been observed eating flesh. They had also been seen performing ritualized "rain dances." Above all, chimpanzees had been seen fashioning tools, a "discovery of the very highest scientific importance," Leakey said, since toolmaking was then thought to be an exclusively human trait.

We promptly dispatched £400 for her expenses, and MBG was back in stride. Goodall's observations would "make a fabulous story for our magazine and we must make every effort to get it."

IN MARCH 1961, the first models of the National Geographic globe with the plastic "geometer" capping it rolled off the Replogle Company's assembly lines. "Boys," MBG said, summoning us to his office when they arrived. "This is great! Look at all you can do with this geometer. It's even unbreakable!" Demonstrating, he dropped it onto the wooden floor. It fractured into a hundred pieces. The look on his face had some of us quickly turning aside to suppress smiles. When MBG presented President John F. Kennedy with a pair of globes, the same thing happened.

Dad dialed up Luther Replogle, chairman of the globe company and an old Naval Academy friend of his; together they improved the plastic. The original 50,000-globe order was upped to 75,000. By Easter Sunday it reached—well, I wouldn't have known or cared, for I was falling in love with Donna Kerkam. The two of us were strolling hand in hand over the grounds of the National Cathedral that weekend when we were spotted by an associate in the business department. I confessed that Tuesday; she resigned on Wednesday.

It didn't bother us. We were already secretly engaged.

ONLY TWO HOURS MARRIED, and I was already hiding something from my bride. As I stripped off my white tie and tails and put on my traveling suit, I looked out the window of the small room on the second floor of the Columbia Country Club in Chevy Chase, Maryland, at the golf course bathed in the long June twilight.

Alec, my best man, had just slipped away to discharge his part of the secret mission we had planned. I crossed the hall and knocked on her door. When Donna opened it, dressed in a new pink outfit, she was simply gorgeous.

Our bags were already at the airport, tagged for Venice, Italy. We had only to run the gauntlet of guests waiting at the foot of the stairs and climb into a waiting limousine, which would whisk us to our hidden getaway car. I had let Donna in on only part of the secret. She was to follow me into the limousine, then slide across the seat after me and exit the limo by the opposite door. That getaway car, I had told her, was a decoy. We would be heading off another way. That was where I had not been totally candid.

Down the stairs we plunged and made our way through showers of rice to the limousine parked in the circle. The driver held open the door for us. I slid across the seat, barreled out the other side, took her hand, and started sprinting for the golf course. I could hear it now, the loud *whump-whump-whump* of the rotors that were already blowing my naval aviator brother's hair all over the place as he waved in the helicopter by hand signals. The craft had hardly touched the lawn when we jumped aboard and secured the door. Then we went up, circling the country club and waving down to our astonished friends and relatives, before peeling off for National Airport.

You just didn't do that back in 1961. I turned to my bride. She was beaming. She had gotten the message: This was not going to be an ordinary marriage. By stepping unhesitatingly into that helicopter, she had agreed to share a roving, adventurous life with me.

The more immediate promise was summer in Europe, part honeymoon and part work. The work part began when we flew to Dubrovnik to update my old Yugoslavia article, which had lain dormant since 1959.

Mate and Jane returned as my translator-guides, so neither of us must have been on too many blacklists. In the three weeks or so we needed to make additional pictures, I enjoyed showing my bride our old haunts and introducing her to old friends. Much of this second trip was mop-up work; she could help me with photographic set-ups and note taking. When she wondered why there were so few men between 40 and 60, I reminded her that World War II still left a deep impress on a country that saw more destruction than practically any other in Europe. She began to get the hang of seeing the world in depth.

AFTER DONNA AND I RETURNED from an assignment in Copenhagen that fall, I was back in my old office in the Illustrations Division—an office now filled with those bound volumes of the magazine from GHG's paneled walls. Gramp had kept his promise. I would cart those cherished volumes from office to office for the rest of my career.

I went downstairs to the second floor and called on Dr. McKnew. I was grateful for his mentoring; we would remain good friends for the rest of his life. When he died at the age of 96 in 1994, I would give the eulogy at his funeral—held, appropriately, in the National Cathedral.

When I returned to the magazine, I was the veritable young man in a hurry. I followed Dr. McKnew's advice and cultivated new friends in accounting; my old friends in editorial ribbed me for being a spreadsheet man. I hoped that would fade once I settled back into my old job and my new marriage.

IN LATE 1961 Bob Breeden was still the quiet one of the Missouri mafia who had arrived at the magazine as picture editors in the mid-1950s. In a world dominated by Bill Garrett, being quiet could mean being forgotten. One day MBG summoned Bob, fellow picture editor Donald J. Crump, and me to his office with a few other editors.

"Boys," he said. "I just spoke with someone from an organization called the White House Historical Association." Uh-oh, we thought. Somebody wanted something. It turned out to be the first lady.

No sooner had her husband been inaugurated than Jacqueline Bouvier Kennedy initiated her campaign to transform the White House from a museum of leftovers from past administrations into the living embodiment of American history.

She had been impressed by the *National Geographic* article "Inside the White House," published 10 months earlier. Might the Society help the newly formed association produce a guidebook to the Executive Mansion? Sales would help fund the restoration, avoiding the need for public money.

MBG looked at us, shrugging helplessly, as if to say, "Well, what else could I have done? It's the first lady!"

Of course we would be happy to prepare the new guidebook—pro bono. But when MBG told us that we needed to pony up a layout in three weeks—Mrs. Kennedy wanted the book out as soon as possible—we all looked at one another.

MBG, however, was looking straight at Bob Breeden.

Once again, my father's extraordinary sixth sense would prevail; Breeden would prove the perfect choice. He had only three weeks to produce a sample mock-up, something that would usually take at least six. Bob assembled a team of two: himself and Don Crump. Don resembled Bob in many ways: He was a big, rangy guy with a good eye for pictures and a personality even more taciturn than his colleague's.

The two men prepared to reckon with that elegant cynosure of every eye: Jacqueline Kennedy.

The challenge was to produce a 132-page book with text, illustrations, and sections on decorative arts and White House history in six months. White House curator Lorraine Waxman Pearce would write the text. Franc Shor would edit it. Illustrations and layouts were heaped on Breeden and Crump, who still had their day jobs.

They finished the book in less than the scheduled six months, in time for the book to go on sale by July 4, 1962. Mrs. Kennedy was delighted.

MBG was ecstatic. Before year's end, more than 500,000 copies would be sold.

WHILE BREEDEN WAS UNDERGOING his baptism by fire, Louis Leakey was back in Washington for another lecture in Constitution Hall. For a grand finale, MBG had proposed that Louis and his wife, Mary, be awarded the Hubbard Medal: the Society's highest honor.

I knew his motivation. The winds of uhuru—freedom!—were blasting a continent too long in thrall to colonialism. No one could predict whether colonial-era projects in places like Olduvai Gorge would be allowed to continue. Tanganyika had just achieved self-government, and Kenya was soon to follow. MBG wanted to steer enough money and attention to them as quickly as possible, should the doors close on Western scientists.

On March 22, 1962, Louis arrived in Washington. This time I met Mary Leakey and their oldest son, Jonathan, a noted herpetologist. Mary Leakey would be only the second woman to ever receive a Hubbard Medal, three decades after author and aviator Anne Morrow Lindbergh.

Hardly had they arrived before Louis announced yet another spectacular discovery: the fossil of a new humanlike creature named *Kenyapithecus wickeri,* roughly 14 million years old and uncovered at Fort Ternan in western Kenya.

Mary, who suffered from stage fright, never said a word. "This medal belongs not to two Leakeys but to five," Louis told our members after the presentation. "Whatever we have done, we have done together."

It was an ever extending franchise; only a few weeks after that ceremony, Jane Goodall first arrived stateside.

She spent only a few hours in Washington, because she was on the way to a conference, but visited the Society and the National Zoo and charmed everyone she met. Mary Griswold had met her in Nairobi the year before and—in a tale she liked to tell on herself—thought her "too frail." Goodall was indeed slender, but her eyes possessed a quiet confidence. She calmly met with the Research Committee before giving a succinct—and well attended—presentation on her work. Only four months had passed since her work had been tossed on the "kill" pile.

BY EARLY 1962 MBG was about halfway through his 10-year reign as president and editor. Times were good: A new globe and atlas were nearing completion, a new headquarters building was on the rise, an improved magazine was on new presses, and Society membership was heading toward three million. Everything was growing, flowering, branching.

In the office, Dad was loved for his unbridled enthusiasm and his instinctive, unerring editing. The questing, roving side of his personality, however, was best seen on the deck of a sailboat. You might call that his Homeric side. His favorite book, after all, was *The Odyssey*.

As he approached, then passed 60, I glimpsed that side of him more and more, the restless Odysseus wanting to return to the sea. He had sold his Star Class boat and, after his remarriage, commissioned a 33-foot sloop christened the *Lady Anne*—ideal for exploring the shallow coves and inlets of the Bras d'Or Lakes. But another decade was fast slipping over the transom.

Whenever I heard MBG's fingers drumming the tabletop in a tedious meeting and saw a faraway look come into his eyes, I knew sea fever had returned, and he was seeing in his mind's eye a map of the isles of Greece, the Caribbean, or Polynesia. He wanted to go down to the sea again—in a bigger boat.

One day in 1962, opportunity came knocking. Blunt White, a member of the New York Yacht Club who had spent the past 11 years racing across oceans in a 46-foot yawl named *White Mist,* had just died. Dad was soon on the phone to me. White's son, Bill, had been my fellow shipmate in the skeleton crew that had sailed *Yankee* across the Atlantic in 1947.

After the estate settled, we drove up to Mystic Shipyard in Connecticut, where *White Mist* rode at anchor. Twelve years old and thousands of miles of ocean behind her, and not a rivet had loosened. The engine, sails, rigging, galley, cabin, and berths all looked shipshape. Dad promptly bought her.

In the years to come, the Geographic's Odysseus couldn't help inviting every single member to vicariously join him on his blue-water cruises, each voyage spinning off a lengthy, always popular article. The magazine staff included many sailors, many skilled navigators among them, who became known as the National Geographic Society Yacht Squadron.

"Thank God MBG didn't take up fire walking," Franc Shor grumbled.

IN MAY 1962 Donna and I were driving the French corniche high above the principality of Monaco. I had been dispatched, as MBG put it in a letter to His Serene Highness Prince Rainier, "to make an extensive series of color photographs to illustrate our account of your country." The idea had been suggested by my brother, who, as aide to Admiral David McDonald—the commander of the U.S. Sixth Fleet, then head-quartered in nearby Villefranche-sur-Mer—had met Prince Rainier and Princess Grace at a birthday celebration for the royal family's children.

Far to the south jutted "the Rock," the promontory with the royal palace, government buildings, the old town, and the Oceanographic Museum, directed by our old friend Jacques-Yves Cousteau. Monte Carlo stretched out across the crowded harbor to the northeast. In between was a narrow, hilly zone dense with business and residential buildings. No translator was necessary. Donna spoke French.

In early June, everyone in the principality was hanging out windows, swarming sidewalks and balconies, and crowding the decks of boats in the harbor to watch Le Grand Prix, the celebrated event when Formula One race cars thunder around those cobbled streets, circling a two-mile course a hundred times.

At the southeasternmost curve—a tight corner known as Gasometer hairpin—I stood on the hay bales protecting a grandstand to photograph the start. Hardly had the lead cars approached the turn on their first lap when I saw through my range finder three cars speeding my way. Sure enough, as they neared, one car skidded into the others, spinning them all in circles and sending a wheel hurtling through the air straight at me.

Instinctively I threw myself to the side and watched, as if in slow motion, that tire fly right over the place where I had stood and smack into an elderly race marshal posted in front of the grandstand. I had spilled onto the pavement and damaged one of my lenses—but that man had been severely injured. An ambulance carted him away.

Donna was on the other side of the course but could see the pileup near the bales and knew that's where I was stationed. I departed the grandstand and navigated the crowded sidewalks, until I reached her and embraced her.

The elderly race marshal hit by the wheel died of his injuries. It had been one of the closest shaves of my career.

The harbor was never without interesting yachts. Onassis's *Christina* was frequently there. So was Cousteau's *Calypso*. Another morning I saw the unmistakable mahogany hull and tan mainsail of the yawl *Agneta* as she threaded the entrance: The international playboy and Fiat heir Giovanni Agnelli had arrived. That very evening, at the Monte Carlo Casino in the *salons privés,* we watched the debonair Agnelli play three roulette tables simultaneously. In just 15 minutes he walked off $25,000 richer—in 1962 dollars—tossing a chip worth $100 to each croupier as a tip.

The most memorable hour in Monaco, however, was the one we spent with Prince Rainier and Princess Grace and their delightful children.

In working out a schedule for our trip, Donna had become friends with Princess Grace's publicist. She met us in the courtyard alongside Georges

Lukomski, who was a palace photographer, an assistant press attaché, and, I suspect, the family bodyguard. He led us on a shortcut from the public and official side of the palace into the private quarters, a warren of rooms richly leafed in gold and hung with velvets. We followed him up and down musty staircases, passing what looked like a torpedo in the hall. Lukomski told us it was Rainier's one-man oceanographic research submarine.

The portrait of Princess Grace by fashion photographer Richard Avedon had just appeared on the cover of the April 1962 *Vogue,* increasing my apprehension. I had no photographic plan in mind, except to capture an informal image of the royal family.

We emerged into a sunlit garden, strewn with tricycles and toy trucks. Near the swimming pool, with its inflated swan and raft, stood a swing set. The owners of these toys could be heard, their piping voices floating above the tall shrubs. Soon the family came into view: Prince Rainier, followed by Princess Grace and the children. They were so engaging and informal that Donna forgot her well-practiced curtsy. Rainier effused a surprising dynamism; I had expected a man worn down by worries about the future. Princess Grace, even lovelier in person than in pictures, wore a stunning aquamarine dress adorned with a diamond brooch.

"Does your *Geographic* article include all the Riviera?" asked Princess Grace.

"No, Your Highness," I replied. "We're photographing only the principality of Monaco."

"That's wonderful!" the prince exclaimed. "I trust you're interested in seeing more than just the casino."

I assured him that we were.

Before we departed, we had a photo shoot. The garden setting emphasized the spontaneity and innocence of the children as they played with their parents. It was the perfect place to capture the extraordinary tranquility of Princess Grace's countenance.

Months later her publicist wrote saying that Princess Grace loved the result so much she hoped she could have some prints.

Long days, long nights, and when the assigned author fell through, Donna and I were tasked with writing the article too.

When Franc Shor caught wind that I was attempting to disentangle the expense account because the Geographic shouldn't pay for Donna, he intervened. After all, he said, she translated for you, kept notes, juggled schedules, and shared the writing. When Franc was married to Jean, he reminded me, they received a double byline. Readers loved stories by husband-and-wife teams.

When "Miniature Monaco" was published the following March, the byline read, "Article and photographs by Gilbert M. and Donna Kerkam Grosvenor." A wife and companion had become a colleague as well.

CHAPTER NINE

WHAT WE DID BEST

n the summer of 1963, on vacation in Beinn Bhreagh and anchored in a cove on *White Mist,* I brought up a bit of Society business. Under Dr. McKnew, I couldn't help noticing shocking invoices for overtime pay in the Printing and Engraving Division because of last-minute changes in layout and copy. I considered that a pointless waste of money and gave thought to improving the editorial process so that the stories we published could be better monitored at each stage from approval to release to the printer.

For a long time I kept quiet. I was already under suspicion for transmitting a budgeting virus from business to editorial—a virus that would supposedly destroy the creative spirit and straitjacket MBG. I never had any such intent and always gave primacy to editorial. But I did want to improve the process. Late picture and text layouts submitted for MBG's approval were the problem, and so to confront it, I envisioned a room not unlike NASA's Mission Control. The new headquarters building rising in the background gave me an opportunity.

On April 20, 1961, we had broken ground on the corner of 17th and M Streets for a 10-story addition to our headquarters. Its clean, modern look, designed by Edward Durrell Stone, was in stark contrast to the Italian Renaissance–style buildings on 16th Street. Dr. McKnew, returning to his roots as a construction supervisor, was in charge. He encouraged input from each employee. If I could secure a room on the magazine's executive floor, perhaps I could install a control center to plan future issues and coverage in an orderly manner. I should never have called it a control center—"control" sounded ominous, but the word was inescapable.

Even talking about a control center would be controversial, particularly from someone far down the chain of command. To get everyone on board required the support of MBG, or at least his acquiescence. I drummed my fingers for days until I devised a plan.

One evening while holed up in a snug Bras d'Or harbor, after carefully stirring our traditional "White Mist special" rum drink, I broached the subject. Dad didn't so much shoot it down as tune it out. That summer he did not want to talk business, and that was final.

I waited until we were back in Washington. One fall weekend I drove out to his home to make the pitch. The money-saving angle would not work, because the Society was growing and flush with cash, which it plowed back into research, exploration, and the bank. I had a trump card ready.

We sat in the den, and after some small talk, I got to the point.

"Dad, I want to talk again about that project I've been working on for several months," I said. "And I'm really excited about it." I went through my litany of concerns: blown schedules, late copy, overtime charges. Caption writers waiting three weeks for a picture layout pushes them behind schedule; they then must produce copy overnight. Stressed researchers—fact-checkers—at the backed-up end of the chain suffered most.

"Frequently, in projection sessions where you review layouts," I continued, "you will improve the coverage at hand by adding three or four pages because the pictures are so compelling. To stay within budget, we're forced to drop another short article because we've exceeded the issue's allotted 148 pages. We rush to make changes well after deadline. Or you'll rightly declare the pictures dull and toss the entire story out. Dad, we are incurring huge overtime costs!"

By this point MBG was tousling his hair, shifting in his seat, tapping his fingers. Finally, he threw up his hands, bolted from the chair, and shouted, "Stop! Stop! You must understand, son, I simply cannot create this magazine from some back office—as though I'm scheduling a haircut! There are too many things that must be considered!"

I had obviously reached him. I sat back and listened.

"Every issue must sing—or harmonize, like a symphony. The pace must change from story to story. A serious lead article should be followed by something light, perhaps a natural history piece, or a short human interest story." He was now pacing rapidly, gesticulating wildly.

"When the reader thumbs through an issue, the pictures must cry out: Stop. Scan the caption. Read the article. Be drawn into the story by sub-heads in the text. That's our job! Get 'em to read the story! I don't give a damn about story length or schedules as long as we keep drawing that reader into our magazine!"

He continued pacing back and forth, his face growing more flushed. "What really matters is that every issue sparkles. Has rhythm and pace—anything to capture and hold the reader. If I have to rip up every issue at the last minute to get us there—that's what matters!"

He paced some more. A hand flew into the air.

"I want that little old lady to slam down the magazine and say, 'By golly, that was interesting! That was fun!' Something for everybody, son, every month! Believe you me, members won't hesitate to tell us we failed! They won't renew. Everything on this planet is fair game for us. God help us if we produce a dull issue—even if the copy was on schedule."

I was quiet for a long while. "Dad, I've never heard it put better. I absolutely agree. I agree with every word you just said. Whatever it takes, whatever it costs, to make an issue sing—I'm with you! But I'm not talking about that. I'm talking about unnecessary costs further up the pipeline: costs due to disorganization." I saw that finger going for that lock of hair again and pulled out my trump card: "Let me give you just one example. Scrambling through just six months of bills, I found overtime expenses exceeded the cost of a map supplement. Dad! Think about it. Another map supplement!"

I watched that finger stop. If the way to a soldier's heart is through his stomach, then the way to MBG was charted on a map. The man adored them. He gave me a long look.

It was grudging support, but I would build a prototype. In the office, the response was predictable: irritation, vexation, exasperation. Above all, a threat to the creative spirit. "Dahlin'," said Mississippi-born Carolyn Patterson, in charge of the legend writers, "you can't confine MBG to a scheduling room! Mess with his style and you'll kill the genius!" She led the charge to dismantle the idea.

I persisted. Knowing the status of text, photographs, artwork, and maps at any given time for any given issue made sense. It would improve, not stifle, the magazine.

With the help of the carpentry shop, I covered three sides of a room on the ninth floor of the new building with metal panels. Then I took aluminum channel stock and adhered it with long magnetic strips, grooved so that you could easily slide in pieces of card stock and move them around. On the card stock was the information—say, "Salmon 052163," for an upcoming story on North American salmon. Information like the issue date, text, illustrations, and page map, along with the production status— progress, potential delays, or special events—were noted. Eventually we added a panel representing pending stories in different subject areas like archaeology and natural history, as well as one for locations: Europe, Asia, Africa, and the oceans.

Once finished, the Control Center featured about three years' worth of approved stories—some 200 titles in all. It quickly became the hub of magazine production and scheduling. Soon all major editorial meetings were held in the Control Center too. MBG realized that this innovation had given him more flexibility, not less.

It was a lot of work to devise and implement—and I still had a job in Illustrations. I took myself off any photographic assignments until the new Control Center had its own director.

And I still had some vacation leave, which Donna and I intended to use.

AS AN EARLY RISER, I was usually up long before breakfast—and well before the command "Saddle up, guys! We're moving out!" rang over the meadows and peaks of Jasper National Park. Outfitter Jim Simpson already had his team tightening the diamond hitches on the 21 horses, including pack animals that carried food, duffel bags, tents, stoves, and panniers for Donna, me, and a group of close friends. Every time I swung into my saddle, another workload fell away. Nothing like a pack trip in the Canadian Rockies for leaving the Control Center and office politics far, far behind.

At times we rode through groves of tall spruce; at times it was golden grass spangled with red poppies. We seldom glimpsed the teeming wildlife I had expected, but that mattered little in Jasper, one of the most majestic places I've ever seen.

One afternoon, after dismounting at a designated campsite, a Parks Canada ranger rode into our midst. "Hello!" was his cheery greeting. "I hear there's a man from National Geographic here!"

Everyone naturally looked my way.

I beamed with angelic innocence, shrugged my shoulders, and looked away, as if to say, "He went thataway." I could practically hear the jaws dropping around me.

The ranger looked crestfallen. He glanced around and then said, "Well, we just wanted to welcome him to Jasper National Park. If we can do anything for you, please let us know." Then he trotted out of sight.

I grinned, and that broke the ice. Everyone had a good laugh. Well, damn! I told myself. I have every right to a great vacation too!

How could it not be a great vacation surrounded by the grandeur of mountains and valleys with such evocative names as the Starlight Range? Whenever we came upon spectacular views—which at Jasper happens at every bend in the trail—one of our gang would adopt his stagiest voice and boom, "He went thataway!" I laughed as heartily as anyone.

I would have been content if that pack trip never ended. But the day came when Jim Simpson and his crew had loosened the last diamond hitch. I carried two things home that I retain to this day. One, that assembly call—"Saddle up, guys! We're moving out!"—became our family summons whenever we had to get the kids into the car. The other was more reproachful.

Even before we had returned home, a small voice whispered: You shouldn't have done that. The ranger was only doing his job. And I wasn't doing mine. I am always on duty whenever the National Geographic Society is involved—especially in a national park.

MBG LIKED TO SAY THAT he had grown up with the national parks, having been present at the true creation of the Park Service. He had been cabin boy on *Elsie,* a yawl skippered by his father and crewed by a Society trustee, Franklin K. Lane, soon to become U.S. secretary of the interior and in charge of parks. Holed up for two days in a cove to shelter from a storm in 1912 on the Bras d'Or Lakes, the two men talked about the need to administer and protect the few parks we then had in existence.

He was proud to have personally known every director of the Park Service from Stephen Mather to Conrad Wirth. It was with Connie, as we called him, that MBG went to Northern California to survey the extensive damage caused by a 1955 flood that had felled 300 giant coast redwood trees in Humboldt Redwoods State Park. Torrential rains had so saturated the soil in the immense clear-cuts surrounding the park that mudslides slipped unimpeded down the slopes and smashed the groves. That happened all through the Redwood Empire, the 500-mile-long, 20-mile-wide belt of giant trees stretching from San Francisco to Oregon.

My father returned from that trip a changed man. He had inherited GHG's seat on the board of the Save the Redwoods League, which over the years had preserved some of the finest remaining stands in a patchwork of state parks, including Humboldt. But protection of a much larger area was needed. Visionaries were already talking about creating a national park in what remained of the Redwood Empire.

GHG had enlisted the National Geographic Society in saving the giant sequoias in the Sierra Nevada. MBG followed suit in protecting the soaring redwoods along that breathtaking coast.

By the early 1960s momentum was building for a park. Stewart Udall, then secretary of the interior, was behind it. So was the Save the Redwoods League, the Sierra Club, and the National Geographic Society. The timber companies that owned most of the remaining groves opposed it.

As usual, MBG glimpsed possibility. He always thought big. Standing beneath those awe-inspiring redwoods, he must have concluded that the best way to promote the idea of a national park to our members was to find the tallest tree in the world.

In 1963 Connie Wirth secured a $64,000 research committee grant allowing the Park Service to make a study of the coastal redwoods—and to find the best place to locate a park. MBG and Connie went there immediately. In Rockefeller Forest in Humboldt State Park, they looked up at a 356.5-foot-tall tree, reputedly the tallest in the world, and Dad casually asked, "Could there be others even taller?"

"Perhaps," someone replied. "We just don't know what may be hidden in the valleys to the north and east."

MBG already had his agent in place: senior staff naturalist Paul Zahl. Paul had been on the Research Committee and was familiar with the Park Service grant. He'd know exactly how to find that tree. "Keep your eyes open," Dad told him. "It would be wonderful to find a record breaker."

It was no surprise to MBG when his telephone rang. "I think I've found the world's tallest tree," Paul told him.

Dad took the next flight out.

They bushwhacked to the site—a grove of redwoods soaring high above a creek bend. The winning tree measured 367.8 feet above the ground. Dad stood on a gravel bar in the creek beneath it and had his picture taken from far away. He splashed that image of a tiny figure standing beneath a stupendous tree on the cover of the July 1964 *National Geographic*. The title had his fingerprints all over it: "Finding the Mount Everest of All Living Things."

Spotlighting that tree worked. The grove, owned by a timber company, was preserved by the company's boss. It also marked a big step to forming a national park. "It's what we do best," Dad told me. "It's what we do best."

ON JANUARY 13, 1963, we celebrated the 75th birthday of the National Geographic Society, kicking off a year of celebrations. But the real gift to our membership came that July: After nearly seven years of labor by 39 cartographers, the first *National Geographic Atlas of the World* was published, and it sold 130,000 copies over the next few years.

My grandfather was more than pleased, and he was proud of his son's achievements—which, in addition to the atlas and everything else, included the new building rising on the corner of 17th and M Streets.

That 10-story building wasn't the only symbolic peak of that celebratory year. On May 22, 1963, Barry Bishop became perhaps the 12th human to reach the summit of Mount Everest. The Society-sponsored American Mount Everest expedition put eight men there, a new mountaineering record—but at a cost. Forced to overnight on the icy slopes, Barry was severely frostbitten; all his toes and the tips of his little fingers were amputated in a New Delhi hospital. Because he had planted the National Geographic flag at the top of the world, Barry came home a hero. Visiting him and his wife, Lila, at their house, his bandaged feet propped up on cushions, we joked about his lifetime sinecure at the Society. But I worried about his future. He was a good, not great photographer, so had limited prospects at the magazine. I pushed him toward Leonard Carmichael's expanding Research Committee, where Barry soon became the secretary. He also went back to school and earned a Ph.D. in geography. Later, Barry would impact my own career as well.

Amid all this, the Research Committee's latest protégée was appearing in the magazine. Like everyone else at headquarters, I watched Jane Goodall at work primarily through the lens of the Nairobi-based wildlife photographer whom we persuaded her to accept at the Gombe Game Reserve: a Dutch nobleman, Hugo van Lawick. Bent over a light table, we'd study 35mm slides of Jane in khaki sitting in the glades at Gombe, armed with notebook and binoculars and simply watching, watching, watching David Greybeard, Fifi, Flint, Flo, and other denizens of what she called "Chimpland." Well into the night on the shore of Africa's deepest and oldest lake, she would write up notes by the fitful glow of a paraffin lantern.

"My Life Among Wild Chimpanzees," in the August 1963 *National Geographic*, became one of the most popular stories of the year and helped launch Goodall on her trajectory of fame.

I was getting restless, meeting people and looking at pictures on light tables that whispered of Africa. I had to see it with my own eyes; so did MBG. We would visit the Leakeys when they returned to Olduvai Gorge in the coming year.

Meanwhile, everyone was planning for our move into the new building on Saturday, November 23. President Kennedy would perform the dedication on December 19.

The day before—Friday the 22nd—Cousteau was back in town for a Society lecture. It was a mild day that grew increasingly blustery by afternoon. When he crossed the street from the Jefferson Hotel, he was carrying a box. In my office he opened it—but instead of neatly arranged transparencies I gazed at an unruly tangle of cut film. He picked out several, held them up to the light, and said, "Hmm . . . this one might do."

He has come unprepared! I thought angrily. More than 7,000 people had paid good money to attend his two lectures, and he's unprepared? Cousteau was a veteran lecturer so could probably pull it off. But we had to do some quick work in the next few hours.

Around 2 p.m., I headed over to MBG's office to warn him that an old friend might be letting us down. But as I entered, I saw his secretary, Gail Carroll, sobbing at her desk. I stopped, stunned, and asked her what was wrong.

"They've shot the president!" was all she could get out.

That's when I first heard the news about Dallas.

All we knew then was that JFK had been struck by a bullet. Someone brought out a television set; soon, we were awash with rumors. The president was dead. The president was wounded. The nation was under attack. At 2:38 p.m. Walter Cronkite famously took off his glasses and told America: The president had been pronounced dead in a Dallas hospital.

MBG, who had drawn closer to the first couple following the phenomenal success of the White House guidebook, was hit hard. Only a week earlier he and his family had been invited to an event on the South Lawn; my sister Sara was about Caroline Kennedy's age.

As far as I knew, no National Geographic Society Lecture had ever been canceled. Cousteau, Joanne, and I were driven down to Constitution Hall to begin rehearsals. Whatever the state of his slides, I knew that Jacques only needed to play up that French accent to charm however many showed up on this dreadful evening.

Our staff people were already in the auditorium, visibly shaken. No one could concentrate. At some point JYC and I stepped outside the main doors and gazed at a city that seemed eerie and surreal—some people going about the everyday business of a Friday afternoon in the week before Thanksgiving, others standing on the National Mall in little knots of fear or sorrow. The great bells at the National Cathedral started tolling, tolling, tolling and would continue until deep in the night.

We looked at one another, our thoughts written in our eyes: The show could not go on. I called MBG, suggesting that we'd reimburse ticketholders. He agreed. I called GHG out at Wild Acres. He also agreed. Leonard Grant, MBG's aide-de-camp, volunteered to stand at those great doors and gently turn people away.

Joanne and I went glumly back to the office. I called Donna for the fourth time that day. Then Cousteau and I headed out for dinner at Harvey's. The white-jacketed waiters clustered before the television set at the bar, watching the 6:45 p.m. arrival of Air Force One, bearing one slain chief executive and another newly sworn-in, at Andrews Air Force Base.

We avoided the obvious and talked about the sea. As people began lining Wisconsin Avenue to watch the hearse, bearing a casket and a glimpse of pink suit, fly by on its way to Bethesda Naval Hospital for the autopsy, we talked about ocean exploration and its challenges, dangers, and overwhelming wonder. We talked about whales and sharks and shipwrecks. But the topic that stands out most in my memory was the fragility of the sea.

That was new to me. Everyone thought that the sea was inexhaustible, the womb of life on this planet—it teemed with life. How could it be fragile? Cousteau just shook his head. I knew he was poetic. I didn't realize he could be prophetic too.

JYC had to fly out the next day. As we walked back to his hotel, an approaching cold front was gusting through the November trees and carrying off the remaining leaves. In Lafayette Square, across from the White House, the wind buffeted thousands of gathered people. Many would remain all night until 4:30 a.m., when the hearse pulled under the portico and the casket and the lady in the bloodstained pink suit were hurried inside, the doors closing behind them.

THE RAIN STARTED AT DAWN and poured down all day, eddying through the dead leaves, sweeping them into soaking piles in the gutters. Never had the weather so reflected the dismal mood of a nation.

The glow of television flickered behind practically every window in practically every house. Much of that historic weekend remains a rain-swept blur. Bob Gilka, our director of photography, sent everybody who could wield a camera into the streets to document the unfolding event, planning our coverage for Sunday's lying-in-state beneath the Capitol's dome and for Monday's funeral cortege and burial at Arlington National Cemetery.

Our photographers covered the ceremony every step of the way—from the mournful procession down Pennsylvania Avenue to the coffin-draped catafalque in the Capitol rotunda to the mass in the Cathedral of St. Matthew the Apostle. Then, ultimately, to the burial at Arlington National Cemetery. And through it all, the sound of muffled drums, the creak of caisson wheels, and at the irrevocable end, the sorrowing wail of "Taps" that lingered in the winter air.

Though it had been an exhausting four days, the tempo accelerated because MBG wanted a major article on Kennedy, his funeral, and legacy for the March 1964 issue. Since it was practically December, we had very little time. We postponed our new building's dedication; President Johnson would officiate the event in January. This meant MBG had to cancel his long-held plans to sail the Nile with Irving and Exy Johnson aboard the *Yankee;* he gave Donna and me his tickets. Despite the sad circumstances, I was thrilled to be sailing with Skipper again. Dad and Anne could still meet us in Nairobi in February to visit the Leakeys.

The March 1964 *National Geographic* with "The Last Full Measure," the magazine's tribute to the late John F. Kennedy, was an acknowledged masterpiece.

A handwritten note was delivered to MBG, on its letterhead a simple "Mrs. John F. Kennedy":

February 16, 1964

Dear Dr. Grosvenor,

I do thank you for sending me and my children the first issues of the *National Geographic* of the President's funeral . . .

As usual, you have done the finest that it was possible to do, and I have seen nothing anywhere that compares with the way you treated those terrible days.

All you did for us, in our years in the White House, in making the Guide Book such a source of pride to the President—And now this—

I am so proud to think that yours is the story that will be saved—and seen by more people years from now.

When I was little my grandfather gave me a subscription to the *National Geographic*—and I used to save them all—until I went to boarding school—and then they were all taken away as there was no more room in my bookcases.

Now every child and grown-up will do the same as I did—only they will never lose that issue—and it will always remind them of all that President Kennedy was—and how tragic for their country to have lost him.

I do thank you with all my heart. Please save some extra copies for his library.

Most gratefully,

Jacqueline Kennedy

CHAPTER TEN

THE AFRICAN MEMORY BANK

When Donna and I stepped off the plane from Khartoum, Wadi Halfa was a somnolent outpost at the foot of the Second Cataract of the Nile, located in northern Sudan, with Egypt a few miles to the north. As we made our way down to the wharf, we saw women washing clothes in the river as they had for generations. But in the town on the bluff above, the villagers were packing up and preparing to move away. The water was already starting to rise.

At Wadi Halfa, the Nile, spilling out of its "belly of stones," starts to become a lake—a 230-mile-long, sinuous lake, thanks to the old Aswan Dam far to the north. In January 1964, the new Aswan High Dam was rearing its massive walls, the first stages completed. When finished, it would impound a lake so vast that Wadi Halfa and its surroundings would be submerged.

We were meeting Irving and Exy Johnson to be among the last to see the storied Nubian Valley, its crags and bluffs crowned with the remains of temples, fortresses, and tombs thousands of years old before it was drowned and lost forever.

DONNA AND I had hardly reached the wharf when the sails of *Yankee* materialized. But it was not the *Yankee* I had crewed on in the summer of

1947. Skipper had her sold in 1958. This *Yankee* was the Johnsons' "dream boat," a 50-foot-long ketch, perfect for cruising during their sunset years. The Johnsons' shakedown cruise in the new *Yankee* was a voyage through the canals of Europe that resulted in yet another *National Geographic* article. After that, they would take on the oldest and longest river in the world.

Once aboard, Donna and I greeted Irving, Exy, and Ted Zacher, a veteran of one of the original *Yankee*'s round-the-world cruises; Winfield Parks, one of *National Geographic*'s best photographers; and Ahmed Fahmy, a Cairo-born, Cambridge-educated former cricket star who would be our guide and interpreter.

Wadi Halfa marked the upstream terminus of *Yankee*'s voyage. We came about and headed north on the return leg. Passing across the border into Egypt, we were surrounded by the grand scenery of the Nubian Nile. Quickly we fell into the rhythm of life afloat on a lake that made for easy sailing. Anchored in some cove, we'd gaze heavenward at immense canopies of stars, musing on time and the river.

Ancient Nubia was the biblical land of Kush, which provided the pharaohs for Egypt's 25th dynasty. Among those desert cliffs, at least 40 teams of archaeologists were working, recording and preserving every site and artifact before the inundation began. Wherever possible, temples and monuments were being dismantled and moved. And before we had logged 40 miles on our northward journey, we landed at the site of the most endangered archaeological treasure of them all—and the one most challenging to relocate.

We could see Abu Simbel from a mile away as we approached, watching it grow ever larger the nearer our arrival. When Irving beached *Yankee* at the water's edge, I jumped ashore. Donna had it easier; Skipper gently lowered her off the bow onto the beach. The towering colossi framing the great temple of Ramses II were as tall as a six-story building and had been carved out of the living rock. To stand and gaze upward at these immense forms that had been sitting in desert wind and accumulating sand for nearly 33 centuries was staggering.

We spent the better part of two days exploring that remarkable temple, dedicated to ancient Egypt's chief gods, and the adjacent smaller temple devoted to the goddess Hathor and Ramses II's queen, Nefertari.

Eventually we had to back off and continue down the river. UNESCO had assembled an international team of engineers who would soon implement an audacious plan to save Abu Simbel. Men were already preparing an artificial site on the top of the cliff, 120 feet above the six-story-tall effigies. Soon they would begin cutting the temples into 30-ton blocks before reassembling them on the new site, safe from the encroaching waters of Lake Nasser.

The river cut through a starkly beautiful desert. Groves of date palms and tamarisks were flooded along its margins; the lake we sailed on was seasonal, highest in January, when the 1902-era dam's sluices were closed. In summer, when the sluices were opened so that the river could inundate the fertile floodplains of Egypt, the Nubian Nile returned to its ancient bed, and the groves and fields reappeared.

The plight of the Nubian people had been well documented in our October 1963 article. But neither Donna nor I had been prepared for the reality. The old Aswan Dam had been bad enough, forcing these people to move from their ancestral villages onto the slopes to escape that comparatively minor inundation. At least they could live close to their original homes and cemeteries.

The new Aswan High Dam was already forcing them to relocate—all 100,000 of Egypt's Nubians were being forcibly uprooted and transplanted far downstream to Kom Ombo. We saw them waiting at the river's edge for the steamers, meager possessions often on the man's back and woman's head.

The scale of these activities became most poignant, however, when we noticed the dogs remaining in the abandoned villages. The people could take farm livestock with them. But there was no room for the village dogs. It really tore at Donna and Exy, because the cruel edict stemmed from a government decree issued by Nasser's minions in faraway Cairo. It became unbearable, however, when we passed places where the starving dogs had clearly turned on each other. The stench of death hung over one such place long before we reached it. Skipper gave the village a hard gaze for some minutes, then said, "We'll anchor upwind."

DAY FOLLOWED NIGHT FOLLOWED DAY; signs of ancient habitation were everywhere along the cliffs, most of them doomed.

We beached *Yankee* beneath a 300-foot rampart with the ruins of an ancient fort and climbed up its craggy slopes. Irving and Exy headed to the very top because he wanted to photograph her from a vantage that also captured *Yankee* beached far below.

Donna and I were climbing a different path, admiring the views, when we heard a thunder of rocks cascading from above. It sounded like a landslide triggered by someone who had slipped off the cliff. A few seconds later the sound of rocks crashing on the beach 300 feet below sent shivers through my body. Had Irving fallen to his death?

I was halfway up the trail where the sound had come from when I heard Exy crying for help. Sprinting to the top, I scrambled through a breach in the wall—only to see, about 12 feet below me, Exy perched on a narrow ledge frantically removing rocks covering what looked like a body—Irving's body.

Rushing to her aid, I guessed instantly what must have happened: Part of the wall on which Skipper had stepped to make his photograph must have given way; as he fell, the rest of the wall collapsed on top of him.

We finished clearing the rocks, but I couldn't tell if he was alive or dead. Even when he finally moaned, I wasn't sure that it wasn't a death rattle. I was just as concerned about Exy, but she appeared unharmed. All this was only inches from the cliff edge. Miraculously, they both hadn't fallen to their deaths.

Irving was seriously injured. We gently arranged him so that Exy could cradle his head on her lap. She and Donna gingerly plucked rock fragments from his scalp. I called out to Ted and Ahmed, standing watch on *Yankee*, and was surprised when Ahmed yelled back that there was a hospital just across the river.

That was a stroke of luck. After racing back up the hill with water and a first-aid kit, Ted and I backed *Yankee* off the beach and motored across the river to the village pier.

The doctor in the clinic, a young man who spoke a little English, scratched up a stretcher and an assortment of stretcher-bearers.

By the time we took *Yankee* back across the river and regained the hilltop, the little circle had grown by the addition of Win Parks and the archaeologists he had recruited while seeking assistance. Skipper needed stitches in his head and was eased onto the stretcher, so the bearers could undertake the tricky process of getting him down the steep hill. Irving, skipper to the core, directed exactly how he wanted to be placed on the foredeck.

We soon became the talk of the village. Inevitably, the district policeman and his assistants came snooping around. He began his questioning innocuously enough: "Was the captain well-liked?" Then, in a more insinuating tone: "Were there problems on board?" and "Did the captain and his wife quarrel?" He then came straight out with it: "Could the wife have pushed the captain off that wall?"

This was annoying enough but compounded our worries. We had to traverse the High Dam's gates in a few days or be permanently marooned upstream. Ted and I could manage the boat if Irving remained bedridden—but not if the police detained us.

Ahmed, overhearing the policeman boast how he was going to order Exy down to the station, muttered something about "stopping Sherlock Holmes." He returned to *Yankee* to use the radiotelephone. Who he called I'll never know. I'm sure they were very well-connected Egyptians.

As evening approached, the policemen faded away.

There was no sign of a concussion, but bruised, bandaged, and with 16 stitches in his scalp, Irving Johnson would need recovery time. The doctor wanted him to stay in that clinic for 10 days. We struck a compromise: Irving would remain in his bunk aboard *Yankee* for 10 days with Exy as his nurse and enforcer. Ted and I would helm the ketch through the High Dam's gates into the impoundment behind the old dam, then motor through the locks until we reached Aswan on the other side at the foot of the rock-strewn First Cataract of the Nile.

At dawn we were under way; it was 150 miles or so to the new dam. Ted or I was always at the wheel. Navigation was simple: Keep to the channel; don't hit any rocks; anchor at night.

But if I gloried in the role of Skipper, I was soon disabused of that notion. Hardly a day had passed when the hatch opened and a bandaged head emerged, one baleful eye giving the topside a careful sweep. The next day about half of that figure emerged. By the time *Yankee* became the last American-flagged vessel to pass through the High Dam's gates, Irving appeared on deck, still wearing his turban of bandages.

The real Skipper was back in command.

In Aswan, an acquaintance of Ahmed's suggested we meet the widow of the late Aga Khan, reputedly the richest woman in the world. Irving guided *Yankee* around the foot of the First Cataract and up the Nile's west bank to the site of the Aga Khan III mausoleum, which loomed over the sand-colored hills. The handsome villa set beneath the imposing mausoleum was the winter home of his widow, Begum Aga Khan, born and educated in France.

A welcoming wave from the distant terrace encouraged Skipper to dock at her pier. The begum was charming and witty, and she spoke excellent English with the lightest of French accents. Since her hobby was photography, she was delighted to be hosting the National Geographic Society, even if Win and I were wearing rumpled sailing togs.

We lingered so late at Nur-el-Salaam that darkness caught us. Skipper started to call the Aswan port authorities to send a river pilot to guide us back through the rapids of the First Cataract to our city mooring. The begum wouldn't hear of it. She declared that she would be our pilot and "knew every rock in the Cataract."

Skipper was dubious, but when she took her position beside Irving at the wheel and began issuing directions with calm assurance, he relaxed, rapt in admiration for her piloting skills. Soon she had us safely back at our berth near the old Cataract Hotel.

North of Aswan we were finally in the Nile of my boyhood imaginings, the river of pharaoh, pyramid, and fellahin. Best of all was the mesmerizing, ceaseless round of the shadoof, lifting water up to the thirsty fields. All too soon, Donna and I were due in Nairobi. We disembarked and said our farewells in Luxor.

AT NIGHT ON THE SERENGETI, those of us sitting in the circle of firelight were surrounded by a majestic symphony. Above the endless fugue of trilling, chirping, and buzzing insects we heard an expansive medley of distant hoots, whines, and howls. A deep undertone, sounding like countless bullfrogs, was the lowing of tens of thousands of nearby wildebeest. They were calving, and we had only to glance at the flicker of lightning beyond Ngorongoro Crater, or look up at the clouds scudding across an immense canopy of stars, to monitor the approach of February's life-giving rains.

Other sounds—a thunder of hoofs, a zebra's sharp bray—betrayed the presence of predators. A maniacal cackle and the endlessly repeated, eerily drawn-out whoops were the telltale sounds of spotted hyenas. A burst of high-pitched yelping meant that golden jackals were regrouping for a kill. A distant, strung-out, almost birdlike *hoo'o! hoo'o!* perked us up: African wild dogs were already becoming scarce. Occasionally we heard the reverberating roar of lions.

For a million years or so, humans had been sitting around such a fire, listening to storytellers. On those nights, however, it was usually just Donna and me, MBG and Anne, photographer Hugo van Lawick, and the impresario himself, Louis Leakey.

Dad had been deeply disappointed not to sail the Nile aboard *Yankee,* so his visit to Olduvai Gorge in Tanzania seemed a wonderful consolation prize.

We learned one thing on the long drive from Nairobi to those digs: A Leakey behind the wheel never misses a pothole. We were relieved to exit the Land Rover upon finally arriving at the camp. A cluster of tents and trailers as well as a shed were perched among the thorn trees and flat-topped acacias on the very lip of Olduvai Gorge near its junction with the Great Rift Valley.

Dr. Leakey, wearing his ubiquitous tan one-piece boiler suit, was the entertainment each evening at fireside—always a stimulating, if not brief, performance. He was at his best with the gorge as his stage and the Rift Valley his backdrop.

Usually, he offered another installment in his fables of adaptation, adapt or perish being the narrative thread linking all creatures great and small. One night it was sparked by the giraffes that hung around the Leakey camp, feeding among thorn trees and acacias. Because Louis had found fossil giraffes with short necks, the tale that night pivoted on how natural selection allowed giraffes to evolve long necks so they could browse the tops of the acacias.

Mary Leakey was always back in the banda, or thatched shed, working on the fossil collection. The ghostly flicker of her gas lamp illuminated an immense pig tusk, the skull of a hartebeest, and the antler—yes, antler—of another extinct giraffe. She had heard enough of Louis's stories.

Hugo, who was photographing African wildlife for Society publications, had been born in the old Dutch East Indies and educated in England. Baron van Lawick—the title was genuine—had spent months filming Jane Goodall's work with chimpanzees at Gombe, and within a month would marry her. "Miss Goodall" would become Baroness Jane van Lawick-Goodall. A few years later, she would add "Doctor" to that, and was one of the few people to earn a Cambridge Ph.D. without having an undergraduate degree. She was at Cambridge when we were visiting Olduvai, her fieldwork best accomplished during summer and autumn.

Wandering in and out of that circle of firelight was a leggy, pipe-smoking 19-year-old in shorts and sandals. Richard Leakey, middle son of the clan, had dropped out of school and now owned Leakey Safaris Ltd. He was helping us distinguish the sounds of the savanna night; I had engaged him for the next month or so to be our guide to the wildlife Donna and I hoped to see and photograph.

The Leakey camp, set high on the bluff above a gorge that in places stretched a mile from rim to rim, was patrolled by Dalmatians on the lookout for snakes, leopards, lions, or rhinos. Only several miles away, the wildebeest herd stretched from horizon to horizon, following a ceaseless clockwise migration set by the cycles of growing grass. Between December and March, the rainy season here, they were always in this quarter of the plain—a half million of them, mixed with zebras, Thomson's gazelles, impalas, and hartebeests; the lush green grass provided ideal calving grounds.

Richard drove Donna and me out to see the show. The calves weren't granted more than maybe 20 minutes to rise up on their spindly, trembling legs—but rise up they must, because the herd would leave them behind. Predators, especially hyenas and vultures, could be seen hanging about the herd's edges. That day we found three starving calves whose mothers had been killed by predators, probably lions. We brought them back to camp with ropes around their necks. The ropes were gone within 24 hours because they were completely tamed. The Leakeys promptly dubbed them Anne, Donna, and Gil. We were bottle-feeding them on the same day one of the nearby giraffes was also nursing a calf.

The Dalmatians had their work cut out for them; animal tracks were all over the tiny compound. One evening when we retired for the night, I closed the tent's back flap; we slept under canvas at Olduvai, our two cots separated by a narrow aisle. A few minutes later, I heard Richard telling me to open the flap. He was making final rounds, checking that his clients were well in hand.

"Sometimes animals wander through the tents at night," he explained nonchalantly. "Must be careful they don't get trapped inside. Don't want them to panic and tear the canvas—or you—to shreds."

"Okay by us," I assured him, reopening the flap to the cool night air. Then Donna and I snuggled into our blankets and listened to our nightly serenade far out on the Serengeti. Soon I was sound asleep.

I awoke at dawn to find Donna sitting up with her blanket wrapped tightly around her.

"Gil! There was an animal in our tent!"

"What do you mean?"

"There was this snuffling right between us! It was some big animal—I saw it! And smelled it! My heart is still racing!"

"Why didn't you wake me up?"

"I tried to! You just kept snoring away!"

Tentatively, I peeked out of the tent. "Well, whatever it was, I think it's gone now." Still wondering if she might not have dreamed the whole thing, I examined the dirt floor between our beds. And saw a muddy print—several of them, running the length of the aisle.

At breakfast we mentioned the episode to Richard, who insisted on having a look. "Hyena tracks, all right," he said, again nonchalantly. "We see them around all the time."

Another morning—perhaps the day Richard took us into the Rift Valley to see Ngorongoro Crater, that showcase of savanna wildlife—I sidled into the Land Rover's back seat. There was a burlap bag next to me, and I thought for a second that something squirmed in it. But I paid it no mind, busily readying my cameras. Then I looked again. Instinct told me that bag contained something ominous. I saw Richard eyeing me in the rearview mirror. Was there a glint of mischief? Eventually he explained that it was just a snake found down in the camp of the Kenyan field staff the Leakeys had engaged.

I involuntarily jumped. Richard put on his best show of nonchalance. "Oh, it's just a puff adder. I'll drop it off in the bushes shortly."

I knew that a puff adder ranked high among Africa's most dangerous venomous snakes, so I was greatly relieved when Richard stopped the Rover, grabbed the sack, walked a short way off the trail, and shook out its loathsome inhabitant. The pipe never left his mouth.

The Olduvai Gorge was yielding enough fossil skulls, teeth, jawbones, tibias, and toes that, taken together, amounted to the momentous discovery of *Homo habilis,* or "handy man." This was a much bigger find than Dear Boy five years earlier. Louis would soon make the news public, predicting it would "shatter the world." It certainly shook up paleoanthropology. The Leakeys were proving Darwin right: Africa, not Asia, was the cradle of humankind.

Olduvai was perfect for paleontological work. It was banded like a layer cake, with the oldest band at the bottom and the youngest at the top, a chronicle of the last several million years in this corner of the planet. I can see them now—Louis in that boiler suit, hair tousled by the incessant wind, and Mary on her hands and knees, digging their way into the history books.

MBG enjoyed playing fossil hunter. He and Louis would crawl around on their hands and knees on the floor of the gorge, each with an identical dental pick and the same serious look of attentiveness. It was obvious why the "village elders," as Richard and I called them, were two peas in a pod. Both were in their early 60s, both silver-haired reservoirs of infectious enthusiasm. Their friendship was intense but all too brief.

One evening, after we had adjourned to that outdoor fire, Richard jumped up and announced that it was "a perfect night for spring-haring."

"Spring-haring?" I asked.

"Yes. Spring hares are these nocturnal rodents living in burrows out there," he said, indicating the Serengeti with a sweep of his hand. "If you drive around at night, you often see them. They freeze when caught in the headlamps. The trick is to capture one by its long, bushy tail before the spell is broken and it darts off, leaping away."

"Does it get hurt?" Donna asked.

"Not at all," Richard assured her. "We merely hold it up for photographs, then release it. They just scamper off."

"How exactly do we capture it?" I asked skeptically.

"You, Gil, must jump out of the Rover before we brake and hit the ground running. Then just scoop him up."

I must have looked doubtful. Was I really expected to run down a wild animal?

Donna, Hugo, and I piled into his vehicle and drove off into grassland so dark it felt a little unnerving. Seated in the front passenger seat, I had lions on my mind—after all, I was the one jumping out into the African night. But that fearful spell was soon broken.

"Eyes! Slightly left!" Hugo yelled, and I caught sight of what looked like a rabbit just as it sprang off into darkness. Several more sightings followed before we mesmerized one of the rodents long enough for me to leap out of the moving vehicle and try to chase it down. Too slow! The critter was gone before I even ran 10 feet. The next attempt also ended ignominiously after I tumbled headfirst into a grassy hollow. Then we saw another pair of headlights in the distance—a Land Rover. After giving it a hard stare, Richard shook his head in annoyance. "Must be the village elders," he said. "There's not another vehicle between here and Seronera."

"Maybe they've come to watch?" I ventured.

"Not likely. I bet they've come to compete!"

I sat, incredulous. The Serengeti Plain was no cricket ground. But there it was, a pair of headlights bouncing on recklessly, stopping suddenly, then bouncing some more. "They'll kill themselves," I muttered.

That's how we continued, two Land Rovers disturbing the African night. Eventually Richard held another hare transfixed in the headlight beam, and I was out of the vehicle, diving into the illuminated circle, grabbing the end of a bushy tail and screaming like a teenager, "I got him! I got him!"

Cheers erupted, and as the grinning village elders pulled up alongside, everyone piled out to inspect our springhare, the only one we managed to catch that night. We stroked its soft, fluffy tail and gazed into the depths of those large black eyes. Then I gently set it down. It darted away.

Later, after Dad and Anne departed for home, Donna and I would climb back into Richard's Land Rover and set out for a three-week safari to the game parks of Kenya and Uganda, adding sightings of elephants, water buffalo, crocodiles, kob, and more to my African memories.

But for that moment, we remained in our small circle of light, laughing and trading observations and gibes, with no way of knowing our family friendship would span three generations and possibly more. It was enough to be out there amid insect song and a medley of distant hoots and howls. Then we headed back to camp, two Land Rovers in the African night, headlamps in the vast Serengeti like fireflies in the dark.

That was nearly 60 years ago. Time passes. Only a photograph holds the moment in thrall. On my bedroom dresser I have a picture of me holding that hare. In that metal frame I am forever and exuberantly young.

Not so much the old fossil looking back at him.

CHAPTER ELEVEN

THE HOUSE OF EXPLORATION

Every time I stepped into the elevator in our new 10-story building and rode to the top, I could see a cross section of the National Geographic Society hive at work. In dedicating the building in 1964, President Lyndon B. Johnson declared it to be a "house of exploration . . . by all nations for all nations."

On the ground floor was our museum, Explorers Hall, with its 11-foot rotating globe, the largest freestanding kind in the world—and, to me, emblematic of our global reach. The second floor, Bud Wisherd's domain, was the finest photographic laboratory in American publishing, buttressed by the film review, camera repair, and custom equipment shops.

Stepping off the third floor made me a happy man; this was—initially, at least—the Cartographic Division. Through its doors was a geographer's Elysium—maps and globes everywhere.

The fourth floor was home to staff photographers like Win Parks, Jim Stanfield, Joe Scherschel, George Mobley, and Jim Blair. The department was under the command of a man with a long, lean face, a lantern jaw, and a crew cut that changed little over the years—and who, on any given day, was keeping tabs on upwards of three dozen photographers on assignment somewhere on the face of the globe. Bob Gilka, the director of photography, had a flinty, tight-lipped, hard-as-nails persona that masked a gentleman who was courteous but direct and economical with words.

He had high standards and insisted his photographers have them too; those who didn't measure up were soon weeded out. Those who did, he nurtured and fostered with a passion. He had a discerning eye for story-tellers with a camera and hired young talent like William Albert Allard, a 27-year-old art school dropout who gained the trust of the otherwise camera-shy Amish and brought back warm, intimate images of that community. There was also Bruce Dale, who skipped college to work for the *Toledo Blade*. Gilka spotted him at a University of Missouri workshop.

The fourth floor also housed the offices of the foreign editorial staff—Luis Marden, Tom Abercrombie, and their ilk. Helen and Frank Schreider, the newest members of that fellowship, had completed an epic 18-month journey down the Pan-American Highway from the Arctic Circle in Alaska to Ushuaia in Tierra del Fuego. They drove a World War II–surplus amphibious jeep dubbed Tortuga. Obstacles they couldn't hack their way through, they simply boated around.

On the fifth floor, accountants scurried among the treasury, payroll, promotion, and procurement offices. Dr. McKnew and Mel Payne occupied the sixth floor, along with the Book Service and the News Service, which churned out press releases.

National Geographic writers and editors kept shop on the seventh floor. John Scofield, an Army officer during World War II, took up photography and mastered it so thoroughly that GHG offered him a staff position after seeing his story on the kingdom of Jordan. Another new hire, Kenneth MacLeish, son of the poet Archibald MacLeish, also had office space there.

Writer-editor Joe Judge was to words what Bill Garrett was to pictures. A shrewd, incisive editor, he would gaze over the rim of reading glasses perched low on his nose, look you directly in the eye, and say precisely what was on his mind.

The picture editors, huddled over light tables, occupied the eighth floor. Bill Garrett stalked among them, rasping out orders and rearranging pictures with a few deft strokes to save another feature—when not shooting with his own cameras. Garrett had that newsy edge; if not in Vietnam, he was high in the Himalaya, where a war had erupted between India and China in Ladakh.

MBG occupied the palatial corner office on the ninth floor; his semicircular desk sat in the northeast corner. We approached him from across an enormous Persian carpet, which sometimes felt like walking the last mile if a set of pictures disappointed him.

Finally, the new boardroom, surrounded on three sides by windows, had drapes that automatically adjusted to the position of the sun crossing from east to west, making an audible *click-whirr*. I found it annoying. MBG loved it.

The top, 10th floor, with its expansive views, housed the cafeteria and executive dining rooms. Luis Marden had inaugurated them with a lavish meal for the prince of Tonga. The bill, Château Lafite Rothschild included, amounted, it was said, to the most expensive luncheon ever held there.

MUCH OF THE TIME, the door to Tom Abercrombie's fourth-floor office was closed, signaling he was in the field. Tom once said that working for the *Geographic* was "like having a magic carpet. You can go anywhere you want." In 1957 it had whisked him to Lebanon, his first foreign assignment. I was his picture editor.

Back then Tom knew so little about that part of the world that he didn't realize that French, and not Arabic, was the lingua franca in Lebanon. He didn't know a word of either. When he arrived, he spoke neither; when he left, he knew both.

He would have assignments in many lands but would make the Middle East his specialty. In Yemen, near the Red Sea, Tom befriended an old man who was nearsighted and effectively blind. Abercrombie said good-bye and moved on. In a port several days' journey away, he found that man a gift. He went out of his way to return and give him a pair of eyeglasses. Tom watched him put them on—and for the first time in years see the stars.

In 1965 Tom became the first American photojournalist to be given wide latitude to photograph Saudi Arabia. He came back a changed man, having quietly converted to Islam. No, he was never conventionally pious—he never gave up wine, for instance. He'd just say it was "more in the nature of an intellectual assent," then shrug, relight his pipe, and get that distant, dreamy look in those blue eyes.

IN LATE 1964 Bob Breeden asked me to join him for lunch: "Gil, I have an idea that I think will intrigue you."

In a restaurant noted for recessed booths and dark corners, Bob told me that a Geographic publications wing producing small-format books might be a promising venture. He sketched out his idea with such persuasiveness that I signed on; persuading MBG would be the challenge.

We ran some numbers. Book budgets were calculated by print order—the more you print, the cheaper the cost per book. We calculated press runs at no lower than 225,000, a figure boggling to modern book publishing but for us a fairly reliable indication of potential sales to our three million members at the time.

Bob wrote to MBG, emphasizing that we might net $250,000 a year—without adding staff. We could market the books in series—say, four volumes a year—and promote all four at once. That was key: selling four books—not just one—on a single promotion. When we pitched the idea in person, I knew instantly that MBG was not into it. He gazed out the window or twiddled with his pencil. Finally, he slumped. "I'm too old for this one, boys," he said. "You can try it after I'm gone. But not now."

It was a long walk over that carpet. Bob and I had nearly reached the door when he called us back.

"Wait a minute, boys. I'm not going to do this. But it's okay with me if you want to try."

When ultimately approved, the Special Publications Division, established in July 1965 with Breeden as director and me as executive editor, issued its first series of four volumes the following year: Jane Goodall's classic *My Friends the Wild Chimpanzees,* along with *Our Country's Presidents, The River Nile,* and *Isles of the Caribbees.* The small-format books were not much bigger than the magazine: 200 pages, richly illustrated, with carefully balanced subject matter.

While it lasted—and it lasted for decades—it filled a niche on our members' bookshelves that no one but Breeden had spotted. Press runs sometimes exceeded 400,000, which meant we could sell 1.6 million books on one promotion. For the first time I could utilize my college education. At Yale I had studied statistical surveying—opinion polling—which I believed was the only way to get a truly representative sampling of the membership. Testing titles before setting the print run eliminated expensive miscalculation.

Even if our seasoned journalists ridiculed surveys, I felt it was important to keep a finger on the membership pulse. It meant you could better serve members. To better serve them meant you could flourish. To know members' preferences didn't mean that you had to cater to them, but to ignore them was potential disaster. Even MBG, who governed by instinct, grudgingly consented to adding surveys to our monthly magazine readership reports. Map supplements always came in with the highest ratings—no surprise to MBG or me, but an eye-opener to some senior staffers.

A little business training went a long way.

CHAPTER TWELVE

THE YELLOW
IN THE LEAF

Most mornings I'd visit the Control Center and study each panel. Afterward I'd walk back to my adjoining office knowing exactly how the next three or four issues were shaping up and what core areas needed attention—and where problems three issues away might need addressing now.

Though the cost of last-minute changes was never entirely controlled, the monthly Control Center meetings were valuable. MBG attended. McKnew and Payne might drop by. Even Carolyn Patterson once pulled me in to point out an impending disaster for her legend writers. "Why, Carolyn," I asked in mock surprise, "I thought you didn't like the Control Center?"

"Dahlin'," she replied, "I'm desperate!"

I'd also think about long-range story development. Nature was often on my mind; so, increasingly, were environmental issues. Adventure and exploration subjects could be especially difficult to find; staffers would often scan newspapers worldwide for promising story ideas.

In 1965 Charles Allmon, an illustrations editor with an eye for the off-beat adventure, handed me a clipping from a Honolulu newspaper about a 16-year-old dropout who had sailed alone from San Pedro, California, to Hawaii. He now planned to make the first solo circumnavigation ever achieved by anyone so young. He was Robin Lee Graham, and his 24-foot fiberglass sloop was named *Dove*.

I was initially dubious until I learned that young Robin, a veteran sailor, had cruised the South Pacific for 13 months with his family on a 36-foot ketch and had mastered navigation before he was 14. He had designed his own self-steering wind vane and could steer from the cabin as well as from topside. Via a mirror system, he could see the compass from the cabin too. We backed Robin for three and a half years. I ran the operation.

Photography was the first challenge. Before Robin even arrived in Samoa with a broken mast, I designed a remote aperture control on a camera to be affixed to the top of his 40-foot mast. Robin could take pictures of himself on *Dove*. That camera, and one mounted aft, saved the story.

Other than surviving catastrophic weather, solitude was his greatest challenge. Although a superb sailor, Robin was vulnerable to anguishing loneliness as soon as he left port. His changing cast of kittens was not company enough. When he docked in Tonga, photographer Bill Allard gave him pointers on taking better pictures; his father met him in the Solomon Islands; in Darwin, Australia, Allmon met him—mostly for company. We urged him to sail leisurely around the world and to visit scenic landfalls along his itinerary as part of the adventure. He also needed to make repairs to *Dove*. Occasionally he took jobs to finance living expenses; he even took time to help a Samoan family recover from a hurricane. He was facile with his hands, adept at any practical task.

We didn't foresee the third, most unpredictable challenge. One day in Suva, Fiji, a friend banged on the boat's cabin top and told Robin that a girl wanted to meet him.

Patti Ratterree, 22, also from California, was drifting around the Pacific, crewing on yachts and working odd jobs. Robin was instantly smitten; by the time she turned up again in Darwin, he was desperately in love.

At headquarters, brows furrowed: Here was the femme fatale who would wreck the voyage. She'd lure him away from finishing, or join him aboard *Dove,* negating the young sailor's unique single-handed voyage

That was unfair. No one should expect a man of 17 going on 18 to stay in solitude on a small boat and forfeit all the joy of youth. His voyage had been an ordeal. He had dodged typhoons, been knocked on beam-ends by a passing freighter, and, during his epic crossing of the Indian Ocean, was swept overboard by a storm and had barely regained the deck when the mast snapped. He sailed half that ocean under a jury-rig, using a cockpit fly, usually rigged to provide shade from the sun, as a sail.

Nevertheless, we had invested in the story and were determined to keep him on course—alone.

ON THE DAY AFTER CHRISTMAS, 1964, my grandmother died at Wild Acres with most of her family gathered around. It was not unexpected; Elsie had been seriously ill for nearly two years. Hardly had a season of subdued holiday cheer passed when all of us—as if of one mind—began worrying about my grandfather.

After their 63 years of marriage, we knew it wouldn't be long before GHG followed her. Even with his hearing aid, it was as if he now lived in a world of murmurings, which sometimes annoyed and confused him. I know he heard echoes of the MBG era at the Society, even if from afar, as the Geographic went from one success to another. I know because he wrote Dad that it filled him with "immeasurable satisfaction."

More and more time was spent at Hissar in Coconut Grove, or at The Point on Beinn Bhreagh. By fall 1965, Gramp was still at The Point, where he had arrived midsummer. He was too weak to be moved anywhere, so he rode out the winter there with Aunt Mabel. Few of us thought he would see that season's end, but Christmas came and went. Family members arrived and departed; each of us said what we knew were our last goodbyes.

His eyes were deep pools of love; mine misted with tears when I took my final departure.

He had been dreaming of journeys and arrivals. So it came as no surprise when, on February 4, 1966, at age 90, he took a nap at The Point and never woke up. He was still chairman of the board and a familiar presence at headquarters, at least before the new building was completed. One of my colleagues had stepped into the 16th Street elevators—and found courtly old Dr. Grosvenor standing there. Gramp, who had been editor of *National Geographic* before the Wright brothers ever flew, exclaimed, "Isn't it wonderful the things Colonel Glenn is doing in space!" Born in Turkey, he died in Canada. His was a truly geographic life.

Dad and Aunt Mabel inherited The Point. Aunt Carol bought *Elsie*. Dad bought Hissar. Wild Acres? The family held on to it for a few more years but sold it after a succession of disappointing tenants.

Probably because of a passionate memo he had written to the board of trustees extolling my skills and in an affirmation of family continuity, I was elected to fill his seat. In that new ninth-floor boardroom only one picture now hung: A portrait of GHG looking over our deliberations as if from a higher sphere.

SPRING FOLLOWED THAT DARK WINTER with its usual burst of cherry blossoms around the Tidal Basin in the nation's capital. But it was slower to arrive in Yellowstone National Park, where it was still winter-coat weather even in May and early June. Donna and I were there to check on one of our most prolific grantees. One morning we saw a sight so arresting that we didn't notice the chill. Frank Craighead whirled around, barking out instructions: "Remember! Pick a lodgepole pine you can climb in case the bear comes out of it early—one thick enough so he can't shake you out but too slim for him to climb."

Donna and I were staring at a temporarily immobilized grizzly bear lying in the grass some 20 feet away. The nearest trees either soared over us with no branch within reach or were too spindly to bear our weight. Evading rogue bears may have been old hat for Frank and his twin brother, John; they had written the textbook on wilderness survival. But it was more problematic for my five-foot-tall wife.

"But Frank, I don't see a tree like that," I protested.

"Believe me, if a bear's coming at you, you'll find one!" he said and turned back to work.

Frank, John, and their assistants slung the tranquilized bear onto an improvised scale on a truck bed to determine its weight. Its length and footpads were measured, its ear tags checked, and its blood, temperature, and stool sampled; it was fitted with a new radio collar. They wrestled the animal into a galvanized-steel culvert used as a cage, secured its doors, and drove off to release it, unharmed, at the farthest point of its known range. No need to shinny up a tree that day.

Frank was still in a dark mood as he drove us back to the project's headquarters near Canyon Village in the heart of Yellowstone National Park. His frown was due not to our conduct but rather to the bear's: It had been removed because it had entered the Canyon Village campground on one too many nights. Once an animal started doing that, it became a "problem" and was probably doomed.

"Can't you just relocate him outside of the park?" I asked.

"No. That's a death sentence too. Sooner or later he'd be shot. They're all shot once they get out there."

Sadly, Yellowstone was the only grizzly sanctuary south of the Canadian border. Outside its boundaries, people were too afraid of bears to let them go unmolested.

At the moment, there wasn't much else for us to see but the glories of Yellowstone, since the bears holed up in dense timber by day and emerged only at night. Frank did take us to the nearby hill on which their tracking antenna stood; this had a much greater range than the small handheld units carried by the twins. At any one time, only a dozen or so bears were fitted with radio collars, since you could keep track of only so many different signals.

Our conversation drifted back to the bear we had seen that morning. It might have been number 202, the only radio-collared one trapped and removed for entering campgrounds that summer. But even if not, Frank said, "the story illustrates all too poignantly the problem of the 'problem bear.'"

Bear 202, a yearling male, had been radio-collared and monitored throughout the previous summer, establishing a 27-square-mile home range encompassing parts of Canyon Village campground—where he never set a paw—but also stretching far to the south. Most exciting to the Craigheads: He had chosen his den that autumn in the valley of the Grand Canyon of the Yellowstone, only a stone's throw away from the den where he had been born: a behavior new to science.

Just a few weeks before Donna and I arrived, the bear had awoken from his winter stupor, swum across the river, and climbed the north bank of the canyon, emerging onto the plateau not far from the campground. And he had found food; it might have been the scraps of a cookout or scraps thrown to him deliberately. "For a grizzly to lose its fear of man requires the cooperation of man," Frank said, "and the initiative usually comes from us."

This bear hadn't hurt a soul. But because they tracked its movements and shared data with the Park Service, everyone felt it needed to be removed.

I later found out that bear 202 returned to the campground area, establishing an enlarged range of 125 square miles with the campground in dead center. He continued to take handouts of food. Though he never acted aggressively, the Park Service deemed him a "problem bear" and the following summer he was shot.

Although the Craigheads were best known for their studies on grizzlies, they also introduced our readers to other magnificent creatures like golden eagles. They would discover that the raptors, though protected, were still being shot by ranchers who believed they were preying on lambs, and that pesticides were contributing to their decline.

I made my own personal discovery on that trip while dangling on a rope 100 feet down the face of a 300-foot cliff in a rugged area near Livingston, Montana, photographing a nest of eaglets tucked into a bluff. Despite assurances from the Craigheads that mother golden eagles rarely attacked humans, this one didn't get the message. She relentlessly dive-bombed me. Flapping my arms and waving my hat failed to dissuade her, and I was roped back up—fortunately, none the worse for the experience.

By 1971 the Craigheads would leave Yellowstone, having terminated their grizzly research after a furious disagreement with the Park Service over bear management. I would be the last of three generations of Grosvenors to publish their stories, but they would always remain part of Geographic family history.

AS SPRING ARRIVED IN 1966, Dad's involvement with the Society began to wane. I'd hurry to his office, hands full of page proofs, and burst through the doors—and pull up short. Sprawled on the carpet, he was poring over his dreaming charts again, lost in a *White Mist* reverie. "My ambition is to ship her over to Tahiti and leisurely cruise around all those places that Herman Melville wrote about in *Typee* and *Moby-Dick*," he said. "Yes, sirree, that's just what I'm going to do."

He never did—a poignant thought now—but having turned 65 in November, he was thinking about retirement. He wasn't about to hang on like GHG did, and he was ready to turn the reins over to the younger generation he had recruited and trained: my generation. The following January he announced he would step down in August 1967.

"Who would succeed MBG as president and editor?" everyone asked. Few in my generation had reached 40. Who could be an interim president and editor? Viable candidates were scarce. Dr. McKnew, the chairman of the board, had no editorial experience. Likewise, Mel Payne, McKnew's protégé. Ted Vosburgh, now number two at the magazine? He had no business experience. Franc Shor? Though he had cleaned up his act to marry a socialite and adopt her twins, he would never win board approval. A committee was formed to recommend a solution.

Was the consensus that MBG was irreplaceable mere conventional rhetoric? Why did so many of us remember Mel Payne alluding to the "end of the golden years"? Payne must have sensed something—a subsonic note in a minor key, perhaps—not audible to the rest of us.

After all, things were going well. The atlas, globe, book programs, and television specials debuting in 1965 with the record-smashing "Americans on Everest" and blockbusters like "Miss Goodall and the Wild Chimpanzees" and "The World of Jacques-Yves Cousteau"; membership had tripled to an unheard-of six million. Even Payne admitted that MBG had been born "under a lucky star."

We thought the Society was green and burgeoning, but in retrospect I think that Mel Payne had spotted the yellow in the leaf: a sign that decline and fall were inevitable.

We brought it on ourselves, though we didn't know it at the time. It happened on the afternoon of June 21, 1967—summer solstice, the longest, brightest day of the year—when the board of trustees, myself reluctantly included, voted unanimously to break up the position of president and editor.

The argument was that Society activities had expanded beyond the range for one person to effectively handle them all. It meant that for the first time since 1920, one person did not hold both editorial and executive power. An editor would run the magazine and be in charge of all Society publications; the president would be, effectively, the publisher, the CEO in charge of the business and research activities. The money side now ruled, a decision that would ultimately lead to the uncoupling of the National Geographic Society and its magazine.

The board elected Ted Vosburgh the new editor. On his recommendation, Franc Shor and I became his associate editors: Franc in charge of text, me in charge of illustrations, books, and magazine production. MBG became chairman; and Dr. McKnew, advisory chairman. Mel Payne was elected president and CEO.

Many seasons of unprecedented growth and achievement still lay ahead. But in the end, Mel Payne was right about the golden era vanishing—not immediately, perhaps, but half a century later.

PART THREE

THE BEST JOB IN JOURNALISM

CHAPTER THIRTEEN

THE TRANSITION

The world of the National Geographic Society did not come to a screeching halt simply because one man retired. The sun rose and set over headquarters, just as it had done the day before and would do the next day. Cars in our parking lot slumbered in the summer heat beneath the magnolia trees, as they had done since the completion of the new building. Employees looked forward to vacations and new assignments.

And Donna and I were preparing to leave on a long assignment—in Afghanistan.

I looked forward to a chance for some serious fieldwork after being office-bound for two years. Ever since I had glimpsed Kabul during the Eisenhower tour I had wanted to return to Afghanistan. We had our visas, tickets, and Land Rover set. My cameras and lenses were ready. Afghanistan was basking in the one brief moment of peace and prosperity it might ever enjoy.

Then Ted Vosburgh, the new editor, called me into his office.

Ted was a methodical man who didn't like surprises. Unlike MBG, he would never tear up the magazine at the last moment; he insisted on knowing the status of every article in the pipeline. Since Franc Shor was away on assignment that summer of 1967, I was to provide Ted with that information, at least until he found his stride as editor. That meant he didn't want me gone for two months too. In short, no Afghanistan.

All that work, all those hopes, up in smoke. Donna was equally disappointed. But I had no choice.

I also had to find a substitute for the Afghanistan coverage. That took a nanosecond; Tom Abercrombie was the perfect choice. I turned over the tickets to him and his wife, Lynn, and they soon departed. In the meantime, I settled down in my office and took on the responsibility of overseeing the illustrations side of the magazine, which Garrett ran on a day-to-day basis because I now had books under my wing as well.

One day staff photographer Bob Sisson invited me over for dinner at his place. He wanted my opinion.

He walked me to the backyard, where a camera with an immense bellows sat on a tripod. He was practicing macro photography, close-up photographs of small critters. They were fantastic and as good as our naturalist Paul Zahl's images. Paul was a biologist who had taught himself photography; Bob was a photographer who had fallen in love with biology. The professional photographer has a better skill set.

I knew that Bob was falling behind in a world of Abercrombies, Allards, and our latest hire, Jim Stanfield. And his recent, demanding coverage of Algeria emerging from its civil war had nearly done him in. Did I think, he asked, that he might become a nature photographer?

Good Lord, yes! I encouraged him. I felt a close bond with this man who had nursed me on that railroad bridge in Connecticut when I was doused with sewage as a cub. I would do anything to help him, and now I could.

Bob Gilka, the director of photography, was impressed with Sisson's work and assigned him a story on salmon. Sisson, in response, constructed an artificial redd, the rocky bed where salmon spawn. It was a half cylinder made of glass strewn with gravel, allowing him to shoot from beneath and make unprecedented pictures of salmon spawning. Bob was off and running—that alone made missing Afghanistan a bit more tolerable.

But it still hurt.

ONE DAY WHEN FEW LEAVES REMAINED on the trees, Tom Abercrombie returned from Afghanistan. He sat down, full of stories, and lit his pipe. He and Lynn had traveled the length and breadth of that fierce, fabled land. Thanks to three decades of strong Society-Afghan relations, he could go nearly everywhere. How far? Umm, about 20,000 miles by Land Rover, camel, horse, and yak. Ten thousand photographs.

Tom had photographed King Mohammed Zahir Shah roaming his estate like any English country gentleman. The queen did not wear a veil; the veil injunction was dropped in 1957. Buzkashi, that violent polo match in which a lamb's carcass is the ball? He had joined the horsemen and "damn near got killed."

Tom had accompanied a nomadic tribe when it left the mountains and headed into the valleys for the coming winter. He had seen the Desert of Death. And seen the Wakhan Corridor, that long finger of territory jutting northeastward into the high Pamirs, usually closed to outsiders.

"Well, let me tell you a story about that," he said, knocking his pipe in the ashtray. On the way back down the Wakhan, he stopped by the house of his guide's father and asked the old man if many outsiders were seen there. The father shook his head: Hardly any. Wait, there was somebody a while back, he remembered. The old man fished around a box and retrieved a grimy rectangle of card stock. Tom mimed squinting at the print in the dim light before slowly making out the words:

FRANC SHOR

NATIONAL GEOGRAPHIC MAGAZINE

WASHINGTON, D.C.

Franc and Jean had traveled there, under armed escort, with the permission of King Zahir Shah, claiming to be the first Westerners to do so since 1838.

A few days later, Donna and I went to the Abercrombies' house in Shady Side, Maryland, for dinner. Tom pulled me aside to thank me because Afghanistan ranked high on his list of peak experiences. His story "Afghanistan: Crossroad of Conquerors," published in September 1968, provided the most complete coverage of that nation most Americans in those years would read.

Sensitive to my disappointment at my canceled trip, Tom reappeared with a thank-you gift. It was an ancient musket, gorgeously inlaid with marquetry of what looked like ivory and lapis lazuli. He had bought it off a Kuchi tribesman near the Salang Pass, just north of the Khyber Pass.

That rifle still graces my mantel today.

IN JANUARY 1968 Richard Leakey came to stay with us. Ours was an unlikely friendship. I was 14 years older, and our two personalities could not be more different. But that visit to Olduvai Gorge in 1964 and our safari together had forged a deep bond.

I always tried showing him something interesting. Once, Donna and I took him to a Super Giant grocery store, where he stood in the pet food aisle gazing in disbelief.

"Do people really buy this stuff?" he asked.

"Of course. How else do you feed your dog?"

"I just open the back door. Ben finds his own food. In the bush."

On another visit, after he assured me he could ski, I borrowed a friend's condo at Stratton Mountain in Vermont and hit the slopes.

Uncertain of his skill, I chose an easy run. At the top, Richard slid out of the chairlift like a pro, pointed his skis downhill, and took off. With the ubiquitous pipe dangling from his mouth and his scarf flapping behind him, he quickly gathered speed. I followed at a discreet distance. Something just didn't look right. With increasing dismay, I realized that he had no experience whatsoever and had no idea how to turn or stop. Cries of "pardon, pardon" didn't exactly give other skiers sufficient warning of impending disaster.

He kept it simple: To halt, crash into something—a trash can, a tree, occasionally another skier. Predictably, that caused a commotion. But if a chap with a pipe, scarf, and crisp Kenyan accent knocked you down, you might be charmed into forgiveness too.

Après-ski was Richard's forte. With a bottle of wine and some hors d'oeuvres, we started spinning stories until interrupted by the telephone. A local reporter was reminding me she would soon arrive to interview us. I had completely forgotten about it but told her to come over in an hour. More wine flowed. When the doorbell rang, I got up to let her in and on a whim introduced myself as Richard Leakey. Richard continued the charade and acknowledged that he was Gil Grosvenor.

She fell for the ruse. We offered her wine, and I began telling tall tales about my fossil-hunting prowess. "Gil" discussed the workings of *National Geographic* magazine. When we got in too deep, however, we panicked and confessed. She was not amused. To make amends, we submitted to a lengthy, in-depth interview.

Richard once claimed fossils bored him, but his genes had the upper hand. He was still running his safari enterprise—but only part-time now, because, like me, he had entered the family business. Soon he was digging away at every likely-looking gulch, gorge, and escarpment.

After Emperor Haile Selassie opened Ethiopia's Omo River to paleontology, Richard joined the 1967 Omo River expedition, funded in part by the National Geographic Society, and returned with a 100,000-year-old *Homo sapiens* skull in hand. He had also flown over nearby Lake Rudolf in northern Kenya, where the Omo River debouches, and noticed that the stark, eroded badlands stretching away from Rudolf's eastern shores looked like promising fossil country.

Richard had come to Washington with his father for the elder Leakey's annual January visit to our Research Committee, on which I now sat as a full-fledged member. When we convened, Louis Leakey told us about his new "Jane Goodall of the mountain gorillas," an American occupational therapist with no credentials for the job. Nevertheless, she was intently determined to set up a camp in the Virunga volcanoes in eastern Congo— in the very same meadow where George Schaller had pioneered the scientific observation of endangered mountain gorillas in 1959. Her name was Dian Fossey.

Leakey felt the need to reassure a skeptical committee because Fossey had just suffered the same fate as Schaller, who was chased out of his meadow when a civil war swept the area. Another bloody insurrection put Fossey in jail before she escaped into neighboring Rwanda. Louis told us she was recovering from her harrowing ordeal and establishing a new research station high on a forested saddle between the peaks of Rwanda's Volcanoes National Park. Because everything Leakey touched had turned to gold, we reluctantly continued our support.

Louis then turned to his widespread paleontological projects, using his considerable persuasive powers to obtain as large a stipend as possible. Then Richard chimed in, stealing his father's thunder by enthusiastically selling the committee on a major expedition to the eroded scarp lands around Lake Rudolf. He, too, was awarded a grant, but his brashness annoyed several members, who issued him a stern warning not to show his face again should our trust in him be misspent.

The outcome? Richard returned from Lake Rudolf carrying a 2.8-million-year-old *Australopithecus boisei* skull—the same species his mother had found at Olduvai in July 1959. But this skull was considerably older:

a major discovery. Richard had the goods! Another Leakey was now embarked on the hunt for human origins.

WINTER TURNED TO SPRING. By now Robin Lee Graham had crossed the Indian Ocean. When I learned that he had reached Mauritius under jury-rig, we had a new mast for *Dove* flown out. With that mast, he sailed on to Durban, South Africa. Nevertheless, by the time he reached Durban, *Dove* was in serious need of repairs. In Washington, the conjecture was that Robin was ready to quit.

I was off to Cape Town, where with growing concern I strode up and down Strand Street waiting for word of Robin Lee Graham's arrival in nearby Gordon's Bay. Undoubtedly, stiff gales and headwinds explained his delay. Then my inquiries turned up something unexpected: There was no Robin Lee Graham in Gordon's Bay. There was, however, a "Mrs. Graham."

That's how I met Patti Ratterree. They were either married, feigning it, or engaged—troubling for a solo circumnavigation. I didn't press the point, because she was so clearly worried about him. Robin had disappeared along that dangerous, shipwreck-littered coast, so I chartered a plane to search for him. When the pilot returned, he told us *Dove* was holed up in Struisbaai, a tiny port not far from Cape Agulhas. The boat was anchored in the bay waiting out a hard gale.

I rented a car. Patti and I drove down that coast. I grew to like Patti, who turned out to be a levelheaded young woman. I was relieved to learn that Robin did intend to finish his voyage—single-handedly.

The sailor Patti retrieved and brought back to our small hotel was a bedraggled, lean, muscular young man with a mop of sun-bleached curls. The boat was in even worse shape: too tiny for him now—he couldn't stand up straight in the cabin. And despite all the expensive repairs Geographic had paid for in Durban, the deck was starting to separate from the hull. The mast-mounted camera looked okay, but I was appalled that he had only a radio receiver with him. I ordered Robin a quality battery-powered ship-to-shore radiotelephone with a generator to power it. That way, he could make distress calls in an emergency and talk to Patti regularly—anything to relieve that awful loneliness.

He was courteous to me but obviously only wanted to be with her. I got it. But I was in South Africa to revise the manuscript with him. He couldn't just wrap himself in her. To his credit, Robin snapped out of it long enough for us to finish it in a few days.

One night at dinner in Struisbaai, he suddenly stood up and said, "I've got to check my boat." The waters of that bay are notoriously tricky; the tide was running out, the wind was up, and he felt the anchor might drag. He didn't think that; he felt it. His sailor's intuition knew that *Dove* was about to be blown out to a sea that stretched for thousands of miles to Antarctica.

Sure enough, when I drove Robin to *Dove,* she was already dragging toward the open sea. He jumped into his dinghy, rowed out to the sloop, moved it to a more sheltered anchorage, and expertly reset the anchors.

After my departure, they were officially married in Gordon's Bay.

I flew home more confident about part one of Robin's article, which was now ready for the printer. But the biggest storm was yet to come.

Every journey has its "middle passage," that darkest, most desperate phase when the mind succumbs to doubts and fears and the odds of success seem longest. For Robin Lee Graham, that corresponded to his crossing of the Atlantic: the 44-day passage from Cape Town to Suriname. It wasn't just that he fell overboard and only barely caught hold of the safety rail around the stern. It was the dejection and depression at being away from Patti. Depression at sea can kill you; the endless horizon of water and sky offers scant consolation in times of deep loneliness. Somewhere out there, his nerve broke. After arriving in Suriname he informed us he would never sail alone again.

I dropped everything and flew to sweltering Paramaribo, Suriname's capital, to reason with Robin, but feared I was too late.

I met the young couple for dinner in one of the crumbling city's best hotels, clutching the October 1968 *National Geographic*. Hot off the press, it featured the first installment of his voyage, with his picture on the cover. I was stunned by what greeted me at the table.

Patti, who seemed a bit tipsy or high, was in better shape than he was. But Robin was dead drunk—and his red-rimmed eyes testified, I thought, to something more than alcohol. He quickly got to the point.

"Gil, I'd rather face a tank of hungry piranhas than ever put to sea alone again. I mean it. I hate that bloody boat!" It was clear that he had outgrown *Dove*, physically and psychologically. Then, leaning forward: "Besides, *Dove's* no longer safe. I don't trust her anymore."

I remembered that deck separating from that hull and knew he was right: *Dove* would not survive another storm at sea, and probably would take Robin down with her. I pulled out my trump card.

"Why not replace *Dove* with a bigger boat? We could advance you the funds you are due for the second and third installments."

Did I see a flicker of interest in those red-rimmed eyes? I wasn't sure. He remained adamant that he wasn't going on alone.

I left Paramaribo thinking that I had failed.

Robin proved me wrong. He did finish. With funds we advanced, he bought a 33-foot fiberglass sloop, complete with self-steering vane and roller-furling gear for setting sail without leaving the cockpit. He and Patti messed about in the West Indies in *Return of Dove,* or *Dove II,* for a year before he resumed his solo voyage where he had left off, in Suriname. He sailed into San Pedro Bay, California, on April 30, 1970, 1,739 days and 33,000 miles after his initial departure: the youngest person at that time to complete a solo circumnavigation.

Today, Robin and Patti live happily together in a log cabin he built with his own hands high in the mountains of Montana. There he started a successful business building houses—about as far away from the sea as you can get.

After that story found safe harbor, and now that he was comfortably settled into the job of editor, Ted released me for a field assignment. Donna and I wouldn't be going to Afghanistan, but to another equally interesting destination.

BALI, "ISLAND OF THE GODS," was not always the paradise of the travel posters. The Muslims who occupied the rest of the 6,000-island chain now known as Indonesia called it the "savage isle," a nod to its mix of ancient religious beliefs and medieval Hinduism. Unlike the rest of the archipelago, Bali resisted conversion to Islam. Located not quite three miles off the eastern tip of Java, it is surrounded by treacherous currents and reefs, and was defended by warriors so resolute that the sultans chose to leave the place alone.

The Dutch finally broke that island's isolation. Their military incursions at the turn of the 20th century led to the violent deaths of thousands of Balinese—many by suicide.

The spiritual universe occupied by the Balinese, as well as the grace and musicality of their dance, inspired Donna and me to explore beyond the well-traveled roads. Anthropologist Margaret Mead and photographer Henri Cartier-Bresson had documented ceremonies like trance dancing, but only in black and white; we hadn't seen any documentation in color.

We had more practical motives too. Sukarno, the father of modern Indonesia, had made Bali, his mother's homeland, the focus of his tourism boost. How would mass tourism affect its unique, fragile culture? How was it faring after the 1963 eruption of Mount Agung, which had killed several thousand people and displaced many more? How well had it recovered from Sukarno's fall in 1965, when perhaps a million Indonesians lost their lives—80,000 of them in Bali's anti-communist purge?

Donna and I spent October and November 1968 in a bungalow not far from the new Hotel Bali Beach, at that time the only luxury hotel on the island. In 1968 Bali was averaging only 40 tourists a day. But with construction of a new jet-friendly runway the deluge was clearly coming. We were anxious to photograph it before that happened.

Siegfried Beil, manager of the Hotel Bali Beach, let me use his refrigerator to store my film and helped get my exposed rolls safely to Jakarta and then to Washington. He also lent me the hotel's four-wheel drive, as our days were spent far away from the beach, up in the hills of the interior. Our guide and interpreter, Njoman Oka, led us behind the scenes. "You must seek out Bali's special moments," he told us. "The Balinese will welcome you, but whatever they are doing, they do for themselves and not for your entertainment."

We had hardly begun to explore the island when Njoman learned that a tooth-filing ceremony would be held in a remote village. Tooth-filing, the ancient practice of filing several front teeth, was a rite of passage to adulthood, a symbolic taming of the primal emotions of greed, anger, selfishness, and lust.

It was rare for a non-Balinese to witness a tooth-filing ceremony—and even more so to photograph it. For one thing, the young people making the transition are deemed vulnerable to the malign influences of evil spirits. For another, the entire ritual—from the initial preparation to the final offering of an effigy to the sea—takes nearly a week. Njoman hoped for permission to document its central feature: the tooth filing itself.

A thatch-topped, mud-brick wall surrounded the compound. Entering it, we had to make a few circuitous turns to divert evil spirits before emerging in a courtyard where several generations of an extended family lived. We sat politely on a cool porch while Njoman introduced us to the headman and explained our mission. The chief nodded and tendered me a bowl of fried dragonfly, which I ate unhesitatingly. Nearby, women were decorating a ceremonial pavilion with palm-frond ornaments and fruit-filled baskets. A coconut-husk fire had been lit to ward off imminent rain; since the sun broke through, it must have done the trick.

Soon we were ushered into the pavilion. Plumes of incense hung in the air; onlookers chanted in rhythm to the gongs and bells of a gamelan orchestra. A frangipani-crowned girl, dressed in a sash of silver and a headdress of gold leaves, was led in, having been isolated for 24 hours. The priest rubbed a gold ring on her lips, and she arranged herself on the couch. He wielded his long file, and soon flecks of enamel were sprinkled over his fingers and her mouth. The six upper front teeth were ground down to an even line. Now she could rest easy: When it would be her turn to die and be cremated, she would be welcomed by the gods and not rejected as a fanged demon.

Several girls and a couple of boys underwent the procedure. All the while, I took abundant Polaroids to give away as keepsakes. My Nikons held the 35mm frames intended for *Geographic* use, but it was clear that the Polaroids were prized by the girls and their families. This ceremony means more than does confirmation or graduation in the West; even calling it "tooth filing" gives it too ethnographic a cast. They were, Njoman explained, laying the cornerstones of their adult lives.

At night we'd often see lamps bobbing about in the rice terraces. Njoman explained that these were the lanterns of eel fishermen; they stalked the paddies, light in one hand and tongs in the other. The lantern would attract the eels. There was something artistic about the scene I hoped to capture—something symbolic about Bali. The fisherman moved like a Balinese dancer, alternately bending down and straightening up, his timeless route through the warren of paddies seemingly as stylized as the movements of the legong dance, for which Bali is known.

I spent three nights photographing an eel fisherman wending his way around in sweeping, Z-shaped patterns, trying vainly for a three-minute exposure that gave the impression of a seamless, graceful, firefly-like movement. It finally came together on the third night, when we captured a sequence on a single frame—although I didn't see it until we were back in the office a month later.

The landscape itself—the immense series of rice paddy terraces stepping down from the volcanic highlands—resembled from the air a carefully hewn piece of sculpture. So I chartered a plane to make aerials.

On previous assignments I was inured to pilots growing bored and pointing at the gas gauge as an excuse for cutting the flight short. But this guy seemed unusually persistent and worried. I soon found out why: Upon landing, the engine conked out on the runway, and the plane rolled to a stop. I walked the rest of the way to the shack that served as a terminal. Because the flight was short, the pilot had only partially fueled the plane.

Besides documenting tooth filing, the most moving ceremony we photographed was trance dancing, which had been high on our shooting list. Njoman discovered an upcoming ceremony, and one morning we drove two hours up to the village of Kintamani, overlooking a beautiful lake that filled the caldera of a volcano called Mount Batur. To document a ritual held sacred by your hosts—a ritual older than the thousand or so years of Hinduism that overlay it—you dress soberly and treat everyone with the utmost respect. Which is to say, you work mostly with long lenses so as not to be intrusive.

In the *sanghyang* form of the dance, two prepubescent girls dressed in traditional Balinese regalia were induced into a trance. In a state of possession, they performed exquisite movements they'd never been trained to do, often standing on the shoulders of their fathers. Though usually a skeptic, I believe that these two tear-stained girls had been transported to visionary realms I cannot fathom.

Bali had cast its spell on us, and must have done the same for many members when "Bali by the Back Roads" was published in November 1969. We had captured a moment when our gentle hosts struggled to preserve their traditional lives in the face of an approaching tourist onslaught that would challenge their culture.

When we left Bali, Donna looked out the plane's window at that receding gem, turned to me, and said, "When we look back on our experience, we must never forget that Bali is not a place, but a feeling."

THE YEAR 1968 ended, in my view, with three great achievements. The first was the flight of Apollo 8 around the moon. Like everyone else, I spent that Christmastide watching the grainy black-and-white images on television or listening to Frank Borman's readings from the Book of Genesis, radio-waved from so far away. I marveled at the iconic photograph, since dubbed "Earthrise": a fleeting image made by Bill Anders as his spacecraft sped around the moon.

The second achievement took place in the Oval Office on October 2, when, in the closing weeks of his administration, LBJ signed three pieces of legislation into law. One was the National Wild and Scenic Rivers Act, a tribute to Frank and John Craighead; another was the National Trails System Act. Both of these were impacted by Laurance Rockefeller's Outdoor Recreation Resources Commission. Rockefeller himself would be instrumental in the third piece of legislation signed that day: the creation of Redwood National Park. He had been the special emissary to President Johnson throughout the campaign to establish that preserve and may have had assistance from an agent within the White House itself: Lady Bird Johnson, a child of the piney woods and bayous of Northeast Texas.

President Johnson presented the signing pen—customarily given to the person most deserving of it—to Melville Bell Grosvenor. In the July 1966 *National Geographic,* he had asked members to write their senators and representatives in support of a park for redwoods. Just as GHG had done with sequoias, MBG had helped save the redwoods.

The third achievement belonged to Bill Garrett, recognized by the National Press Photographers Association as Magazine Photographer of the Year. Garrett's prize pivoted on his coverage of the Mekong River, which he traversed from the Chinese border to the South China Sea during a time of insurrection and war.

Bill was never afraid of the fighting, whether accompanying U.S. Marines on foot in the swamps of the Mekong Delta, pursuing the Vietcong on U.S. Navy patrol boats, riding helicopter gunships, or debating pro-war hawks on the Washington cocktail circuit. Word of Garrett's outspoken opposition to the war probably drifted back to Mel Payne, who already thought him too liberal.

By 1969 we were all torn apart by that conflict—me especially, because of my own experience in South Vietnam in 1955 and because my brother was risking his life there every day flying F-4 Phantoms in the skies above Hanoi. I had a chance conversation with a sergeant recently returned from the fighting. Remembering my own psychological warfare years, when I had steeped myself in the culture and geography of Vietnam, I asked what impressed him most about the people there.

"There's two kinds," he replied. "The Charlies shoot at us. The Friendlies shoot with us—but what help is a guy who can't even talk English?"

My suspicions were confirmed: We Americans did not know the first thing about the people we were fighting at such a cost. That's when the idea of publishing a map reflecting the cultural diversity of Southeast Asia was born.

We could have printed more articles, even a book. But maps made National Geographic distinctive. I mentioned the idea to Bill Garrett, who jumped all over it, initiating one of the standout cartographic-editorial projects of the following decade: our "Peoples and Cultures" of the world series.

AS SPRING 1969 SLID INTO SUMMER, Donna and I finally got away ourselves, joining a Research Committee field trip to Greece and Turkey. If the ancient road from Halicarnassus to Aphrodisias was as appalling as the modern one, no Caesar riding in his chariot would have failed to send a few heads rolling.

It took us three hours to get from Bodrum, successor to Halicarnassus, to the site of Aphrodisias—three hours on a bus twisting and turning around the bare brown hills of southwestern Anatolia, three hours of choking on the Turkish dust and bouts of carsickness. Donna and I wondered how the older members of the Research Committee were faring. Craning my head around, I managed to scan the rickety bus. Those gray-headed gentlemen and their wives looked unperturbed. Dr. Alexander Wetmore, secretary of the Smithsonian Institution before Dr. Carmichael succeeded him, was dozing in his seat. Someone noted a grayish crow glimpsed out in the fields. Without opening his eyes, America's foremost ornithologist stated, "It's a hooded crow. *Corvus cornix.* Widespread in Asia Minor."

Donna and I tried ignoring our nausea and affected an equal show of nonchalance.

All was forgotten once we finally rolled down a road lined with pear trees and the 16 soaring columns of the ruined temple of Aphrodite, focal point of a lost city once named for that goddess: Aphrodisias.

There we met Dr. Kenan Erim, the Turkish-born, Princeton-educated archaeologist who had been excavating this extraordinary place since 1961, mostly with the support of New York University and the National Geographic Society.

These ruins were what remained of the once opulent capital of Caria, a Roman province in Asia Minor. Boasting 50,000 residents, it had flourished from the first century B.C. to the sixth century A.D. before a series of earthquakes and wars toppled it. In its heyday, it resembled a modern university town: a place that cultivated the arts and sports.

The marble blocks and broken statuary invited you to imagine its former beauty and elegance. Isolation had preserved it; a half century earlier, it took three days on horseback to get there and back from the nearest railway station. Scant archaeological work had been done until Kenan arrived, assisted each season by a team of scholars, graduate students, and people from the local village.

He showed us the stadium—one of the finest Roman ones still extant—which had held 30,000 spectators. Those with more luxurious tastes might have reclined in the now roofless Baths of Hadrian or gossiped in an agora, the marketplace long buried in juniper and poplar.

Kenan could bring a pile of stones to life. Marble in the nearby hills had given Aphrodisias its reputation for superb statuary and attracted sculptors from all over Europe. Kenan would caress a statuette rescued from a pile of rubble and explain how some long-forgotten student had marred the face with a clumsy chisel, relegating the piece to the junk pile. He told tales of gambling, prostitution, and thievery, adding the full plethora of human experience to the ruins around us. He was especially mesmerizing when telling of the pilgrims who came from far and wide to visit the temple of Aphrodite.

This place had probably been a Great Mother Goddess cult center since the Bronze Age, Kenan said. She had probably been some version of Astarte or Cybele, the Near East fertility deities of biblical times. By the Greco-Roman era, she had been assimilated by the then dominant Aphrodite or Venus, the dazzling goddess of life and love. Women who made the pilgrimage to the far-famed Carian Aphrodite sacrificed their hair to her in the annual mourning for the death of Adonis.

Kenan's narrative was spellbinding. We were in a dusty corner of Turkey, where red poppies dozed in the nearby fields and wild thyme, olive, and fig sank their tendrils into the tumbled masonry, chunks of friezes, and statuary unseen for centuries. It was as if the goddess and a sense of fecundity still dwelled in this place.

A month or two later, Mel Payne hosted a Research Committee reunion dinner in Washington and asked everyone to bring his or her favorite memory or memento from the recent trip. Donna hung a cardboard sign around her waist that read "My favorite treasure from Aphrodisias," the arrows pointing to her swelling belly. We had been trying to have children; being pilgrims to the shrine of fertility did the trick. On March 29, 1970, our treasure from Aphrodisias arrived: Gilbert Hovey Grosvenor II.

IF I COULD PICK ONLY ONE rocket launch at Kennedy Space Center to witness, Apollo 11—that "giant leap for mankind"—in July 1969 would be it. So did a million other people, cramming into every available motel room or simply car-camping alongside every road margin providing a view. Grandstands three and a half miles away from the massive Saturn V rocket at its gantry had been erected for VIPs and journalists. While every National Geographic Society grandee, including Payne and Vosburgh, had qualified for the former distinction, I was there in the interests of photojournalism. I wanted to join Jack Fletcher, known for his technical expertise, at work.

Fletcher had invented a camera triggered by the light of the rocket ignition alone, since no human was allowed close to the Saturn rocket. We spent most of July 15 setting up those tripod-mounted cameras at selected vantage points, each with motor drive and a magazine full of film, which meant slogging around in deep sand and battling mosquitoes.

Several other *National Geographic* photographers and picture editors were also around; we had planned a major package for our December 1969 issue. As associate editor in charge of illustrations, I was coordinating their efforts, including those of a picture editor with a special interest in space-related subjects: Jon Schneeberger. MBG liked him and sometimes shanghaied him to crew on *White Mist.* Jon had a unique way of expressing things, along with a stubbornly rebellious streak. Like his best friend Bill Allard, he could win the confidence of anyone.

Our photo lab personnel were managing the photo pool, a consortium of press services, and NASA to coordinate the photography of this historic launch. The team would work out of a converted motel room in nearby Cocoa Beach to process the film and distribute images to the world's press.

On the morning of July 16, 1969, Donna and I headed to the bleachers. At 9:32 a.m., everyone put on sunglasses and craned their necks to get the best view.

First came the flash—I hoped those cameras began firing away. Then, thunder, mounting in crescendo as the shock wave hit and the rocket began majestically rising from the pad. It became a burning orb, a miniature sun disappearing into the heavens with Neil Armstrong, Buzz Aldrin, Mike Collins aboard.

Then it was over. Jack Fletcher would collect those cameras and exposed film. Our technicians and those from *Life* would make thousands of color duplicates to be distributed all over the world before the mission was even completed.

Four days later everyone with access to a television set watched that booted foot ease down that ladder, tentatively touch the lunar surface, pull back up, and settle back down—that "one small step for man." Many were still watching when the command module *Columbia* splashed down into the Pacific east of Wake Island and the helicopter from U.S.S. *Hornet* retrieved the astronauts. Aboard that aircraft carrier with President Richard Nixon and a host of dignitaries were two *National Geographic* photographers documenting the recovery. We still had the inside track with NASA.

Afterward, select duplicates of the mission photography made in NASA's color lab in Houston were handed out to every media representative, including our photo editor, Jon Schneeberger. Later that night Jon returned to a back entrance to that lab and walked away with high-quality copies of all Apollo 11's photography. His initiative was affirmed when

NASA selected the Society to be one of only three repositories for copies of all its mission photography.

On February 16, 1970, in our 10th-floor dining room, at a small black-tie dinner to celebrate the presentation of the Hubbard Medal to the three Apollo astronauts, I shook hands with Neil Armstrong, Buzz Aldrin, and Mike Collins, who would become a Society trustee. In gratitude, Armstrong presented us with a two-by-three-inch framed National Geographic Society flag he had carried on the lunar surface. The Poles, Mount Everest, the Challenger Deep (the Mariana Trench), and now the moon.

LIKE LEAVES IN AUTUMN, older colleagues were dying or retiring. W. Robert Moore, former chief of the foreign editorial staff, succumbed to leukemia; he had ranged the world with large-format cameras and glass plates. Tony Stewart, in his heyday our legendary chief photographer, retired.

That fall, when we dedicated our new Membership Center Building—a modern facility that was equal parts mail, computer, fulfillment, and customer service center near Gaithersburg, Maryland—questions of succession surfaced again.

Ted Vosburgh was 63 when he took command of the magazine; his was understood to be a caretaker editorship. In October, when he announced his intention to retire, the guessing game began anew. Franc Shor? Though next in seniority, he would never pass muster with Mel Payne or Dr. McKnew. Me? Because of my name, I was in Mel's sights too. Bill Garrett? Too liberal for Payne, though Bill's pictorial genius and charisma had "editor someday" stamped all over him.

Meanwhile, Ted called me into his office to help plan the transition. He was particularly interested in the direction the younger staff might take. I replied that we hoped to cover topical subjects like the environment and pollution. Ted thought that controversial issues might alienate many members. I suggested that if we kept it balanced and objective, it wouldn't.

Pollution was controversial in the 1960s. Although an advocate of national parks, MBG was averse to what he called "kooky" environmental activism, the kind that "blocked the path of progress." He was sure that the little old lady in Dubuque felt the same way.

But pollution was congruent with our conservation ethos and had been a topic simmering among younger staff since Rachel Carson's 1962 best seller, *Silent Spring*, helped launch the modern environmental crusade. We received letters from members, government officials, and experts, wondering why, as our chief designer Howard Paine put it, "we appear to ignore the subject, or to be unaware of it."

I encouraged Howard to write Vosburgh a memo. "I am dismayed," he wrote, "in this age, to hear arguments like 'It's not for us,' 'We don't want to upset the readers,' 'It's too big,' 'It's too complicated,' 'It can't be illustrated,' 'It belongs in other magazines.'" The contamination of man's natural environment was no bigger or more complicated than many subjects we covered, he argued, and certainly could be illustrated. It undoubtedly belonged in our magazine.

Ted agreed, and in November 1969 he set up a task force to plan our coverage. The Cartographic Division began preparing an updated world map—backed by artwork illustrating the sources of pollution. "Jolt and educate," picture editor Mike Long suggested. He recommended a "ghastly portfolio to begin the story." Our new generation was gathering momentum.

CHAPTER FOURTEEN

THE THIRD GENERATION

O n the morning of June 11, 1970, I was up early, presentable in my best dark suit, white shirt, and tie. My hair had been cautiously cropped and combed—a deliberate attempt to look as conservative as possible. "The consummate undertaker," Donna said, smirking.

At the Geographic, everyone sensed the impending drama. I buried myself in work until the board of trustees meeting convened. I gathered my papers and—passing colleagues who whispered, "Good luck!"—strode down the hall into the boardroom, where I took my place at that long table.

MBG was seated in the center, gesticulating to Ted Vosburgh on his right. To his left a ramrod-straight Mel Payne sat still as flint, gazing inscrutably down at his folded hands. While I arranged and rearranged my papers, I looked around. Leonard Carmichael, Laurance Rockefeller, Connie Wirth, and the rest of the old guard chatted casually. I hoped they would be in my corner. I knew Dr. McKnew would back me. A handful of new trustees brought on by Payne, though, might line up behind him, should matters take a wrong turn.

MBG, still chairman, banged the meeting to order. The first business consisted of housekeeping chores: quarterly reports from the president and the editor, followed by a question-and-answer session. After lunch in the executive dining room, we reconvened to address the issue that many of my colleagues on the magazine thought might mark a watershed for the *Geographic* and their own careers: electing an editor to succeed Ted Vosburgh.

Would the board turn to the younger generation? Most of us were barely 40. Would the trustees play it safe by electing a caretaker editor for a few more years? Or, God forbid, hire a headhunter to dig up a big-name candidate with no institutional knowledge?

MBG called us to order and announced Ted Vosburgh's impending retirement before launching into a heartfelt eulogy of Ted's saintly attributes. The sun kept marching across the sky and—*click-whirr!*—the drapes automatically adjusted themselves.

Finally, MBG sought the board's wisdom and guidance in selecting a new editor, and my heart beat a little faster. I knew I was in the pole position—a subcommittee had recommended me—but Mel Payne was the wild card. He was the president and chief executive officer and might exercise the right to choose the editor he wanted, subject to the board's approval. But in the four years since the splitting of responsibilities, it was still an organization with two heads; he had not yet made a move to consolidate his newfound power. The board was still electing the editor as well as the CEO.

Ted spoke on my behalf, extolling my leadership in establishing the Control Center, which saved the magazine large sums of money and led to my becoming chairman of the editorial council. He effusively praised my diligence as associate editor and my management of Bob Breeden's Special Publications Division. He pointed out how my coverage of President Eisenhower's trip abroad proved I had the mettle as writer and photographer.

Dr. McKnew chimed in, lauding my intensive education in the business department. "He knows our magazine and Society business very well," he said—cracking a slight smile: "After all, I trained him."

MBG spoke, slowly at first, before adrenaline overtook him. "This magazine enjoys the finest collection of young journalists in America!" Banging his fist on the table, he continued, "This is their day! Let them skipper this ship! They're ready."

Stone-faced, Mel Payne sat not uttering a word. Perhaps other trustees wondered why. I welcomed his silence with relief.

My election as editor was unanimously approved by voice vote, with my tenure to commence on October 1, 1970.

Now it was my turn. I thanked the board members for their confidence and assured them there would be no radical changes in our journal. I reiterated my belief that "evolutionary changes are essential; revolutionary ones are often fatal." I announced my wish to keep Franc Shor, 56, as one of my associate editors and to balance him with a second associate editor, John Scofield, 55. The board concurred.

I promised to work closely with Payne—hoping he was reassured by my dark suit and conservative demeanor.

Meeting adjourned, I lagged behind, receiving the congratulations of each trustee as they filed out. Eventually it was just MBG and me. A warm handclasp and embrace, that old grin breaking through his dignified composure if only for an instant—but an instant I will cherish for a lifetime. I was now a third-generation Grosvenor editor of *National Geographic,* and I would give it my all.

It was the happiest day of my professional life.

THE NEWS SPREAD FAST. Even before I was back in my office, colleagues lined up to shake my hand. Once in my office, Bill Garrett and Joe Judge, among others, offered handshakes, backslaps, and questions: "Who voted with us—or opposed us?" "What did you tell the board?" "Who carried the day? MBG?" I could respond only that it was very undramatic.

First, I wanted to see Franc Shor and John Scofield. Franc was a known quantity; John was quieter. As the one responsible for assembling the package that went off to the printer each month, John would be the glue that bound us: authors, copy editors, issue editors, researchers, engravers, and me. His support would be critical.

Before we convened in the Control Center to celebrate, I slipped into Ted's office to thank him for his support. The December issue, to be sent to the printer in August, would be the first one to bear my name atop the masthead. That was exciting: December would carry our pollution package. I wanted to send an immediate message about our direction. I made it the cover story and prefaced it with an editor's note so that our members understood its significance. Ted thought I was moving too fast, but with the transition under way, the issue was my baby.

At the celebration in the Control Center, we shared our hopes, dreams, and aspirations along with the wine. My announcement that the pollution package would showcase our tenure met with cheers from the staff. No one could have predicted that my decade as editor would mark the Society's greatest growth in our history, with 4.3 million new members.

I sought stronger photojournalism in our pages—in-depth reporting on pertinent issues with a geographical context. I'd enlarge the breach made in the Iron Curtain by MBG. I vowed to keep the Middle East in focus, to include more environmental stories, and to publish more exploration and adventure. I vowed to fight for more creative map supplements, such as the "Peoples and Cultures" series, even if I had to barter editorial pages or create more advertising to finance them.

My senior staff were top-rate professionals, some pushing 50 or spilling over its edge. Ken Weaver was still the chief science writer. Carolyn Patterson remained head of legends. Bob Gilka, the director of photography, was already becoming famous. Bill Garrett and Joe Judge would be my wingmen.

In depth and breadth—not to mention the occasional flash of flamboyance—ours easily rivaled any magazine staff in the country.

That night, having given my wife and infant son a warm embrace, I fell promptly asleep but awoke early. I was still elated but faced some sobering truths.

I was still haunted by the collapse of the *Saturday Evening Post;* now *Look* and *Life* were rumored to be in financial trouble. The magazine industry was unforgiving, and the margin between success and failure was perilously slim. I thought of Dr. McKnew's "sweet spot" in a magazine's heartbeat: stable circulation. In cutting subscription prices to boost circulation and advertising, the *Post, Life,* and *Look* had fallen away from their sweet spot, leaving an erratic heartbeat in its wake.

No way would I let that happen to our magazine. I realized how prudently I would have to manage the journal. Evolution, not revolution. We could not afford to alienate a single member if we could avoid it. Unlike the other publications, we were not dependent on advertising and not run by for-profit companies all too willing to cut their ties to a leaking ship. Another trip wire was television, widely blamed for the woes of magazine publishing. I wasn't so sure. Greed seemed a bigger culprit.

And there was the additional worry of a new rival—just a few blocks away.

Two months before my election to the editorship, S. Dillon Ripley, a famed ornithologist and distant cousin of GHG's, became secretary of the Smithsonian Institution and debuted *Smithsonian* magazine. He had lured Edward K. Thompson, the former managing editor of *Life,* to Washington and went after our membership by publishing similar stories on similar topics. The Society and the Smithsonian had been tight as ticks for decades, but Ripley felt competitive with the *Geographic.*

Beset by so many challenges, I would have to make every issue of *National Geographic* sing. Ensure every issue was balanced. Finally, I would closely monitor the renewal rate and publish stories that members, not necessarily editors, wanted to read—particularly at renewal time.

At that, I finally fell back to sleep.

THE NEXT MORNING I reentered the world of reality: Mel Payne requested my presence in his office. He shook my hand in congratulations, indicated a chair, and sat down across from me.

"Gil, you should know you were not my choice for editor."

Although I suspected as much, his bluntness took me aback. "May I ask why?" I managed.

"I think you'll be unduly influenced by Bill Garrett," he replied.

I wasn't surprised—his dislike of the brash, liberal-leaning Garrett was well known. I was angered and let that show. But I decided not to step into the trap and countered by asking whom he would have appointed.

"Joe Judge?" he mused. "Or maybe we should have conducted a nation-wide search."

"Mel, Joe knows nothing about pictures. The *Geographic* is a picture magazine first and foremost. Text is important but certainly not as crucial as photographs. Be assured, Joe will be my primary wordsmith."

No response. I probed further.

"Why didn't you speak up at the board meeting?"

"Ted supported you so enthusiastically, as did Tom McKnew and MBG, that I realized the board as a whole supported you. A long time ago I learned never to paint myself into a corner." He paused. "Anyway, I had always thought you would take my job when I retire."

I was so vexed by this point that I stood up and prepared to leave. "I respect your honesty, Mel," I said on my way out. "But I vow to prove you wrong."

Only years later did I come to respect his candor. He could have chosen to say nothing.

Meanwhile, I had a job to do. As editor-elect, I worked for the next six weeks putting our December issue together. The pollution package—"Our Ecological Crisis"—featured a stupendously good "ugly picture": Cleveland's Cuyahoga River, so befouled by oil and sludge that it actually caught fire in 1969. We made the wide-angle shot a gatefold, an unmistakable statement that our new team had tossed aside the rose-colored glasses we'd always been accused of viewing the world through.

At the end of July, I showed the layout to Ted Vosburgh, as a courtesy. Surprisingly, he liked it—so much so that the next day he asked, bashfully, if I would keep his name as editor on the December issue. That way he would retire having ushered in the beginning of our coverage of the environment.

Our generation's signature entrance became Ted's swan song, I thought ruefully. But I couldn't turn him down. He had supported me every step of my advancement over the past decade. I could do no less for an old, trusted friend.

Another old friend, Bud Wisherd, was still coming in every day despite his recent retirement. That photo lab was his life until one terrible day in late August 1970 when I answered my intercom.

"Gil, you better get down here," Carl Schrader, now chief of the photo lab, said. "Bud is lying on the floor of the men's room in the old wing. He's dead, Gil."

I went flying down the steps. I could tell in a glance he was gone; the life had gone out of his 69-year-old eyes. Heart attack or stroke, I'll never know. Once the police and the ambulance arrived, and the news began spreading through the building, I remember getting into the car with Carl. We had to tell Carrie, Bud's wife.

As anyone who has done so knows, making such a call is a searing thing. We rang the doorbell at the modest house, and in a minute or two she opened the door. She looked at Carl, then me—and realization dawned in her eyes.

"It's Buddy, isn't it?"

They had been married since the dawn of creation, so we weren't telling Carrie anything she didn't know when we emphasized what a beloved figure Bud had been and what a beacon for young technicians joining our ranks. The hardest part is the leave-taking. A day that had dawned like any other ends in a lonely house forever darkened by grief.

I could already recite my own tribute to Bud. I had just wanted to borrow a camera to take to Holland on that long-ago day at Yale. He persuaded me to think about a *Geographic* article. I could fairly say that Bud steered me into the course my life would follow.

August turned to September, and on October 1, I became editor. Hardly had I moved GHG's bound volumes into Ted's old office when I became entangled in an embarrassing mess of my own making.

In summer 1947, when I was aboard *Yankee* somewhere between the Azores and Bermuda, a balsa-wood raft with a bird painted on its single sail was nearing the Tuamotu Archipelago in the South Pacific. I was headed for boarding school; Thor Heyerdahl and Kon-Tiki were headed for fame.

GHG had been the first to publish an article by Thor Heyerdahl in English, an account of the young Norwegian explorer's sojourn at Fatu Hiva in the Marquesas. That had been before the war. But after the war, when Heyerdahl approached the Society, hoping it would sponsor his voyage across the Pacific by raft so that he could demonstrate the feasibility of Polynesia having been settled from South America, GHG and the Research Committee turned him down at the last minute with the curt dismissal: "Sheer nonsense." Heyerdahl was still smarting.

I suspect the committee members thought the premise behind the voyage was as unsound as the raft; Heyerdahl's notions about the settlement of Polynesia from the east, rather than the west, were too unorthodox for them. For once, GHG neglected the adventure angle. Instead, *Life* snapped up the rights to the epic story; a young Kenneth MacLeish edited that riveting account, making Thor Heyerdahl a household name. His famous book followed, selling 20 million copies in 63 languages. That made Thor wealthy enough to buy his own medieval village near the Italian Riviera. The Society, needless to say, was embarrassed.

In March 1968, John Scofield received a letter from Thor Heyerdahl. The explorer had seen one of John's photos in our August 1966 issue depicting the reed boats on Lake Chad. He asked Scofield for advice about visiting Lake Chad. That made for a good topic of discussion at lunch, but then we learned something more interesting: Heyerdahl had noticed the similarity between boats constructed of papyrus-reed staves depicted in ancient Egyptian tombs and the craft found on Central Africa's Lake Chad and on South America's Lake Titicaca. The light clicked. The reed boats, pyramids, and calendar systems found in pre-Columbian America all resembled those found in ancient Egypt. Might the Egyptians have exported their culture across the Atlantic? Could they have traversed the ocean in seaworthy reed-built boats?

The idea sounded preposterous, but Heyerdahl built an exact replica of an ancient Egyptian reed boat—papyrus staves bound together with hemp rope—and prepared to sail it across the Atlantic to prove his new thesis. There wasn't a lot of difference between a raft built of balsa and a boat made out of grass when it came to buoyancy and safety, and soon the media—including *National Geographic*—were scrambling to cover the "Kon-Tiki of the Atlantic."

Once again, Thor sailed into the prevailing winds of historical orthodoxy, but this time we chased the adventure angle. Outside of a rubber raft, a radio, and a generator, *Ra*—named for the Egyptian sun god—was equipped as in the days of the ancients, with figs, dates, honey, and rice in ceramic pots. With a crew from seven different nations, Thor set sail from a beach in Morocco. But before they reached mid-ocean, the boat became so waterlogged that it disintegrated.

Undeterred, Thor made a few adjustments and, by the time I was editor, built *Ra II,* 50 feet long and 12 feet wide. In summer 1970, he again set sail from Morocco, steering for the Canary Current and the trade winds. Landfall? Anywhere between the West Indies and the Amazon—it didn't matter.

This time they spent 57 days wallowing across the ocean on what amounted to little more than a floating island of vegetation. But the boat was seaworthy enough to survive the 30-foot waves several gales kicked up, and it eventually beached on Barbados, demonstrating it was possible for ancient seafarers to cross the ocean in reed boats.

The voyage had been heavily covered in the press while we were going toe to toe with *Life* and, oddly, the *Ladies' Home Journal,* for North American magazine rights. We finally landed them in August, around the time Heyerdahl washed ashore. I was excited by the possibility of redeeming our past mistake. Since the agreement entailed us publishing as soon as possible, we slated it for January 1971. We looked through the pictures taken during the voyage, made selections from the logbook that Thor had lent us, and sent the layout to him in Italy for approval.

I was thrilled to hear that he was greatly satisfied with the mock-up. That's when I made my big mistake.

As mid-October approached, we had to move the story to the printer. At the last minute I decided to monkey around with the layout. I thought the mix of captions and logbook extracts looked too cluttered and combined them in one stream of prose, each spread self-contained. Not a word was changed, only rearranged. I thought it looked cleaner, though I betrayed my own principles by remaking the plates, a costly move. Out the door it went, and we moved on.

A few weeks later, Heyerdahl saw the final dummy and sent word that he was not happy.

My heart sank. We hadn't changed a word from the version he approved.

I put Carolyn Patterson, who had worked with him on the text, on the telephone to find out what was wrong and make amends. In short, Thor was distressed to see it as one continuous stream of text because that's not how he would have written it. He felt using so many log entries for copy made him look amateurish. The earlier version made it clear that the copy was merely log extracts, so no one could mistake them for polished prose. He was afraid readers would think him an incompetent writer.

I felt even worse when she told me he was ashamed to be listed as author. He seemed to insinuate that we pulled a fast one—just as we had done back in 1946 when our committee declined to support him.

This was my fault. I could feel John Scofield, Bill Garrett, and Joe Judge looking at me and thinking, New quarterback. Fumble on the first snap.

I flew Carolyn to Italy to smooth things over. Heyerdahl was a perfect gentleman. He was moved that I would go to such lengths to assuage his feelings. When he reviewed the advance copy, he admitted the article looked better in print than as a dummy. And he was very happy that a picture of *Ra II* made the cover.

LIVING UP TO OUR rich mapmaking legacy was one of my highest priorities when I became editor. In March 1971 we released the "Peoples and Cultures of Southeast Asia" map that Bill Garrett and I dreamed up after my chance conversation with the sergeant newly returned from Vietnam.

A few weeks later Bill and I went to the University of Miami, where I was to address a conference on visual journalism. The audience, largely composed of New York's leading art photographers, reporters from *Life* and *Look,* and photojournalists from the Magnum agency, tended to look down on our journal. At the last minute we decided to carry a box of those maps. I've never forgotten the avidity with which those high-flying New Yorkers snatched up copies of "Peoples and Cultures of Southeast Asia."

Our members raved too. One day I was in Chicago taking a taxi to O'Hare Airport. When the driver found out that I was the editor of *National Geographic,* he glanced sharply at me in the mirror. Ten seconds later he pulled to the side of the road, turned off the engine, and faced me.

"Don't worry, I'll get you there on time," he said. "A few years ago I was in Vietnam with the Seabees. We were building camps for the Special Forces in the back of beyond. I didn't know where the hell I was, except it was mountains all around. But you published a map not long ago. I read every damn word on it and learned I was with the—who were they . . . the Yards—something like the Yards?"

"The Montagnards?" I ventured.

"Yes! Yes!" He turned back, put the car into gear, and declared over his shoulder, "That was a good map!"

I later heard that a South Vietnamese soldier, after the fall of Saigon, bought a copy of that map on the black market for the equivalent of $200 and used it to lead 100 refugees to safety across the Laotian border. I still shake my head with wonder. You never know the afterlife of something you publish.

We went on to publish a series of these "Peoples and Cultures" maps. Titles included "The Indians of the Americas" and "The Peoples of the Middle East." The most important ones focused on regions where public ignorance of differing cultural and historical experiences might lead to conflict.

That Middle East map was accompanied by a wide-ranging article by Tom Abercrombie on the history and geographical footprint of Islam. "The Sword and the Sermon," published in July 1972, was the result of a 1971 journey that covered 22 countries and filled three of Tom's passports.

Our story and cultural map provided superb background for Society members in understanding the tangled complexities of that part of the world. As MBG might have said, "It's what we do best."

MEANWHILE, MBG's brilliant gold strike, the Leakey dynasty, continued its own evolution. Louis's heart condition was slowing him down—to the point where Richard Leakey was soon directing the Coryndon Museum, renamed the National Museums of Kenya.

Richard's first marriage to an archaeologist ended shortly after it began. In 1970 he married Meave Epps, a former assistant soon to become an expert on fossil humanoids. Meave would continue the Leakey legacy, becoming a good friend as well. The golden age of paleoanthropology inaugurated at Olduvai in 1959 would reach a new apogee, the Leakeys again in the lead.

In 1972 Bernard Ngeneo, working Lake Rudolf's eastern shores for Richard, found "Skull 1470"—*Homo rudolfensis*—the oldest complete cranium dating back nearly two million years. Readers of *National Geographic* in the 1970s and '80s received a full accounting of early-human stories. In addition to being the "magazine of record" on the subject, we became the target of letter campaigns from anti-evolutionists.

About this time, Louis Leakey played his final card: Biruté Galdikas, who, with a master's in anthropology, ironically had the best qualifications of the three female primatologists he brought to us.

Her project, studying orangutans in Borneo's Tanjung Puting Reserve, was only narrowly approved by the Research Committee. Galdikas was the first person on record to observe the apes coming out of the trees to feed on the ground.

Shortly before Louis died in October 1972, he dubbed Goodall, Fossey, and Galdikas the "Trimates," also known as "Leakey's Angels" or the "Leakey syndicate."

As the midwife at the birth of modern primatology, the Society also supported the work of other primate researchers. There was Francine "Penny" Patterson, an animal psychologist who had taught Koko, a lowland gorilla born in captivity, a modified form of American Sign Language, which she called Gorilla Sign Language, or GSL. According to Penny, head of the Gorilla Foundation, Koko had a vocabulary of 1,000 signs and could understand twice as many spoken English words.

Koko's compound was in the Santa Cruz Mountains of California, and when I arrived for a visit in the late 1970s, Koko was throwing a tantrum and signing that Penny was a "dirty toilet bird." Demure Penny Patterson never would have taught her that combination of words. Though some scientists had doubted the gorilla's ability to communicate, that convinced me. Koko clearly selected three words she knew and arranged them in a unique way to express a thought.

Koko made our cover twice: Her most beguiling appearance was a self-portrait she made by pointing the camera at a mirror. "Make sure Koko gets paid the regular cover picture rate," I said at that unusually well-attended projection session—and she was.

Dian Fossey, a field researcher like the other two Trimates, had profound antipathy for anyone who studied captive gorillas—Penny Patterson included. The early 1970s were Dian's finest years with the National Geographic Society. Having established her Karisoke Research Center in Rwanda, she settled in to study the furtive mountain gorilla.

To illustrate her work for the magazine, we found Robert Campbell, a photographer in Nairobi, and dispatched him to Karisoke. Dian was tall and dark-haired, and her behavioral observations incorporated imitation: she'd wallow in the sodden nettles, scratch herself, and belch as a gorilla would. She never actually engaged with them, despite 2,000 hours of observation, and refused to pressure them.

That presented a problem. The only pictures we had that depicted any contact between Dian and gorillas featured her with two orphaned ones awaiting shipment to a European zoo.

Campbell, anxious to get a publishable coverage, pushed Dian closer and closer to her subjects—and in January 1970, the same month she made her first appearance on our cover, finally captured "the touch," the moment Dian's outstretched finger made contact with that of a male she called Peanuts.

Stalking our halls with a stage-prop spear, Dian was a formidable-looking woman, but her heavy smoking and drinking had rendered her health anything but robust.

PRIMATES ASIDE, there was one other highly intelligent species in Africa whose fate really alarmed me: the elephant. I'll never forget the first time I saw one. I must have been five years old when my mother took me to where the circus was disembarking from the rail cars and parading into the fairgrounds in Washington, D.C. There were clowns, trapeze artists, and sword swallowers, but I was awestruck by the elephants—not just for their size but also for their grace. They stepped so softly on the hard-packed surface. I was mesmerized by how their toes spread out as each pad settled delicately into the dust. My foot couldn't do that! Forever afterward, elephants would be my favorite land animal.

Decades would pass before I realized just how imperiled they have become. Tourists demand jewelry and trinkets made from African and Asian ivory. The Japanese consumption of elephant ivory for *hankos,* or carved name seals, was another contributing factor.

Such dismal developments are deeply rooted in geography, and we reported them in our balanced, carefully fact-checked manner. We turned to a friend of Richard Leakey's, zoologist Iain Douglas-Hamilton, and his wife, Oria, to bring this sad report to our members.

The Douglas-Hamiltons were perhaps the first researchers to study and census elephants and identify individuals by their unique signatures of tusk and ear. Their formative work took place in Tanzania's Lake Manyara National Park. They also worked in the thickets of Tsavo National Park, compiling life histories of elephant families in a race against Somali poachers. Finally, supported by the World Wildlife Fund, the New York Zoological Society, and the International Union for the Conservation of Nature, they undertook the first comprehensive, continent-wide census of elephant numbers. We reported the results in the November 1980 *National Geographic.*

Their careful count added up to 1.3 million elephants left in all Africa. Seventy-five years earlier, there may have been a hundred times that number. The animals were hard pressed by ivory poaching on one side and habitat encroachments on the other; the latter, in my opinion, is the gravest long-term threat. Man will always win the battle for habitat.

One of Iain Douglas-Hamilton's first research assistants was Smith College graduate and *Newsweek* correspondent Cynthia Moss. She became so enamored of these animals that she quit her job and co-founded the Elephant Research Project in Amboseli, a small Kenyan national park in the shadow of Mount Kilimanjaro. One of her assistants, Joyce Poole, had grown up in Kenya and at the age of 11, after hearing Jane Goodall speak, decided she, too, would become an animal behavior specialist. When she was 19, she volunteered at Amboseli, to work for Cynthia Moss; she also graduated from Smith, then worked on her Ph.D. at Cambridge. Joyce and Katy Payne, a musicologist and acoustic expert, would go on to do Society-sponsored work in how elephants communicate over vast distances infrasonically, below the level of human hearing.

I'll never know how we had overlooked Cynthia Moss in the pivotal early stages of her Amboseli Elephant Research Project. But I kicked myself from the moment I climbed into her four-wheel drive and she drove me around that small gem of a national park. It was picturesque Africa itself, snowcapped Mount Kilimanjaro dominating every scene. Because the fierce, cattle-herding Maasai warriors who lived around Amboseli's borders kept poachers at bay, the shrubby savanna was alive with elephants.

As we bounced through thornbush and tall grass, Cynthia pointed out the progeny of such famous matriarchs in the annals of elephant research as Teresia, Slit Ear, Torn Ear, Tania, Tuskless, and Echo. The park was small enough that it was possible to identify every pachyderm there by telltale patterns in ears, tusks, and tails. As we rode among elephants that I once would never have approached any closer than 100 yards, I learned how tightly females bond in extended families or clans, and how affectionate they are with one another.

If there were any place in Africa where elephants had right of way, it was around that research camp. There, under the shade of the acacias, I heard about elephants as fellow sentient beings. Joyce Poole, whom Richard had just appointed to head the Elephant Program of the Kenya Wildlife Service, might have come down from Nairobi. But there were other knowledgeable observers too. I listened to their stories about elephants' long lives and deep memories, about their superb intelligence and complex societies, about their astonishing empathy and altruism, careful rearing of calves, concern for injured or dying comrades, and regard for the bleached bones of their ancestors—even about their capacity to grieve, perhaps weep.

Joyce and Cynthia were convinced that elephants share the full range of emotions that humans do. Yet it looked to me like some human beings were doing their level best to destroy such ancient lineages within the span of one human lifetime. Human and elephant populations—both territory demanding—are clearly on a collision course. And then there was poaching, which reached a crescendo in the 1980s—that lamentable decade when fully half of Africa's remaining elephants were slaughtered.

It was Richard Leakey—the most forceful advocate for Kenya's wildlife—who came up with an audacious idea to confront the ivory trade. With Kenyan president Daniel arap Moi's blessing, the Kenya Wildlife Service, which Richard ran, rooted out corruption, strengthened the ranger corps, and turned those men into paramilitary defenders of wildlife, backed by a shoot-on-sight policy targeting poachers.

Richard convinced President Moi to make a grand gesture: the torching in Nairobi National Park—in full view of the world's television cameras—of 12 tons of confiscated elephant tusks. It was a declaration of war against the illegal ivory trade: a statement that Kenya would keep no stockpiles to cash in when all the fuss blew over, and a challenge to other nations to do likewise. I watched it on the news and shook my head in admiration and fear for Richard's life.

He was a field marshal directing a "bush war" against heavily armed Somalis marching into Kenya, primarily targeting Tsavo and Meru National Parks. Men on both sides were frequently killed. So were tourists. A grim situation was escalating.

At the same time, talk turned to banning the trade in ivory altogether. In my view, what resulted ranks with the moratorium on whaling as one of the two or three most dramatic conservation measures of the late 20th century. And I had a seat at the table: the boardroom table at the World Wildlife Fund U.S. headquarters in Washington, D.C. Two conservation giants, Russell Train and William K. Reilly, tracked through as CEOs while I served on the board. There I heard all sides of the issue and was aware of the deep division in public opinion.

The countries of southern Africa—especially Zimbabwe, Botswana, and South Africa—held elephant herds that were actually growing in numbers. They needed the money obtained through the sale of legally harvested ivory from authorized culls. Many conservationists, moreover, believed that an outright ban was a death sentence for elephants. They believed that as underground demand skyrocketed, prices paid for tusks would increase, as would the death toll.

Marshaled on the other side were Richard Leakey, Iain and Oria Douglas-Hamilton, Cynthia Moss, Joyce Poole, and the African Wildlife

Foundation, among others. Such was their prestige—especially Joyce's argument that ivory poaching destroyed the fabric of elephant society—that those of us sitting around the board table at WWF-U.S. sided with them, and the rest of the World Wildlife Fund affiliates followed suit. In 1989 the Convention on International Trade in Endangered Species (CITES) banned all trade in elephant ivory worldwide.

Even so, I predict that the day of the free-roaming elephant will soon vanish. Elephants are prisoners of geography. Because they consume hundreds of pounds of food a day, they need vast tracts of land and are extremely destructive to groves, orchards, and crops. With human populations expanding in Africa and Asia, the pachyderms are increasingly forced to forage on farms and in villages, trampling fields and people alike. Even the most intelligent ecosystem-management plan probably can't overcome such pressures. Most elephants will be fenced within existing sanctuaries because we'll never find enough unutilized land to accommodate healthy herds, which depend on those clans and complex societies mixing, mingling, and interacting.

The Maasai believe the elephant to be the only other creature possessing a soul. It will be profoundly tragic if that wild, stately tread is seen no more.

BY LATE 1971, Donna, our son Hovey (as we called him), and I moved out of the District of Columbia to McLean, Virginia, to a house perched on the Potomac River cliffs. It had one drawback: Loud jets making their western approach to National Airport flew right down the path of the Potomac. That would take getting used to.

At home my thoughts turned to how best to educate Hovey. Whenever he quit playing with his toys on the carpet, I had only to glance up from the newspaper to see him transfixed by the flickering images on the television set. That troubled me. Our kids, in the age of television, were becoming passive spectators rather than active participants.

Bob Breeden and I threw ideas around. Children's publishing was a big field, but we were searching for something different, more stimulating and hands-on than other kids' books.

We concentrated on children between the ages of four and eight, focusing on animals because kids naturally identify with them. We wanted to offer books with big print, durable bindings, and engaging activities. In the first three years, our "Books for Young Explorers" series sold more than three million volumes to members.

As if I needed reminding of the perils of publishing, another giant had crashed. *Look* magazine—a near-*Life* clone—had kept pace with *Life* throughout the 1940s, '50s, and '60s but began losing advertising revenue to television and suffered from postal increases. It lost a million subscribers in just over a year, finally shutting down in October 1971.

Despite the turmoil in the industry, our magazine was still the jewel in the Society's crown. Shortly thereafter, I received an invitation to meet the wearer of a real crown: Elizabeth II, Queen of the United Kingdom.

Donna and I were thrilled, even if it meant flying to London on a Wednesday and returning home 40 hours later on Friday.

Walter Annenberg, the former publisher of the *Philadelphia Inquirer* and the *Atlantic,* was U.S. ambassador to the Court of St. James's in London and had just refurbished both Winfield House, his official residence in Regent's Park, and the embassy chancellery on Grosvenor Square. To celebrate the occasion, he decided to hold a banquet and invite a cross section of Americans, including the media. Dick Pearson, our diplomatic affairs liaison, who knew Annenberg, suggested me and Donna.

At the banquet, we found ourselves seated with, of all people, Dillon Ripley of the Smithsonian Institution and his socially prominent wife, Mary Livingston Ripley. My fears that I would be subjected to Dillon's insistent probing into what was going on at the *Geographic* were relieved when Sir Michael Adeane, private secretary to the queen, and Lady Adeane took their seats at our table. I had long sought permission to publish a story on Britain's royal palaces, and Sir Michael was the perfect person to discuss it with.

GHG was an anglophile. In 1935 he had published an article on George V's silver jubilee. His 50th anniversary issue—April 1949—was titled "The British Way." And the Royal Family was reportedly delighted with the September 1953 *National Geographic,* with its photographs of the coronation of Elizabeth II.

I was planning my approach while Donna and I awaited the evening's pièce de résistance: Her Majesty's personal greeting to each guest. When our turn came, we moved into an adjoining reception room. The sovereign sat at a small table and rose to greet us. After welcoming the Ripleys, she turned to us and warmly congratulated me on becoming editor of *National Geographic,* a magazine for which she had the greatest respect. Then, seating herself, she engaged us in exactly five minutes of conversation.

By the time she turned her gaze on me, I drew a blank. The queen, obviously accustomed to dumbstruck presentees, initiated the conversation: jet noise. She lamented the incessant roar of jets following the flight path over Windsor Castle on the way to Heathrow. I complained about the low-flying jets following the Potomac en route to National Airport. Then she shifted the conversation to—illegal drug use. We discussed young people, drugs, and her concern for her own children. Out of the corner of my eye, I saw Dillon's wineglass slip from his hand. I watched in horror as its contents, as if in slow motion, splashed into the royal lap. No sooner had the liquid landed than Dillon turned to an attendant and said, "Mrs. Grosvenor needs another glass of wine, please." At which point Donna rounded on him and exclaimed, "No, thank you. I don't drink wine."

The queen remained perfectly composed. She behaved as if nothing had happened.

Although discomfited, I ignored it too, and our five minutes were up. Seated again, I unveiled my request to Sir Michael. *National Geographic* magazine, I told him, wanted to publish an article of quality on either Buckingham Palace or Windsor Castle. I mentioned our past pieces on the royal family and pointed out that we were the journal of an esteemed geographical and educational institution.

After feinting us off with "Indeed?" and "Quite so," Sir Michael said he doubted *National Geographic* could get the kind of behind-the-scenes access denied even to British publications. If the *Geographic* did get the nod, it would be for Windsor Castle, not Buckingham Palace.

After years of delicate negotiations, we did get permission to photograph Windsor Castle. Published in November 1980, the article by royal biographer Anthony Holden featured photographs by Jim Stanfield. We never heard a word from the royals or the British Embassy in Washington in response to the piece. But it was rewarding to learn that the queen personally selected one of Stanfield's pictures—the cover shot, showing Prince Philip driving a four-in-hand carriage through the snow-covered grounds of Windsor Castle—for her official Christmas card.

ONE DAY IN JANUARY 1972, we hosted a lunch in our 10th-floor dining room for two members of NASA's top brass, Director James C. Fletcher and Deputy Director George Low, to discuss astronauts and photography. Everyone agreed those master copies of the mission photography entrusted to us contained an unrivaled, scientifically important record of man's greatest adventure. The Apollo program was entering its final year; time was running out to get one more knockout photograph to wrap up this great chapter in the space age.

In a February 1972 story about Apollo 15, we had included a picture with that monochrome cratered surface in the foreground: a breathtaking view of a jewel-like crescent Earth hanging in the velvet black background.

"That is exactly what it looks like!" astronauts reviewing the layout had exclaimed.

From our perspective as the magazine of record, a full-on portrait of Earth in space could have an impact that would last for generations. The Apollo astronauts might be the only humans for decades to voyage far enough into space to capture the entire planet in one frame. Might such a picture be possible? I asked.

The NASA chiefs agreed. Two missions remained. Apollo 16, set to launch in April, wouldn't work because of time constraints. Apollo 17, slated for December, would probably be the last chance for astronaut-made photographs of Earth for quite some time—more than half a century, as we now know.

Apollo 17's trajectory would offer an excellent, if fleeting, opportunity for a full-on shot of our planet. Fletcher and Low promised that NASA would train each crew member—Eugene Cernan, Ronald Evans, and Harrison Schmitt—to use a specially engineered Hasselblad medium-format camera.

BACK ON EARTH, we pulled another eminent field biologist into our orbit. I'd met George Schaller in the 1960s, when I served on the board of the New York Zoological Society. He had already undertaken the study of mountain gorillas in the former Belgian Congo that led to Dian Fossey's similar project in Rwanda. In the mid-1960s he studied lions in the Serengeti, which led to his first major *National Geographic* article, "Life with the King of Beasts."

Schaller employed many of the Craigheads' techniques, including ear tags and radio tracking. He knocked the lions out with hypodermic darts, then worked feverishly over the unconscious cats to measure their temperature and take blood samples before retreating to the safety of the Land Rover. The family angle was there too. George, his wife, Kay, and their two sons lived among the lion prides in Serengeti National Park.

I had hardly become editor when George, who would work closely with us for decades, presented us with another coup: telephoto frames of an exceedingly rare snow leopard he had glimpsed during a wildlife survey of Himalayan fauna, sponsored by us and the New York Zoological Society. The first photographs ever published of a snow leopard in the wild appeared in our November 1971 issue.

AT 5:39 A.M., ON DECEMBER 7, 1972, some 18,000 miles above the planet, astronaut Harrison Schmitt lifted his Hasselblad and, pointing its lens outside the window, squeezed off two or three frames of the rapidly receding Earth. He put the camera away and concentrated on his other duties aboard Apollo 17's command module.

The module splashed down in the Pacific on December 19, in view of the U.S.S. *Ticonderoga*. Soon the astronauts were back safely—as was the Hasselblad and a frame of film exposed at just the right time, in just the right place, for the most successful geographical picture of my lifetime. The fruit of that January meeting with the NASA high command was developed and labeled #AS17-148-22727. History has come to know it as the "Blue Marble."

That image may be the most reproduced photograph in history. It has appeared in books and on T-shirts, bumper stickers, dinner plates, playing cards, and screen savers. It is an icon of our age. In those days the Society simply had the clout to dial in an order for a picture of Earth—and—presto!—it was delivered.

We were riding high, but a cautionary tale was unfolding in the publishing world. "To see life; to see the world; to eyewitness great events . . ." had been Henry Luce's promise when he debuted his new picture magazine in 1936. Though more news-driven than *National Geographic*, *Life* could lay fair claim to being the magazine of record for its time. At its peak it had eight and a half million subscribers—and that's when the trouble began. Luce kept writing off the losses from *Life en Español,* marketed to Latin America, Florida, and California since 1952. Although that edition died in 1969, damage was done to the flagship magazine. Advertising revenues dried up; circulation eroded. A spike in postal rates was the final blow.

"So why must we stop?" was the question in the final issue, December 29, 1972.

"The painful fact is that LIFE's costs have been steadily outrunning our income ... LIFE has been losing money for four years. We have persevered as long as we could see any realistic prospect ... of a turnaround. We no longer see such a prospect."

A sobering assessment. The Geographic had to avoid that fate. So far, we had. Our membership was rising by about half a million each year; we were nearing eight million now. I hoped we could continue our upward trajectory.

CHAPTER FIFTEEN

A LITTLE DÉTENTE

We boarded our train for a 24-hour journey on the Trans-Siberian Railway—that long, steel backbone of the Soviet Union—one mid-morning in Irkutsk, gateway to Lake Baikal.

Our party—Donna, myself, staff photographer Dean Conger, and his wife, Lee—took our seats in a curtained cabin. Only one other person was in it: a beaming young soldier returning home from the Chinese border. Dean, an old Russia hand who could speak the language, struck up a conversation.

There was a reason for the young man's undisguised happiness. Married a year earlier, he had been rudely jolted from his honeymoon, forced into his ill-fitting uniform, and marched off to conscripted duty. He had been shivering in Manchuria when his son was born—a son he was eager to see for the first time.

We liked him immediately. He was guileless and readily answered any question. Hour after hour, as we rolled westward through the forests, stopping briefly in small towns, we forged a friendship: the camaraderie of the rails. At some point in the journey, our friend took the enameled red star off his uniform and gave it to us as a token of friendship. I gave him my National Geographic lapel pin in return.

I can't remember where exactly our friend left us, but I remember leaning out the window and watching him lift a pretty girl off her feet in a fervent embrace, and how tenderly he held the son he had never seen. We waved until the train carried us away.

BY 1969, tensions had relaxed following the Cuban Missile Crisis. The ensuing détente was promoted by President Nixon and Leonid Brezhnev—and so we had planned a Soviet Union book, prompting my trip.

Furthermore, Dean Conger already had a foot behind the Iron Curtain. He was drawn to the Soviet Union; it became his beat, the place where he downed countless vodka toasts and KGB challenges over the course of 26 journeys. Compiling the best of his photographs and new material into a book was a natural.

Dean was committed to the project, though he cautioned that it would take considerable time and finesse to meet the challenges of Russian bureaucracy and security.

As it turned out, time would not be our problem. Scrutiny was.

The Soviet response was initially enthusiastic, but negotiations proved excruciatingly protracted. Blocking our progress was that vast communist apparat, the Novosti Press Agency. Its Washington front man was Georgi Isachenko, managing editor of *Soviet Life*, a glossy photo magazine for U.S. readers. He worked just around the corner from Geographic headquarters, and his job may have included KGB work as well.

We had numerous sit-downs to gauge the depths of Soviet suspicion. Magazine articles on places like Leningrad and the Volga River, where access was tightly controlled, were quickly approved. But the proposed book required access on an unprecedented scale; we wanted to visit all 15 Soviet republics and upwards of 43 cities, to cover different ethnic groups, attend major festivals, and even view research sites in the far north.

I guessed at one reason for Soviet resistance: National Geographic's supposed relationship to U.S. intelligence agencies. In 1948 Pravda had absurdly accused us of being a "nest of spies."

Although Time-Life publisher Henry Luce had hired the notorious "turned" spy Whittaker Chambers to be a foreign news editor, and *Washington Post* publisher Philip Graham was rumored to be running a CIA campaign to infiltrate U.S. newspapers and magazines in the 1940s and '50s, I didn't think any National Geographic journalist was the tool of an intelligence service. It's true, though, that one time the FBI had used one of our corner offices to surveil people visiting the Soviet Embassy.

It was our patriotic duty to offer our services if asked, but "government cooperation" could derail tricky negotiations for the access we hoped for in the Soviet Union. This was driven home one afternoon when I met Isachenko in our building lobby. We stepped into an elevator shortly after I assured him that we did not cooperate with U.S. intelligence agencies. Unbelievably, in walked a uniformed officer prominently displaying an Office of Naval Intelligence badge. Georgi sized him up and gave me an enigmatic wink.

Not long afterward, Dean Conger was detained while working in Russia. That was my primary reason to steer clear of "government cooperation." In a police state, the slightest suspicion of a hidden agenda could mean incarceration for a journalist.

After a heated debate, the board of trustees agreed to allow Society employee intelligence gathering only in times of congressionally declared war. Despite the elevator incident, we got word from Moscow: Come on over, they said. Since I had not seen the country with my own eyes, I took them up on it.

DONNA AND I ARRIVED IN MOSCOW just after President Nixon left; he'd given détente a big push by signing the Anti-Ballistic Missile

Treaty. The Congers and Donna and I checked into the sumptuous Hotel National for a day or two of acclimatization and sightseeing—and vodka.

Dean had warned me that vodka accompanies any business or social occasion in Russia, and to be prepared: The Russians will put you off-balance—literally. The toasts started almost immediately. My defenses were butter and guile: the butter to coat the stomach and slow the absorption of alcohol, and the guile to water any nearby potted plants with vodka without being caught.

After Moscow, we made the long flight east, over the Urals into Asia, landing in Irkutsk, Siberia. Lake Baikal, dazzlingly blue, dwarfs all metaphors; it is bigger than Belgium and deeper than a mile, with one-fifth of the world's freshwater. It is also polluted.

Northern Siberia is a harsh land, much of it underlain by permafrost. We took another long flight, to brown, treeless Yakutsk to visit the Permafrost Institute. The city sits atop frozen ground from 570 to 1,300 feet deep. It's the coldest city on Earth.

"Nearly half of the Soviet Union is underlain with permafrost," Dr. Pavel Melnikov, the institute's director, told us. Oil, gas, and valuable ores lay beneath it, he explained, but the severe conditions required special techniques to extract its riches.

Melnikov had his own détente going. He had approached U.S. permafrost researchers in Alaska but was rebuffed because of security concerns. So instead he was cooperating with Canadian specialists. "If scientists could work together, perhaps politicians and generals—and journalists too—might follow suit," he said. Just as I got a feel for Siberia, it was back to Moscow by air.

Moscow was buzzing with excitement—not at our arrival but because of a state visit by Marshal Tito, whom Brezhnev wanted to coax back into the Soviet fold. The next morning, Dean and I left for Novosti's offices in Pushkin Square for our first long day of negotiations for the book. When

◀ Trance dancing was a Balinese custom seldom witnessed by Western tourists when I photographed this tearstained girl, transported into a self-induced reverie, in 1968. (Gilbert M. Grosvenor)

▼ In my most challenging photographic time exposure, a Balinese farmer carrying a lantern traces a sinuous path through a rice paddy while stalking eels at night, 1968. (Gilbert M. Grosvenor)

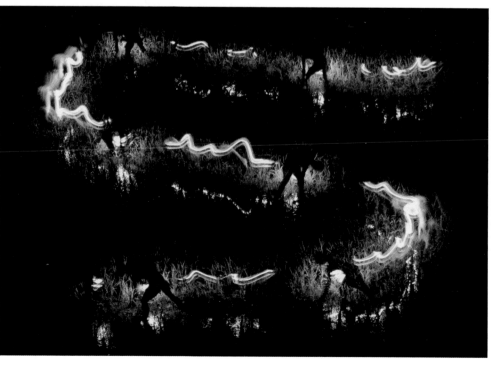

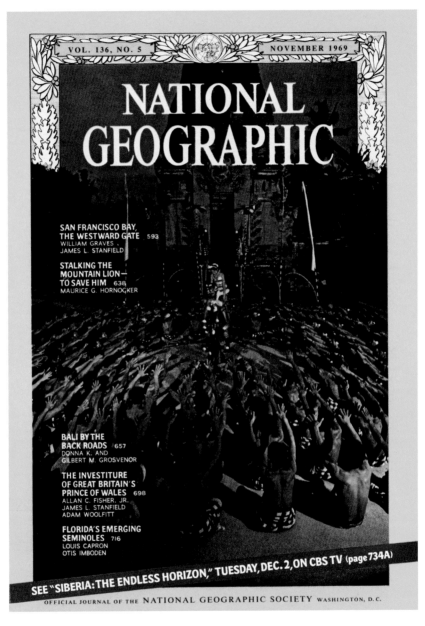

SEE "SIBERIA: THE ENDLESS HORIZON," TUESDAY, DEC. 2, ON CBS TV (page 734A)

OFFICIAL JOURNAL OF THE NATIONAL GEOGRAPHIC SOCIETY WASHINGTON, D.C.

My picture of the *kecak*, or "monkey dance," in Bali would never have made the magazine's cover in November 1969 had it not been for an approaching thunderstorm that gave the sky a dramatically lurid glow. (Gilbert M. Grosvenor)

◀ Mel Payne and I—pictured here in 1969—had a mutually wary relationship when he was the Society's dynamic president and I was on the track to the editorship. We agreed on two things: our love for the Society and our reverence for its principal architect, my grandfather GHG, depicted in the portrait above us. (James A. Sugar)

▼ Star picture editor Bill Garrett had the finest photographic eye of any journalist I ever encountered; here, we consult in 1969. The previous year, Bill won the coveted Magazine Photographer of the Year prize from the National Press Photographers Association for his coverage of the Mekong River during the Vietnam War. (Gordon Gahan)

Before the shadows lengthened in the Virunga mountains, Dian Fossey—pictured here in 1969—became one of the first human beings to actively engage with mountain gorillas in their wilderness home. Her tragic murder in 1985, portrayed in the award-winning biopic *Gorillas in the Mist,* spurred such attention to the cause that in the end, I think she really did save these beloved animals. (Robert I. M. Campbell)

Paleoanthropologists Louis Leakey and his pipe-smoking son Richard examine a fragment of monkey skull at the Koobi Fora research camp in northern Kenya, 1969. National Geographic Society support for the Leakeys helped change the narrative of human origins. And along the way, Richard became one of my best friends, as well as my "eyes and ears" in Africa. (Gordon Gahan)

Far below Great Lameshur Bay in the U.S. Virgin Islands, Sylvia Earle shows a sample of submarine algae to a fellow participant in Tektite II, a NASA-funded underwater laboratory program, 1970. I consider Sylvia to be the most eloquent champion of ocean conservation since the days of Jacques Cousteau and Rachel Carson. (Bates Littlehales)

The "Blue Marble," one of the most famous photographs ever made, is the defining image of my decade as *National Geographic*'s editor, from 1970 to 1980. As a "magazine of record" with close ties to NASA, we played an important role in the genesis of this image, created during the final Apollo mission in 1972. (NASA)

In early 1975, I was surprised to learn I had been voted 1974's Editor of the Year by the National Press Photographers Association. But the credit was all due to the staff, including Bill Garrett (seated to my left) and Bob Gilka (over my shoulder). Gilka harnessed a stable of photographers second to none, including two of the very best: Jim Stanfield (with dark beard) and George Mobley (with white beard). (Joseph J. Scherschel)

A gleaming new printing plant in Corinth, Mississippi, was the happy result of audacious business decisions made by Mel Payne (the silver-haired figure at left consulting with Bill Garrett). Here, we watch the June 1977 *National Geographic* come off the line. The issue contained a controversial story on South Africa that would provoke a confrontation with Payne, resulting in the biggest challenge to the magazine's editorial integrity during my long career. (Winfield Parks)

◄ At a dive hole in the ice near the North Pole, I hold Robert E. Peary's sledge flag, 1979. I had just enjoyed one of the peak experiences of my life: plunging beneath the polar icecap at a Canadian research camp with Joseph MacInnis (behind me) and underwater photographer Al Giddings (not pictured); geologist Steve Blasco looks on. Since that moment, the Arctic and its fate have captivated me. (Emory Kristof)

▼ As our scope of operations expanded, we realized the National Geographic Society needed a new building. Here, Mel Payne, the chairman of the board, and I, the Society's new president, preside over the 1981 groundbreaking for the last major addition to our Washington, D.C., headquarters complex. (Joseph H. Bailey)

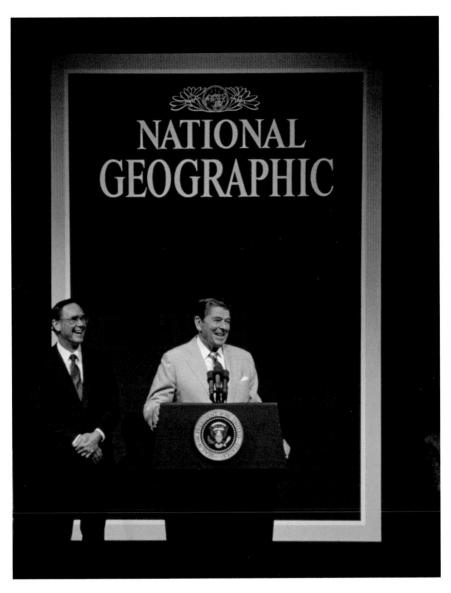

No less a figure than President Ronald Reagan would dedicate our new building upon its completion in 1984. "I guess you have trouble storing your old *National Geographics,* too," he quipped, bringing down the house. Most of our members would never throw an issue away. (James P. Blair)

This celebrated portrait, known as the "Afghan Girl," is arguably *National Geographic* magazine's most famous photograph. It epitomized Bill Garrett's editorship from 1980 to 1990, much as the "Blue Marble" did mine. Hidden away in a workbox, where it had been banished by a photo editor put off by its intensity, the shot was rescued by Garrett and elevated to the cover of the June 1985 issue—and the rest is history. (Steve McCurry)

Underwater explorer Bob Ballard was tailor-made for National Geographic. Exuberant, exciting, engaging, he had the knack for making big discoveries—none bigger than his quest for the *Titanic,* shown here in 1985. But in my estimation, his 1977 discovery of hydrothermal vents in the deep Pacific was even more important because it revolutionized our understanding of life on Earth. (Emory Kristof)

During the centennial of the National Geographic Society in 1988, we capped a festive year with a banquet honoring leading figures in exploration and discovery. Sitting, left to right: nautical archaeologist George Bass, photographic pioneer Harold Edgerton, oceanographer Jacques-Yves Cousteau, cartographer Barbara Washburn, paleoanthropologist Mary Leakey, and twin wildlife biologists John and Frank Craighead. Standing, left to right: astronaut John Glenn, deep-sea explorer Bob Ballard, archaeologist Kenan Erim, cartographer Brad Washburn, primatologist Jane Goodall, me, paleoanthropologist Richard Leakey, lecturer Thayer Soule, and mountaineer Sir Edmund Hillary. (Sisse Brimberg)

▲ In the 1980s, the Society launched a nationwide effort to improve geography instruction in American schools. The initiative took me to classrooms across the country—including this 1989 trip to Miami's Shenandoah Middle School. I often appeared with a giant pencil and always shared an inflatable plastic globe with each pupil. (Pete Souza)

▼ In 1989, the Society began a National Geography Bee, long moderated by *Jeopardy!* host Alex Trebek (left). Winners—including the first champion, Jack Staddon of Great Bend, Kansas (third from left)—received college scholarships. Alex became a very close friend of mine; his efforts on behalf of geography would win him a Gold Medal from the Royal Canadian Geographical Society in 2010. (Sisse Brimberg)

▲ Sailing the waters of the Bras d'Or Lakes off Beinn Bhreagh, 1990. Joining me on this summer day are (left to right) my second wife, Wiley Jarman Grosvenor, and my two sons, Gilbert Hovey Grosvenor II and Graham Dabney Grosvenor. (James P. Blair)

▼ Anchored just offshore the Dominican Republic, I hold the ceramic dish chiseled out of the coral-encrusted remains of the 17th-century Spanish galleon *Nuestra Señora de la Concepción,* lying some 30 feet beneath the boat on which we sit. Sitting between me and extraordinary treasure salvor Tracy Bowden is my daughter, Alexandra, known as Lexi. When she joined the National Geographic Society's board of trustees in 2009 as Dr. Alexandra Grosvenor Eller, she represented the sixth generation of my family to serve that beloved institution. (Jonathan S. Blair)

we returned to the Hotel National late that evening, Dean opened the door to his room and stopped: A strange man stood by the window. Lee pointed at me and said, "There's one in your room too."

Sure enough, a man in a leather jacket stood guard by the window. Donna looked at me and shrugged. "They just barged in," she said. "Been here about an hour."

Dean spoke to the man in the leather jacket. After a few terse words, the man turned back to the window while Dean pivoted to us. "Tito's at the Bolshoi tonight. His motorcade will be returning to the Kremlin via the Leningrad Prospect"—pointing down at the avenue our rooms overlooked—"and I think these guys are some kind of security detachment. They'll leave once the fuss is over."

Soon we could hear the wail of sirens from the Bolshoi Theatre up the street. The motorcycles and black ZIL limousines flashed by and vanished.

The men at the windows abruptly walked out of our rooms.

I asked Donna if the man in the leather coat had harassed her. "I could have ripped off my pajama top, and he would never have noticed," she said. "He was fixated on that window."

"KGB?" I asked Dean. He nodded.

The next morning, back in Pushkin Square, I mentioned the incident. Hoping to lighten the atmosphere, I quipped, "In what chapter will that episode be featured?" All I got was a few wan smiles. We spent two more days and two more vodka-swashed nights, to no avail.

I returned to our hotel none too sanguine about the book. Novosti insisted on drafting a proposal that both sides would find amenable. We waited. And waited—but no proposal. We all knew why: The Soviets insisted upon censorship—for me, a nonnegotiable point. Donna and I flew home . . . with no agreement.

In early December 1972, I was invited to the Soviet Embassy to celebrate the 50th anniversary of the Union of Soviet Socialist Republics. Was there something ironic about feting the dictatorship of the proletariat beneath the crystal chandeliers of an elegant old mansion? Before I had time to parse that thought, the new editor of *Soviet Life*, Anatoly Mkrtchian, approached and told me that the Novosti book proposal was under review and would soon be in my hands.

It was July 1973, more than a year after my trip to Russia, when Novosti's proposal arrived, making it clear the Russians still wanted ultimate control. I walked away again, frustrated.

Meanwhile, I had China in my sights.

IN HIS FIRST TERM AS PRESIDENT, Richard Nixon played the "China card" in a bid to squeeze and deter the Soviet Union, hinting that the United States might establish full diplomatic relations with the People's Republic of China. Secretary of State Henry Kissinger dined with disguised representatives of the PRC at the Yenching Palace, the Chinese restaurant where I'm sure they did not order the crab au gratin. Kissinger followed up with a clandestine visit to Peking in 1971.

We already had a report from China in our December 1971 issue by Audrey Topping, wife of *New York Times* correspondent Seymour Topping. Audrey was born in China when her father was a Canadian diplomat there. He remained close to Premier Zhou Enlai, Chairman Mao's handpicked successor. She obtained a rare visa as a "Canadian housewife."

Topping wasn't permitted to travel far or stay long, but her "Return to Changing China" provided a rare glimpse inside the secretive communist giant. Two months later President Nixon flew to Peking. The resulting Shanghai Communiqué held the promise of diplomatic relations and established "liaison offices" in Peking and Washington. I waited, ready to pounce.

Two old adjoining apartment buildings on Connecticut Avenue near Kalorama Road in Washington were purchased, gutted, and connected behind their facades to create the Chinese presence. I hatched a strategy.

The Chinese delegation took occupancy in May 1973. Though the news media was camped out on the sidewalk in front of the new "chancery," the Chinese diplomats hardly ventured outside—though occasionally a venetian blind might be cracked as someone peered out. I launched my plan.

We would quietly invite the delegation to our headquarters without any fuss or announcement. They could explore without being exploited. It might help get our foot in the door.

I rehearsed my telephone call to Huang Zhen, head of the Chinese delegation. To win the confidence of the Chinese government without compromising our principles would be a major achievement. We had to convince them that the National Geographic Society, with its history and reputation for fair and objective reporting, was the best route to showcasing their land and culture.

I dialed the number. Huang Zhen, chief of the delegation, was on the other end.

"Hello, my name is Gilbert Grosvenor, and I am the editor of *National Geographic* magazine. I would very much like to welcome you to our great capital city. It would be my pleasure if you and your delegation joined us for an evening reception at our Society's headquarters."

I kept the sentences short and sweet. It felt like talking to air—there was little in response. I plunged on, detailing our long history of portraying China to the American people. I mentioned five generations of my family's involvement and the Society's eight million members (a gasp from the phone). Finally, Huang responded.

"Let me look at my schedule, and I will call you back tomorrow."

That was encouraging. I suspected he wanted to check with Peking first. The following day he called back and accepted. I was ecstatic.

We planned the reception in our 10th-floor executive dining room with its superb views, mapping out the reception minute by minute from greetings to goodbyes. We would have a cocktail hour—or should we? We decided to offer orange juice, soft drinks, and wine. Carefully we chose the staff attendance list—not only senior staff but also those best equipped by experience or personality to chat with the Chinese delegates, many of whom probably didn't speak much English. I was committed to making sure each guest had a good time.

Since the Chinese valued stable relationships steeped in history and genealogy, and since we had compiled so much material on their land, I decided that we should display a copy of everything we had ever printed on China—hundreds of items in one impressive display. I was amazed by the mass of material, which required a long table covered in green felt. When that proved inadequate, we stacked the publications three or four deep. Surely this would send the message that we were bona fide recorders of China's history and geography.

When the limousines pulled up to our doors, I went down to welcome Huang Zhen, a short, graying man in a Mao jacket. The greeting seemed cordial, and the delegation was escorted to the 10th floor.

I made my introduction, gave a brief history of the National Geographic Society, and summarized our past work in China, gesturing to the table stacked with publications. I concluded with my family's past visits to China.

Guiding Huang to the bar, I noted he chose orange juice. After a lingering look at the chardonnay, so did I.

So did everyone. Fortunately, a few staffers instantly saw the problem of the vanishing orange juice and made other choices. I showed Huang a table piled with copies of our latest book, *Vacationland U.S.A.*, telling him we had a copy for each member of his delegation: a welcome-to-Washington gift. He flipped through a copy, studying the pictures. "It looks beautiful," he said.

Receptions end when everyone runs out of polite conversation; Huang was the first to leave. As I accompanied him down the elevator, I noticed he didn't have a copy of *Vacationland U.S.A.* with him. Five other senior Chinese guests who had flipped through that book left empty-handed too. Was that a sign that editorial cooperation would not be forthcoming?

When the last limousine departed, we broke out the wine. Everyone agreed that our guests had left happy. But what of our own offer of détente—the gift book? Only one lower-level employee had taken one with him. Was that single copy being analyzed for acceptance? I went home puzzled.

The following morning my phone rang early. Huang Zhen called to thank me for the reception and offered his apologies for forgetting his copy of that beautiful book. Would I be so kind as to forward it to him? Within minutes a driver was on the way to his office with a copy. Soon the phone was ringing off the hook: Everyone wanted their copies of the book too. I dispatched a truck full of books to the liaison office.

A few months later, Luis Marden reported his conversation with the diplomat. The hang-up to cooperation would be our maps and atlases, which showed the Republic of China—Taiwan—as an independent country. That limbo would last another five years, until diplomatic relations would begin with the People's Republic of China.

That didn't stop Luis from obtaining one of those hard-to-get visas. Working through his friend Van Lung, proprietor of the Yenching Palace and a man with important connections in the PRC, Marden in 1974 became the first National Geographic staffer since 1949 to visit mainland China. He was admitted as the author of a story on the world's most versatile plant: bamboo.

ULTIMATELY, WE WON OUR GAME of brinkmanship with Russia. Novosti came back with an acceptable contract. It reserved right of review but gave us final say on text and pictures. The trade-off was recognizing that publishing anything they disagreed with would jeopardize our chance for any future access.

We signed off and set to work on a "Peoples and Cultures" map, a television documentary covering the Volga River, and our long-cherished book. We paired Dean with writer Bart McDowell. It took them the better part of two years and at least a dozen trips, but they succeeded brilliantly.

Despite Soviet obstinacy, restrictive itineraries, and countless objections of *Nyet! Ne fotografirovat!* the book dummy presented for my approval looked great and was strong on human geography. Now we had to show it to the Russians for their endorsement.

We asked Georgi Isachenko to review the layout. Breeden told me that after doing so, Isachenko quipped that the subtitle—"The Soviet Union Today"—should be changed to "The Soviet Union Yesterday." There were too many pictures of onion-domed churches, he warned. Moscow would want more scientific or technological images—icons of the modern, industrialized state.

Once more we prepared to face the nitpicking censors in Pushkin Square.

I'd experienced that before. One day I was summoned to the Soviet Embassy. Ambassador Anatoly Dobrynin had a comment on one of the courtesy copies of an upcoming magazine article. Although he spoke excellent English, he kept hammering on and on about "skinny coos." I was baffled. Finally, he pointed out a photograph of cows being herded down a village street. Isachenko could barely suppress a grin.

So when our negotiating team flew back to Moscow, I prepared myself for the call saying the project was dead. It wasn't.

Journey Across Russia: The Soviet Union Today, published in 1977, was honest, informative, and by far the most interesting book on the U.S.S.R.

Within weeks of its release, our members snapped up nearly 400,000 copies.

We had enlarged that hole in the Iron Curtain. The opening in the Bamboo Curtain, however, was still too small to squeeze through. Years would pass before we would find our way in.

CHAPTER SIXTEEN

ENRAPTURED BY THE DEEP

One day a beluga whale turned up in the harbor of Guysborough, Nova Scotia.

Everyone called her Wilma. No one knows why; the name just fit. She was a gregarious little cetacean, about 12 feet long, who eagerly approached every boat in the harbor when she appeared sometime in 1993. She seemed to crave human companionship, which raised the question: Why did she arrive in Guysborough alone? Why did she stay?

Her DNA told marine scientists at nearby Dalhousie University that Wilma came from a disjunct population of belugas that, ever since the last Ice Age, had lived in the estuary of the St. Lawrence River—unlike the vast majority of belugas farther north in the Arctic Ocean. Some of these adolescents have a wandering penchant, swimming upstream as far as Quebec or as far south as New York Harbor.

Was Wilma another such adventurer? Or was she orphaned when an orca took her mother, leaving her lost and bewildered until she found a haven among her new two-legged friends?

While Wilma would make forays out of Guysborough's little harbor into Chedabucto Bay, which opened onto the Atlantic, she always came back. The Dalhousie folks insisted on one rule: Thou shalt not feed Wilma. Otherwise, people could fraternize with her. She became a media sensation.

It was a two-day sail from Beinn Bhreagh across the Bras d'Or Lakes to Guysborough—but we went every summer Wilma was with us. Hardly had we anchored in the harbor before Wilma found us. Each of us in my family swam and played with her.

Wilma was innocent and trusting, despite the scars left by powerboat propellers. She had some strange attraction to them; maybe they reminded her of her own rapid, clicking language. She'd recognize the sound of individual boat motors, then swim out to greet the boats she knew. She gravitated to one particular boy's little outboard; even from far away she'd bolt in his direction to find him, and the two would be inseparable for the rest of the day.

Then one day she was gone. Wilma was never seen again. I like to think she met up with another wandering beluga and made her way back home, where she lives to this day. I fear, however, that an orca got her.

I wonder if she might ever have lived a fulfilled whale's life anyway, if only because her kin—dolphins and porpoises—are increasingly ravaged by bladder cancers, ulcers, tumors, and toxic poisoning by PCBs: all the ill effects of living at the outflow of a river carrying industrial effluents to their home waters. Many others ingest the plastic waste now littering the oceans or die entangled in cast-off commercial fishing gear. Some are slashed by boat propellers or fatally struck by ships in highly trafficked waters.

Wilma was emblematic of so many unanswered questions. Despite their size, whales are among the least understood of Earth's creatures.

When I was growing up, not much was known about them. Whales, along with dolphins and porpoises, were among the most difficult creatures on the planet to study in their own environment. Information on whales came almost exclusively from the whaling industry; the particulars concerned only the most commercially valuable species, leaving out dozens of smaller, less visible toothed and beaked whales. Even today cetologists aren't certain how many species there are; the working figure is around 89.

Remington Kellogg of the Smithsonian Institution was America's premier cetologist. He was also a member of the Society's Research Committee and the author of a 1940 *National Geographic* article with paintings of all the better-known whales, porpoises, and dolphins in color: a publishing first.

Kellogg could cite an important statistic: Fully three-quarters of a million whales had been killed since 1900, which meant that they were vanishing as fast as the plains bison had. Fortunately for their survival, their behavior and migration routes remained a mystery.

That 1940 article had been our last survey of the state of the world's whales; the few articles on orcas in the pipeline were largely photographed in marine mammal parks, since photography of the great whales in the ocean was considered impossible then. A new survey would again be illustrated with paintings.

One of the greatest conservation victories of the 20th century was in the making: the effort to save the whales. That turn of the tide surged through the pages of *National Geographic* when I was editor, and I like to think it had an impact on the Save the Whales movement—especially after Dr. Roger Payne entered our fold.

Few names are more familiar in the annals of whale conservation. Trained at Harvard and Cornell, Dr. Payne pursued studies of echolocation in owls, bats, and moths but ultimately picked whales as his focus. He went with his wife, Katy, to Bermuda to study the wintering humpback whale population. There he met Frank Watlington, an engineer working for the U.S. Navy, whose secret job was to drop hydrophones into the ocean.

Most likely he was listening for Soviet submarines. But he recorded something else: strange whoops and moans when humpback whales were in the vicinity. He told no one about these sounds, thinking whalers might use the information to pinpoint remaining stocks. But after worldwide protection was given to humpbacks in 1966—if not before—he shared them with the Paynes. The following year the Paynes, too, were dropping hydrophones into the sea off Bermuda and listening to the choiring in the deep.

Listening to humpbacks off Bermuda in spring 1967, the Paynes traced out what sounded like long sonic arrangements of repeated sequences, lasting up to 30 minutes, which they could describe only as "songs." Or, as Roger put it, "alien oratorios, cantatas and recitatives."

Some scientists were skeptical, but the Paynes' record *Songs of the Humpback Whale*, released in 1970, was a tremendous hit. Those marine choristers provided the anthem for the Save the Whales movement—strains soon incorporated into pieces composed by Judy Collins and referenced by Crosby, Stills, Nash, and Young. The humpbacks had become a pop sensation just as debate about their future was roiling the International Whaling Commission.

Starting in 1971, Roger worked at Península Valdés, Argentina, where endangered southern right whales came inshore during the austral spring to breed. His entire clan would descend upon that promontory: Roger, Katy, and their four children lived in that charmed spot in tents, ate meals on a picnic table, and fell asleep each night to a serenade, as Roger put it, of "grunting, mooing, moaning and sighing"—the sounds of the whales milling about in the sea beneath the Paynes' temporary clifftop home.

We started work on an article profiling the family and its whale-watching.

After sunrise Roger would peer through telescopes, study the cetaceans, and identify individuals by characteristic marks in fluke or fin—or even in callosities, the wartlike masses that often encrusted their bodies. Sometimes he'd go down to the beach, slip into a kayak, and paddle among them. The giant creatures were so intent on playing, mating, and nursing that they seemed largely indifferent to his presence. "During that first season, we discovered extraordinary evidence of right whales' restraint towards humans," Roger wrote in the October 1972 *National Geographic*. "We had become convinced that the true disposition of the right whale is at variance with its centuries-old reputation for smashing boats and men."

If whales were that accommodating, why not put photographers in the water with them? We signed on Charles E. "Chuck" Nicklin, a professional underwater photographer who had been one of the first humans to swim among whales, along with the former Navy photographer William Curtsinger. Together, they pioneered a new, demanding kind of photography, and I approved creating a major package on the world's whales for publication.

When published four years later, that two-part package contained an overview of whales, whaling, and conservation efforts, along with a comprehensive piece on population biology by the American cetologist Dr. Victor Scheffer. It also featured the first widely distributed map of every known whale-related breeding ground, calving ground, and migration route—arguably the most definitive such map to this day.

We would return to whales with a different twist in 1979. *Symphony of the Deep: Songs of the Humpback Whale* was in our January issue along with two articles on those "gentle giants." Roger narrated the record, and the joke was that with 10.5 million pressings, humpbacks had "gone platinum"—the designation for records that reach sales of one million. We had exceeded that factor by 10. It long remained the largest single press run of any vinyl recording.

"As we inch closer to understanding these fascinating creatures, we must search for ways to cement our ties with them and co-exist peacefully," Roger Payne wrote. Judging by my experience with Wilma, I sometimes wonder whether cetaceans haven't been working longer at forging bonds with us.

In my life I witnessed only the turn of the tide now heading in the direction of understanding. I hope my grandchildren will be swept up in its full flood.

IN THE LATE 1960S Jacques-Yves Cousteau had furled the National Geographic banner and sailed off in *Calypso* to start another chapter in his remarkable story. Filmmaking had been his first love, and he was returning to it after 15 extraordinary years pioneering underwater archaeology, marine biology, submergence diving, and submersible design.

He was exceptionally brilliant and, sometimes, exceptionally infuriating. Whenever he could be cajoled to visit Society headquarters and give the Research Committee a progress report on his many funded projects that had seemingly stalled midstream, he would, with Gallic charm, bewitch everyone. He'd written some of the most popular *National Geographic* articles we'd run—and started some that might have been popular had he bothered to finish.

Cousteau was truly *Homo aquaticus,* the visionary of an age when humankind would simultaneously explore both the continental shelves and the moon. The "Columbus of the depths" would be hard to replace—but replace him we must.

Cousteau had been the first to use scuba to excavate an ancient shipwreck—a Roman-era vessel off Marseille that took eight years to excavate. In the late 1950s, when I was earning my scuba license to dive on shipwrecks, we already had several explorers scouring the seafloor that way.

Edwin Link, the aviation pioneer, and the noted navigator Philip Van Horn "Vanny" Weems explored the drowned remains of Port Royal, the pirate town in Jamaica so quickly destroyed by a 1690 earthquake that its church bells were said to ring beneath each tide. In 1958 Peter Throckmorton, a New York photojournalist and sailor, went to Turkey to investigate rumors of shipwrecks littering the seas near the forelands of Asia Minor, an age-old trading coast. Working from old sponge boats, he recovered 3,300-year-old spear points and copper ingots from one shipwreck he thought might be the oldest yet found—a story told in "Thirty-Three Centuries Under the Sea," in the May 1960 issue.

I helped Peter put that story together. He realized that he wasn't qualified to excavate that wreck properly and sought help from dry-land archaeologists. At the University of Pennsylvania Museum of Archaeology and Anthropology, he found the new discipline's true founder.

George Bass was a 27-year-old archaeologist embarked on a career excavating classical sites. But after some quick diving lessons in a swimming pool, he set off for Cape Gelidonya, where Peter's ship lay in 90 feet of water. In a single season, George successfully transplanted the standard techniques of land archaeology—mapping, gridding, marking, documenting, excavating—to the seafloor, where he made archaeological history: Cape Gelidonya was the first wreck site to be excavated entirely underwater. The Bronze Age ship was the oldest one found at the time.

We were fast becoming the magazine of record for underwater treasure hunts too—which drew criticism from the nautical archaeologists we sponsored. George Bass did not mince words when he claimed that treasure hunting was "tomb robbing." But I disagree, provided it is done responsibly. If the seafloor is the greatest historical archive on earth, littered with perhaps a million shipwrecks, archaeology will be centuries getting to them.

I suspect that most criticisms aimed at treasure hunting are directed at buccaneers like Mel Fisher. It was Fisher, draped in gold chains, who became the poster child of the greedy treasure hunter in 1985, after he finally found the remains of the *Nuestra Señora de Atocha,* a galleon loaded with 40 tons of gold and silver sunk by a hurricane in the Florida Keys in 1622.

In 1973, while underwater photographer Bates Littlehales was covering Fisher's operation, his 11-year-old son, who had accompanied him, was tragically sucked into a boat propeller and died before reaching the hospital. Two years later Mel lost both his son and his daughter-in-law when their boat capsized. There was something unlucky out there.

Still, Mel continued his quest. "Today's the day!" he would say. By the mid-1970s he had amassed a significant haul of treasure. We coupled our first article on Fischer, written by Eugene Lyon, an expert on Spanish colonial Florida, and published in June 1976, with an exhibit in Explorers Hall, followed by a television special with the enticing title "Gold!"

All three were enormous successes. The exhibit attracted half a million visitors, including Queen Sophie of Spain, and featured a clever display allowing visitors to reach in and heft a gold bar—but only your hand could be withdrawn.

Mel Fisher came too. On one visit we were invited on the *Harden and Weaver Show,* a top-rated radio show in Washington. On the appointed morning we met at the studio on Jenifer Street. Mel, declining a lift, said he would meet me there and walked in carrying his breakfast—a substantial one, it seemed, from the size of the McDonald's bag.

Midway through that interview, Mel reached into the bag. I thought he was going to pull out an Egg McMuffin and eat it right there. Instead, he removed a long, solid-gold chain recovered from *Atocha,* one of 43 found on that wreck. Needless to say, once we admired it on a live microphone, there was no returning it to the bag and walking down the sidewalk. He allowed my driver to take him safely back to his hotel.

In the May 1976 issue we explored a fleet of 60 sunken warships, sent to the bottom of Truk Lagoon in the Pacific when U.S. bombers caught part of the Imperial Japanese Navy napping in a supposedly impregnable anchorage. The text was written by Sylvia Earle, a scientist-diver so charismatic that she became our new Cousteau.

She'd earned her degrees in marine botany, so knew ocean ecology, and broke into the boys' club in 1964 as the only woman to join the 70 men aboard the *Anton Bruun* in the International Indian Ocean Expedition. The Truk Lagoon story showcased her talent.

Three years later Sylvia would climb into a "Jim" suit: a body shell developed by Oceaneering International as a diving system. Though pressure-rated for 2,000 feet, it had never been used that deep; the operator was always lowered and retrieved on a tether from a ship.

Six miles off the coast of Oahu, Sylvia was carried into the depths by a submersible from which she could detach and, wearing the suit, walk untethered across the seafloor. For two and a half hours she ambled through a forest of coral 1,250 feet beneath the surface: the first human to walk untethered that deep. Anything could have happened—a nudge, a bump, a puncture. It was quite a feat for "Her Deepness," as she became known.

Brave? Unquestionably. Most of all, though, I think of Sylvia as a fierce guardian of the planet who believes in the resiliency of nature but warns we must never be casual about it.

IN SUMMER 1974 a research flotilla assembled over the Mid-Atlantic Ridge some 400 miles southwest of the Azores. Project FAMOUS— French-American Mid-Ocean Undersea Study—was a multiyear effort culminating in the first manned descents to the still unseen rift valley known to lurk two miles below. Onboard one vessel, the Woods Hole Oceanographic Institution's R.V. *Knorr,* was a marine geologist named Robert Ballard.

We would cover the expedition and include a first-person account of what it was like to descend in a submersible down to the Mid-Atlantic Ridge. Ballard, who had spent six years diving in *Alvin,* the tiny submersible used to map the seafloor off Maine, would write the piece.

Our May 1975 package on this epochal expedition—the first full-scale use of manned submersibles for deep ocean research and the first color pictures of its discoveries—marked Bob Ballard's entrance onto the *National Geographic* stage.

In 1976 the National Geographic Society, Bob Ballard, and *Alvin* descended into the Cayman Trough, a deep gash bisecting the Caribbean Basin, in search of hydrothermal vents—underwater hot springs—which should have been found, along with magma, upwelling through rifts. Alas, only one extinct vent hole was found and photographed: evidence they existed somewhere. Even so, staff photographer Emory Kristof's crew produced superb pictures of the operation with ever more ingenious camera rigs. Published that August, it was Ballard's second *Geographic* story, "Window on Earth's Interior."

In early 1977 Ballard and *Knorr* went on another quest for vents—this time in the eastern Pacific, on the Galápagos Rift, several hundred miles north of that archipelago.

One day in February a telephone call was patched through informing me that they'd found those sought-after vents.

The ship had been traversing the rift and was towing a deep-water sophisticated camera sled when a temperature spike indicated the presence of warm water. The scientists retrieved the sled and removed the 400-foot-long roll of color film. When it was developed, the scientists saw—clams? What were they doing there? Supposedly, the deep, black sea was abiotic.

The next day three men descended in *Alvin* for a firsthand look, dropping 8,000 feet into darkness until arriving at the clam-strewn spot dubbed Clambake. It was a hydrothermal vent.

The expedition would identify four more vent sites holding a profusion of clams, mussels, crabs, lobsters, fish, and ghastly undulating tube worms. "Like something out of science fiction!" I heard again and again.

Deep-sea hydrothermal vents and unexpected clams, whale songs and underwater gardens of coral—all were part of what Sylvia Earle would one day call "the rainforest of the ocean, this complex ecosystem that drives our life support system."

"The wonder . . . ," Sylvia had said, musing on "the flash, the sparkle, the glow, the cosmic universe" that William Beebe must have seen out the small window of his bathysphere in 1934. Beebe, the first oceangoing scientist welcomed into the fold of the Society, was succeeded by other explorers of the deep, like Sylvia and Bob Ballard.

Sylvia's lifelong pursuit of illuminating and preserving the world's oceans was known as Mission Blue. To unveil that hidden world for readers would become our mission as well.

CHAPTER SEVENTEEN

MINE WAS THE MIGRATING BIRD

S ometimes a story idea would literally walk in the door. I was sitting in my office one day when staff writer Harvey Arden called. Could he bring someone for me to meet? Of course, I replied. What crossed my threshold entered not on two legs but on four: The most striking dog went straight into my executive bathroom and began lapping up water from the toilet bowl.

He was followed by his owner, a young man with long, red hair, wearing sweatpants and green high-top sneakers. "Gil," Harvey said, "meet Peter Jenkins."

Peter was from Greenwich, Connecticut, but had hiked to Washington from Alfred University in western New York State. Furthermore, he intended to continue walking all the way across the country. When I asked him why, he replied that the Vietnam War, Watergate, the environmental crisis, racial tensions, and other disputes then dividing the country had left him disenchanted with his native land. A friend had suggested, "Why not go see for yourself?" Peter liked that idea, so he was stopping by the Geographic to gauge our interest. As his professor said, "What have you got to lose?"

I thought we had nothing to lose by loaning him a camera. He actually might do it, I thought. He seemed self-assured, open-minded, neither egotistical nor bashful. That half-malamute dog, Cooper, clinched it. "Stay off interstates; linger along the way. Send us the film. Cooper will lead you to interesting people and photographs," I told him. We fixed Peter up with a camera, lenses, and film, and sent him off. My staff looked at me, convinced I had finally lost my mind.

I won that gamble. Looking again at the two articles that journey produced, it is clearer to me now why this saga had such great appeal.

Unlike Robin Lee Graham's odyssey, Peter's was closer to Walt Whitman's "I Hear America Singing." Because his challenges were less severe, Peter easily moved from a wary, if cheerful, skepticism to a wholehearted embrace of the United States. His encounters included a mountain hermit in Virginia, a welcoming African American family in North Carolina, a farming commune in Tennessee, and lonely ranchers on the wide sweep of the western prairie. Peter was a remarkably fine photographer, especially of portraits. It was a bravura performance by a rank amateur.

"I guess wherever you go, you find some kind of reflection of yourself," he wrote. As he walked his way across the country, he sawed lumber, fed roughnecks on offshore oil rigs, and waited tables in Dallas. He trapped gators in Louisiana and ran cattle in the Great Basin. If he had a "middle passage," it began with the death of that wonderful dog, Cooper, accidentally run over by a truck.

His only admission of despair was the single sentence: "I had never been so alone." He found redemption along the Gulf Coast, among blooming azaleas and the astringency of salt air. At a revival in Mobile he became a born-again Christian; in New Orleans he fell in love and married.

That's right, married—in journey's midst, just like Robin Lee Graham. But the solitary aspect was not as crucial to Peter's wanderings as it was to Robin's quest. He and Barbara walked every step of the way to the West Coast, approaching every new encounter without prejudice or preconception: the secret of his appeal to readers.

I flew out to join a small group for their march down an Oregon beach, when they waded into the Pacific, nearly six years after his first step. "A Walk Across America," published in our April 1977 issue with the memorable line "I started out searching for myself and my country and found both," was voted the most popular story of the year by our membership.

Peter Jenkins navigated by a spiritual compass: He'd pause on the road until, he wrote, "my soul started spinning like a weather vane, and where it finally pointed, I would walk." His mode was unerringly generous: "I wanted to share every environment with the people who were rooted in it." A perfect summation of the life geographical.

David Lewis, another voyager whose adventures enthralled our readers, had a compass that included the sea, sky, and stars. He was born in Devon but grew up in New Zealand and Rarotonga, the South Sea island then part of the British Empire. Lewis thought of himself as half Polynesian, and in Rarotonga first heard the Polynesian seafaring sagas that left a deep mark on his imagination and soul.

In 1960 he had come in third on the first single-handed transatlantic race, despite being dismasted in its early stages. What really made sailors sit up and take notice, though, was Lewis's three-year circumnavigation of the globe with his wife and two young daughters—the first ever undertaken by a double-hulled catamaran.

On the leg from Tahiti to New Zealand, the path the Maori had followed to the North and South Islands eight centuries earlier, Lewis stowed his compass, charts, and sextant and sailed it the way the Polynesians of old had. He followed *kaveinga,* the "star path," and landed only 26 miles away from his projected landfall.

Those of us who thought the epic of Polynesian migration ranked among the greatest geographical subjects in history grappled with how to present so sprawling a theme to our members. Historians and mariners had long wondered how the far-flung isles of Oceania had been settled;

and how, centuries before the cross-staff and compass had come into use in the West, the Polynesians in their sacred 100-foot-long, double-logged canoes unerringly found atolls and islands across the vast Pacific.

We decided on a package with charts, diagrams, and paintings, supplemented by a "Peoples and Cultures" map titled "Islands of the Pacific and their Discoverers." Since the Polynesian way-finding arts were so integral to the presentation, we turned to David Lewis.

Lewis had first glimpsed the *kaveinga* when he asked an old Tongan how best to negotiate a dangerous coral reef; he realized the answer lay in age-old sea lore many Westerners had assumed was lost. After that, he took a lead role among scholars convinced that the ancient art of Polynesian navigation still lived in the remoter archipelagos, kept in trust by wise, elderly men.

When we met, David's bristly hair and goatee were going gray; his manner was polite and unassuming. The tattoos hidden beneath his suit were the real thing, inked by Polynesian artists in palm-frond huts and infused with symbolic meaning. He flashed a crinkly grin.

We sent him and photographer Bill Curtsinger to the Caroline Islands, where one of the last big canoe fleets still followed the ancient rhythms of wind, wave, star, and bird. The old Polynesian navigators could read the waves, particularly long oceanic swells; they could feel them beneath their feet and determine the direction from which they came.

The star path was the route marked out for the helmsman. If traveling east, the path was delineated by a succession of stars rising one after another out of the sea above the horizon; if traveling west, it was indicated by stars setting one after another out below the horizon. The navigator need only keep his prow pointed toward those spots, discarding each star when it rose too high in the sky, then picking out the next one rising from a nearby point. As a check, he could glance at the Magellanic Clouds and the Southern Cross, his North Star equivalent. Lewis found the Caroline

Islanders possessed an unbelievable memory for where stars would be even in daytime; when they emerged into view at twilight, they were always right over the canoe's prow: an incredible feat of dead reckoning.

Birds were messengers, rather than omens, to these ancient mariners—not pelagic birds like the albatross, but land-based birds like terns and boobies, which rarely strayed more than 20 miles from nesting colonies on islands. Their flight patterns often indicated the way home. There were other signs: patterns of ocean phosphorescence or distinctive clouds that typically form above islands.

David's "Wind, Wave, Star, and Bird" was the centerpiece of the award-winning Polynesian package in the December 1974 issue. Those navigators were in close touch with their interior mapmaker. Since there is no such thing as a featureless landscape, it follows that the more observant we are as we travel, the better we can appreciate and cherish the world.

TO APPRECIATE AND CHERISH THE WORLD is a lesson best learned while young. Donna and I had another child, a daughter, Alexandra Rowland Grosvenor, whom we called Lexi, adding even more urgency to my passion for education. That summer in Beinn Bhreagh, I realized the best way to promote active learning among children was to transform our *School Bulletin,* the mini–*National Geographic* disseminated through public and private schools. Why not fill its pages with projects kids would find challenging and fun? Why not send it to their homes rather than to their schools?

I scribbled notes and canvassed family and friends for what might appeal to kids; not many illustrated children's magazines were being published. *Ranger Rick* was closest to what I had in mind, since it featured animals and nature and was illustrated by color photography. But I thought our publication should be more geographical.

Bob Breeden, still in charge of the Special Publications Division, built a prototype, which I took to our board of trustees, who rejected it. I remember Ted Vosburgh's scathing, if ironic, comment: "It's downright childish." Back to the drawing board.

This time I went to the staff for suggestions. We decided on a few themes: a larger format than the *School Bulletin* had; a focus on animals, because children had a natural affinity for them; and the inclusion of games and projects to compete with "couch potato" TV viewing.

Breeden's group came up with a winning format on our second try, which the board approved. After extensive testing, we called it *World* magazine. Following a splashy announcement in the July 1975 *National Geographic* and a mass promotion to our 10 million members, we signed on a million subscribers. Those first issues included a multiple-piece world globe, a punch-out cardboard pterosaur that actually flew, and a pinhole camera that worked.

We never had to market *World* beyond our membership. Grandparents, aunts, and uncles looking for birthday and holiday gifts for their young relatives guaranteed a strong circulation.

In July 1974, Franc Shor suddenly died. He was only 60 years old but had been spinning downward since his marriage had broken up a few years earlier. He had started drinking heavily again, and while his claim to have visited every country on the planet was never verified, the rumor that he had his own corner of the wine cellar at the Ritz Paris turned out to be true. The wine was cleared out and shipped back to Washington, and a wake was held in his memory. I would miss Franc for years to come.

METICULOUS EDITING BY STAFFERS like Franc Shor and John Scofield was only one part of the publishing process. To ensure unimpeachably accurate reporting, every story we printed—every sentence, every word—was subjected to rigorous fact-checking by our research department. But occasionally current events outran us.

A dust storm of controversy was stirred up when Robert Azzi, an Arab American photojournalist, produced an article on Damascus, Syria.

Its religious makeup included Sunnis, Druze, Alawites, Christians, and a handful of the once numerous Jews. Although not permitted to leave the city without a permit and forbidden to immigrate to Israel, every Sephardic Jew had "rights like any other citizen," according to a prominent rabbi Azzi had interviewed, including "freedom of worship and freedom of opportunity." That passed muster with local diplomats, the Syria desk officer at the State Department, several rabbis, and our researchers.

Scarcely was that April 1974 issue off the press than four Damascene Jews were brutally murdered by Arab Muslims. The world's attention turned to the plight of this group trapped behind the Syrian lines—and suddenly our article, "Damascus, Syria's Uneasy Eden," sparked a firestorm. The American Jewish Congress launched an attack, blaming us for "shocking distortions"; at the same time, I learned our issue was banned in Syria for being pro-Israel.

The orchestrated letter-writing campaign began—not just a handful, but thousands. Most were ugly in tone; one threatened my life. I learned a hard lesson: Finding the middle ground in the Middle East could be hazardous to your health.

Spring turned to summer, and I worried that, like a grass fire, this might burn into our membership rolls. One June afternoon someone told me to look out my office window. Sure enough, a long line of protesters waving signs was shuffling up and down the sidewalks of 17th and M Streets. The American Jewish Congress was picketing us. That got my attention.

I asked the researchers to review the fact-checking trail once more. They came back to me with what I feared: Some experts were qualifying their approval of the sentences about the Damascene Jews; recent events had modified their tune. Furthermore, the rabbi whom Bob Azzi had talked to might have been too guarded in his choice of words. We had unwittingly stumbled.

In response, we inaugurated an Editor's Note in our November 1974 issue. "We have erred," I concluded, addressing the issue of the Damascene Jews. Nevertheless, we would still report on sensitive areas of the modern world, "sticking not to our guns but to the facts as we find them."

It was the first admission of error in *National Geographic*'s history. Undoubtedly, we had made mistakes before, but our reputation for accuracy meant the retraction was given wide play in the press. Nevertheless, I don't remember either Mel Payne or the board—MBG was still chairman—ever bringing the matter up in a critical context.

On January 1, 1975, we broke the nine-million-member ceiling for the first time. We must have been doing something right.

A FEW MONTHS LATER I received word that I had been named Editor of the Year by the National Press Photographers Association for the leading role *National Geographic* had played in the use of news pictures.

Only a few of the many stories I reviewed from 1974, the year represented by the honor, qualified as "news" stories. Besides Damascus, there was "East Germany: The Struggle to Succeed" and "A Rare Look at North Korea." The latter was a coup because its author-photographer, Edward Kim, was a *National Geographic* picture editor. Born in Seoul, he moved to the United States and played family connections on both sides of the Demilitarized Zone to become the first American photojournalist allowed inside the Hermit Kingdom in a quarter century.

I was saying, "That's great! That's great!" practically every hour of the day. I said it when Bob Sisson showed me his pictures for "Life on a Raft of Sargassum." I said it again when I read Ken MacLeish's lovely piece on Canterbury Cathedral and when I saw the layouts of "Awesome Worlds Within a Cell." Because they were great.

The "world and all that is in it." The mix. The blend. The symphony. The Editor of the Year award was really a tribute to the men and women who bent over light tables arranging Kodachrome slides, who edited text, fiddled with layouts, organized projection sessions, drafted maps, drew illustrations, answered member queries, processed their dues, and spent hours on the phone with those out in the world producing those words and pictures. It should have been conferred on them, the *National Geographic* staff: my Geographic family.

In "Wind, Wave, Star, and Bird," David Lewis invoked one of his Tuamotu sacred chants, an ode to the ancient Polynesian voyaging canoe:

> *Mine is the migrating bird*
> *Winging over perilous regions of the ocean,*
> *Ever tracing out the age-old path of the wandering waves. . . .*

In those years when I was editor, *National Geographic* magazine was my migrating bird, my voyaging canoe—the one that took me, like the sea kings of old, to unknown lands. It did that every hour of every day, and it was marvelous.

CHAPTER EIGHTEEN

THE SIEGE

Mel Payne turned 65 years old and was retiring in May 1976—about the same time as Luis Marden. "Retirement" was a relative term to Luis. The year before he did so, he witnessed the coronation of King Birendra of Nepal, attended the visit of Emperor Hirohito to Woods Hole, and discussed the fantastic notion of locating the remains of the *Titanic* with Bob Ballard. To top it off, he received two thank-you notes from Jacqueline Kennedy Onassis: one for giving John Jr. advice about scuba diving; the other congratulating him for his article on Tuscany.

Mel and Luis had been close in the mid-1930s, when both had joined the Society's staff. They took flying lessons together and spent weekends fishing the Potomac and its tributaries. Both had wives named Ethel. Ethel Payne was as wonderful in her way as Ethel Marden.

Inevitably, they began drifting apart. Mel was buttoned up, austere. I think he grew more judgmental and conservative the higher he rose in the Society's hierarchy, while Luis never removed his metaphorical pith helmet. They never actually ruptured, just diverged. Mel was a superb steward of the Society's resources, which Luis spent too freely. They were two faces of one Society.

Mel Payne was an enigma. When I reached out to him after his only son was killed in a motorcycle accident, I might as well have reached out to a marble statue. Shortly afterward, Ethel Marden went over to visit the

Paynes; Luis was away on assignment. Mel was sitting in the den, watching football. The two Ethels were in the kitchen. When Ethel Marden stepped into the den, she pulled up sharply: Mel was watching the game, tears streaming down his cheeks.

I had watched Mel pull off one of the most audacious business decisions in the Society's history. He threw off the yoke of our printer—the best, most famous one in the country—and engaged another one with a more down-market, raffish reputation.

Chicago had long been this country's printing headquarters. That's where R. R. Donnelley, our printer since 1957, was located. It was indisputably top of the line but drove a hard bargain. Mel hated the annual contract negotiations. He became convinced Donnelley was taking us for a ride. He decided to look elsewhere.

One of Donnelley's crosstown rivals was W. F. Hall, Inc., founded as the printer of Montgomery Ward catalogs. It had upped its game and, when Mel came calling, was printing Sunday supplements, *Playboy*, and Bantam books. Mel knew that only a few printing processes provided acceptable quality for us. One was letterpress and offset: another was gravure, which was newer and messy but improving rapidly.

Payne struck a deal with Hall, transferring our printing from Chicago to Corinth, Mississippi. Two four-story-tall gravure presses were installed in a dedicated plant near a good rail network and an inexpensive rural labor base. It promised to be the biggest technical changeover in the history of our magazine. The transfer—like moving an automobile plant from Detroit to Dallas without missing a muffler on the assembly line—would begin in summer 1977.

Mel, uncharacteristically, was gambling our entire stake on one throw of the dice—ultimately, a brilliant move. The increased efficiency and improved economics permitted us to hold at bay the ever increasing costs of printing *National Geographic* for years to come.

I applauded him with everyone else at a celebratory banquet. At the board meeting that spring, we voted in a new management team. MBG would step aside as board chairman and become chairman emeritus while retaining the purely ceremonial title of editor in chief. Mel Payne would become chairman of the board. Our new president and CEO, entrusted with overseeing the transfer of printing from Donnelley to Hall, would be Robert Doyle.

Bob, liked by me and everyone at the Society, had the added virtue of having no editorial experience and thus no desire to tinker with the magazine. Until then, Payne had left me alone to run the magazine. I knew Bob would too.

I left the boardroom with a lighter step. As I returned toward my office, I had no idea I was walking into a trap.

WHEN MEL PAYNE RETIRED as president and became chairman of the board, he set up a board subcommittee on management continuity—largely because Bob Doyle would turn 65 in 1980, only four years in the future. By then we would need to have groomed a replacement. It looked like our new chairman was using the continuity committee to go after my family.

The first target was MBG. The committee recommended that he not retain the title editor in chief but be named editor emeritus instead. GHG's name would remain on the masthead—a sign of continuity at the Society. Mel would never touch that one but would aim at MBG. He didn't like Dad receiving a stipend, however small, for an empty title and knew that removing the title and stipend was the first step in steering the Society away from the Grosvenor family. The next two steps, I thought, were aimed at me.

One recommendation was that after Payne retired as chairman, the next chairman should come from outside the organization. That would ensure I would never accede to that title, however far in the future that might lie. Going outside our Society was such a bad idea that the board immediately rejected it. A final recommendation was accepted: The two positions of president and editor would remain separate. Never again would one person hold both offices concurrently.

I had hoped that the board would revisit the 1967 decision to break them apart; I still didn't see how the two-headed arrangement would work in the long run. It had worked well enough so far, but a clash was inevitable—especially if our fortunes took a downward turn. Mel knew what I was thinking and had scotched it.

When the board met in autumn 1976, I discussed our upcoming issues. January 1977 would feature the recent Viking lander's descent to the surface of Mars, Castro's Cuba, and Puget Sound. February would highlight Harlem, along with Rajasthan, the Ohio River, and John James Audubon. March headlined Tom Abercrombie's piece on Egypt. April? The separatist fever in Quebec, the first installment of Peter Jenkins's walk across America, and others.

I don't remember a single objection being raised. Certainly not from Mel Payne.

I probably did not mention another story in the pipeline: on South Africa. That was proving troublesome for two reasons. One was the nature of the apartheid regime itself: increasingly a pariah state that provoked strong emotions. The other was that regime's new policy of brutally attacking any media outlet that even slightly disparaged the system.

We had every good reason to publish on South Africa. It was an important economic success story in Africa, thanks to vast deposits of precious and strategic minerals. Also, a violent, chaotic tide of revolution was breaking. Portugal, after a protracted guerrilla war, relinquished Angola and Mozambique. Rhodesia was embroiled in a "bush war" and seemed about to submit to Black majority rule. Would South

Africa take that course, despite its powerful military and whip-wielding police?

We hadn't published a country profile of South Africa since November 1962. That piece, an extended travel brochure, showcased the scenic beauties of South Africa: spectacular Cape Town, gorgeous beaches, breathtaking wildlife—a mostly white South Africa. No coverage of Soweto. We dispatched staff photographer Jim Blair and staff writer Bill Ellis to produce a balanced article.

Jim had striking portraits of South Africans: Alan Paton, author of *Cry, the Beloved Country*; Harry Oppenheimer, the De Beers diamond kingpin; Gary Player, the champion golfer; and Steve Biko, the anti-apartheid activist and martyr celebrated in *Cry Freedom*. He had also captured pictures of Black life lived under the oppressive heel of apartheid: squalid rooms, haunting eyes engulfed in defeat and despair.

Bill Garrett mocked up a cover depicting a Black diamond miner's face looming out of a sea of darkness: a searing image of hopelessness. Bill Ellis's text complemented the pictures. Several reviewers—including Walter Cronkite and Jim Hoagland of the *Washington Post*, who had won a Pulitzer for reporting in South Africa—pronounced the final result accurate and fair. That was the feature I carried over to the South African Embassy on Massachusetts Avenue.

We always sent mock-ups of our country profiles to their respective embassies. Informed that the magazine was preparing a story on South Africa, its government tried to influence us with offers of deluxe all-expenses-paid tours, which we politely ignored. I met Ambassador Roelof "Pik" Botha, explained our objectives, and left him the dummy.

By December, the January issue was in members' mailboxes. "Inside Cuba Today" was sure to be the attention-grabber; Fred Ward, a thorough-going professional with camera and pen, had negotiated three months of unfettered travel in the island and scored an interview with Castro. I expected Cuban émigrés in Miami to bridle but was annoyed when one of our own board members, Crawford Greenewalt, took his issues with the coverage to Chairman of the Board Mel Payne. Greenewalt, former president of E. I. du Pont de Nemours and Company, had lost a plant in Cuba when Castro nationalized industries. People and corporations lost millions, including DuPont. Greenewalt was angry that the organization he served as trustee would even consider publishing a story on Cuba.

Meanwhile, Pik Botha summoned me back to the South African chancery. He shredded the dummy, complaining that Black South Africans were only portrayed as living in poverty, which falsified the actual state of affairs. When I took issue, Botha stubbed his finger at a picture of Black miners in their sordid dormitory, thundering, "If that's not squalor, then I don't know what is!"

I said something about the picture depicting a situation stemming from apartheid's employment restrictions but opted not to get into a shouting match. We offered a few adjustments—clearly too few for the ambassador.

Walking back to headquarters that mild afternoon, I remember thinking that Botha had been a little too stagy. We made the small adjustments as promised; our researchers fact-checked everything for the umpteenth time; I worked on a carefully worded Editor's Note and dispatched the story to the printer.

The February issue was now in members' hands. Sandwiched between accounts of John James Audubon and the longest manned balloon flight was "To Live in Harlem . . . ," a name that to many white Americans symbolized a location better avoided than entered. We chose to enter. Overdue, but editorially tricky: It had to be authentic without looking like *National Geographic* was trying hard to be hip and relevant. Harlem was the country's most famous and influential African American community.

The author, Frank Hercules, had been living in Harlem for three decades, writing novels and the prophetic *American Society and Black Revolution,* which argued that racism was the core of American ideology. It was a place he deeply loved. The photographer, LeRoy Woodson, Jr., was a journalist whose mother had worked in our archives. Woody had grown up in Paris, where his father was a diplomat, and before reaching 30 had established himself in the New York scene, photographing celebrities like John Lennon and Yoko Ono.

Hercules exalted Harlem in words that were often sheer poetry. Woodson's photographs portrayed it as a distinctly American community that held many surprises for our mostly white audience. I thought we hit it about right.

But our New York advertising office overhyped it, taking out full-page advertisements in the *New York Times* and *Wall Street Journal* announcing, "It's Time You Took Another Look." To celebrate the article, they threw a big bash, which Mel declared in "bad taste." He was livid.

New York's literati snickered at "*National Geographic* does Harlem"; conservative columnist Kevin Phillips mocked our "radical chic." Reed Irvine, head of the ultra-right Accuracy in Media, dusted off the Cuba article and, coupled with our recent television special on the Volga River, accused us of being soft on communism—which didn't brighten the fervently anti-communist Mel Payne's mood either.

Ten days later the board of trustees held one of its quarterly meetings. That's when I grew alarmed.

THAT INANE AUTOMATIC SHIFTING OF the drapes in the board-room was the background music to a six-month ordeal wrestling with a proposed "editorial oversight."

The April 1977 issue was in most members' hands, and one of its articles, "One Canada—or Two?," reignited Crawford Greenewalt's anger. One of his friends—a Montreal businessman and son of a former DuPont president—had read that piece on separatist fever in Quebec and complained it was full of distortions.

The idea of distortions in Peter White's text puzzled me. Peter was probably the most thorough writer on staff, a meticulous researcher for whom the smallest detail was not too trivial to chase down. The article was verified by our army of fact-checkers. Distortions seldom survive that kind of scrutiny.

That was one brick too many for Mel Payne. At that board meeting in March, he suggested that an editorial oversight committee be formed to look into changes in the magazine's editorial policy.

"The magazine is not changing," was my response. "The world is changing." I was doing exactly what my predecessors had done.

Mel Payne could transfix you with his gaze alone. I could see the cold fire banked behind his pupils. "Several trustees have lodged objections," he replied calmly. "It's a board matter now."

Ted Vosburgh saved the day. He quickly motioned for a vote of confidence in me as editor, and it passed unanimously. Mel didn't seem angered or upset. He was biding his time.

In March, advance copies of the June issue arrived in my office; per custom, I sent one over to the South African Embassy. I knew I wouldn't have to wait long for the summons.

It came a day or two later. I appeared as requested. Arranged on Pik Botha's spartan desk were a *Time* magazine and the advance copy of the June *National Geographic* I had just sent him. I hardly had a second to take that in, because he was on me and furious. He jabbed at me with his finger.

Tiring of this fusillade, I held up my hand and asked, "Mr. Ambassador, why are you hitting us so hard?" Pointing to his desk, I added, "*Time* pulverized South Africa."

Botha, crimson-faced, picked up our advance copy, slammed it down on his desk, and fairly roared, "You don't understand! People believe what you write!"

I sat stunned, then felt elation. "People believe what you write": He had inadvertently put his finger on the pulse that made us tick. Of course! I thought as I walked back to the office, momentarily heedless of whatever dire threat he had launched. It was a two-beat pulse: One was accuracy and the other was trust. The first is invested in staff; the second, vouchsafed by the membership. Accuracy, balanced and nonpartisan accuracy—and trust. We must never lose that trust.

I would hold on to that throughout the troubled days ahead. In the meantime, Carl Noffke, information counselor at the embassy, wrote me a blistering letter taking us to task for an unbalanced, unfair story that seemingly singled them out for biased treatment. "We will take every proper step to protect our interests," he threatened.

Mel Payne would not like that letter.

SIX WEEKS LATER, on May 12, 1977, Mel chaired a meeting of the Executive Committee, composed largely of Society executives and trustees who lived in town. During that session, he mentioned the need to convene an ad hoc editorial oversight committee to determine whether the magazine had strayed off the course set by GHG's editorial principles— especially the one proclaiming that "nothing of a partisan or controversial character" would be printed. "There has been too much emphasis on disagreeable aspects," Payne declared. "In the future there won't be so much emphasis of that nature."

That sounded like a shot across my bow. The June issue was in the mail, and I knew my problems would soon be compounded should the South African Embassy launch a public attack. Which it did on May 26.

That Thursday evening, readers of the *Washington Star* opened their newspaper and saw a full-page advertisement courtesy of the South African Tourist Board: "National Geographic Magazine has always been an objective camera trained on the world. In its June 1977 issue, however, the camera uses a distorted lens, giving a heavily slanted political and racial bias to its picture of the Republic of South Africa," it said.

Not only was the *Geographic* accused of deliberately distorting, even omitting facts about government achievements and racial progress; it was also tainting South Africa, it averred, with the brush of "journalistic racism—anti-white racism."

That editorial oversight committee was certainly coming. The chairman of the board didn't like to be embarrassed in the pages of his favorite newspaper.

At the June 9 board meeting, Mel Payne opened his attack. Referring to the increasing volume of indictments, he said that it seemed appropriate for the board to determine whether or not the charges were justified.

I sat quietly waiting my turn to respond when Ted Vosburgh came to my defense. He reminded everyone of membership growth the past seven years under my leadership: We had started at a little more than seven million and were approaching 10 million. That was the voting booth that mattered. By that measure, my editorship had been very successful.

MBG stirred into action. He looked directly at Payne and growled, "Looks like a railroad job to me!" Neither man blinked. The tension was apparent.

Wagging his finger, MBG declared the mound of critical letters little more than a "flea on an elephant's back."

"We knew we would have trouble over the South Africa article," he said. "I have read it several times, and I think it explains fairly both sides of the question. We simply can't neglect important areas of the globe because we don't like their government." He surveyed everyone at that long table. "If the editor does not do his job, the board can fire him. But I would not serve as editor with a committee looking over my shoulder!" He sat back.

Crawford Greenewalt spoke. "The magazine has been subject to criticism," he said. "If the board has nothing whatsoever to do with editorial policy, then I, for one, can't see serving as a board member."

"I read the article," opined new board member Chief Justice Warren Burger. "It would never have occurred to me that anyone except the most intense partisan could take exception to it."

"The question," Payne countered, is if "some element not properly a part of the National Geographic Society's mission is creeping into the magazine." He won that round: An ad hoc investigative committee was authorized.

I was not pleased—or surprised. If the magazine was found to be drifting off the straight and narrow, it might put the Society's nonprofit status at risk. As trustees of an august institution, it was their duty to ensure its journal was not seen as veering off in a radical direction. If that meant an ad hoc oversight committee, so be it.

Meanwhile, I had a battle plan.

DETERMINED NOT TO LOSE editorial control of *National Geographic,* I set up a task force—Joe Judge (whom Payne liked), Kent Britt (the June 1977 issue editor), and senior researchers. Bill Garrett (whom Payne disliked) stayed in the background.

My battle plan was simple: Drown the ad hoc committee in paper. I would drive them crazy with details and the endless fact-checking materials for the Cuba, Quebec, and South Africa stories. I would show how every assertion, quote, and statistic in those pages had been verified many times over. Board members would learn the extraordinary lengths our researchers went to get it right. If we could prove that all charges of bias and distortion were baseless, we would win half the battle. The other half—Payne's opposition to "controversial" subjects—would take more time and thought.

The first meeting of the new ad hoc committee convened on June 27. Its chairman, Lloyd Elliott, president of the George Washington University, had been recruited as a new trustee by Mel Payne, so I knew where his loyalty lay, at least in the beginning. Mel was on this committee too, but I don't remember him at this first meeting.

I looked around. Along with me and Bob Doyle were Jim Webb, Louis B. Wright, and Crawford Greenewalt. Webb, a former NASA administrator, had no editorial experience but was thoughtful and fair. Crawford, a titan of industry, was a leading hummingbird photographer and had published three articles in *National Geographic,* so he had been through the editorial process.

Louis Wright also had two *Geographic* stories to his name; though as former director of the Folger Shakespeare Library, he was more scholar than student of magazine journalism.

When Elliott said this was "not a witch hunt," I concluded it was. My first order of business was to demolish any charges of willful distortion or sensationalism. I had instructed my team to ostentatiously wheel in a large cart filled with files. They also brought in stacks of documentation assembled by the researchers backing up every statement in the Cuba, Quebec, and South Africa articles. Every word had been intensely scrutinized, double- and triple-checked, before publication—our policy for every word in every issue.

I put that committee through hell. I made them study every single page in every single document until their eyes glazed over. The automatic drapes clicked and whirred through several cycles. I made it as painfully tedious as possible. We broke for lunch, returned and kept going. Greenewalt was practically climbing the walls. I quit only when they revolted. Okay, they said, we get the point.

Although everyone was now irritable, the nagging question of the criticisms still had not been resolved. I said that we prided ourselves on providing solid background information on sensitive areas of the world: increasing and diffusing geographic knowledge. Criticism is inevitable. "We publish 87 stories a year," I pointed out. "One or two may give us problems." The South Africa article reflected an extraordinary situation.

"You cannot run a 'hearts and flowers' story about South Africa when everyone watches daily television news about riots in Soweto," I said.

Lloyd Elliott tried to outflank me. The criticism might be on target, he said. It might reflect "an unwitting shift in editorial policy."

We were fighting a different battle now. There had been no radical changes; the *Geographic* had not abandoned its core nonpartisan principles.

Was an oversight committee really needed? Jim Webb wondered.

"The editor should be able to control the magazine," I responded. "You cannot have a committee decide editorial content. If you don't like the magazine, appoint a new editor."

Louis Wright sprung another worrisome beast: our tax-exempt status. "That is a problem if you go political."

"I will never go political," I retorted. "That would destroy our members' trust." Perhaps our trustees had not been reading my Editor's Notes, which always championed nonpartisan objectivity.

Wright agreed that an oversight committee might not be necessary but still wondered if editorial policy was being changed "unwittingly." That would be a matter for the trustees.

Crawford Greenewalt spoke up. I was prepared for the worst—he had started this fuss by complaining about Cuba. Surprisingly, he seemed to side with me. He thought the board should weigh in only when its advice might be needed. He obviously wanted to get out of that room because he offered everyone a way out. "Why not write up an amendment or clarification to existing policy to review at our next meeting?" Everyone hastily agreed. We adjourned until August.

WORD OF THE EDITORIAL OVERSIGHT committee leaked to the press. "*Geographic* Faces Problem of Portraying Harsh Reality" appeared in the July 17 *Washington Post*. "The dispute," it said, "goes to the basic question of how boldly the society, with its tradition of Victorian delicacy, will pick its way through a global landscape where life's harsher realities, as one staff writer put it, often 'leap right out at you.'"

It was the first of many articles that tried prying open our boardroom doors. I worried it would provide more ammunition for Mel Payne.

At the August meeting of the ad hoc committee, Mel, present this time, was clearly displeased with results of the previous one and irked by the newspaper articles. Since our main order of business was to debate a draft editorial policy statement, I thought we had turned the corner.

Wrong again. Payne didn't like the statement. He still stubbornly hoped to stop the perceived drift into the thicket of controversy and wanted the board to have the right to approve upcoming stories.

Crawford Greenewalt spoke up. "That would never work. "You can't predict whether a subject will prove controversial. The cat's out of the bag by the time an article is ready to read. Leave it to the editor to carry out a policy with full faith and trust."

That carried the day. I took the draft policy statement and walked back to my office with Joe Judge. We sat down with Bill Garrett and refined a few words in the draft. In 15 minutes I returned. Copies were circulated, read, and approved for submission to the full board. Payne looked crushed. "Since this reflects board policy, I think the chairman should sign as well as the editor and president," I said. Heads nodded. Mel smiled. I had saved face for him at no cost to me. We would meet in September, prior to the board meeting, to wrap it up.

Ultimately, their report would declare, "We find no evidence of any intentional change in policy and we reaffirm editorial policy and commit ourselves to following it." When delivered to the full board, the succinct statement was unanimously approved. Mel Payne never again posed a threat to me or to the editorial process.

Editorial integrity had won.

MY PROFESSIONAL TRIUMPH was overshadowed by a devastating personal loss. In August, Donna asked me for a divorce. The mutual flame we once shared had been flickering for a while. Being editor was time-consuming. She was pursuing her own career, photographing animals and children and becoming quite good.

And our paths had diverged. Donna had vehemently opposed the Vietnam War at the same time my brother was flying missions across the dangerous skies of North Vietnam. Then came her enthusiasm for women's liberation. Most painful of all, her interests shifted to other places and people—especially men.

We had two young children, and the thought of losing them devastated me. Ultimately, the divorce was amicable; we even shared the same attorney. Although we had joint custody of the children, they lived with me for the next few years, as Donna was focused on self-actualization. Best of all, we remained good friends until the day she died in 2021.

I'll always remember Donna at her loveliest, her wide smile and flashing eyes, her charisma, the way she touched people from all walks of life. She could converse with anyone, from a princess in Monaco to a mussel fisherman in Italy, and charm them all. And I'm pleased that her picture of a Balinese dancer was chosen by Carl Sagan in 1977 for the "golden record" of images and sounds from Earth to accompany the two Voyager spacecraft. One day, a million or so years hence, an alien civilization might intercept those craft and glimpse something of what our world was like. Donna could probably have found a way to talk to them too.

Inevitably, place and setting played a huge part in the resurrection of my spirit and being. It took place near Beinn Bhreagh, across the mountain in the neighboring property known as Poker Dan's.

CHAPTER NINETEEN

INDIAN SUMMER

Throughout the 1960s and '70s, whenever I spent my August vacation in Beinn Bhreagh, I would bump into our neighbors, Dabney Jarman and his family, who lived nearby at Poker Dan's.

At the Jarmans' annual August party, I couldn't help noticing that Dabney's youngest daughter was no longer a little girl; I was alone now, so I looked at life a bit differently. Wiley was still freckle-faced but clearly a beautiful young woman. She was now a primary school teacher in Denver. Since I saw her only at Baddeck in August, that's about all I knew of her; our conversation had been the pleasant if inconsequential chatter between old neighbors.

Back home, on a whim, I retrieved her Denver telephone number, but did nothing about it. Thanksgiving came and went, as did the Christmas holidays; then one day, when planning a business trip to Los Angeles, I impulsively booked the flight through Denver.

My layover was maybe three hours. If Wiley didn't answer, I told myself, it was no big deal. But she did, and she drove out to the airport for a quick visit. Snow began to fall, faster and faster, deeper and deeper. Soon the city, highways, and airport were shut down. We gathered that night with other stranded passengers in the airport's lounge, talking, laughing, walking, catnapping, and endlessly sitting around—just the kind of night to foster a camaraderie that might last a lifetime.

THE YEAR 1978 dawned with healing in its wings, chilled by a gust of foreboding.

The board's management continuity committee reached out to me. Lloyd Elliott, its chairman, invited me to lunch. Bob Doyle, our president, would be retiring in two years; the Society needed a succession plan in place. Would I be interested in his job? I would be the third Grosvenor and fifth in my family to hold the position.

I would be the first Grosvenor to do so while not being editor as well. Unless... but any suggestion of recombining the positions of president and editor was met with a very firm no by Lloyd Elliot. "Take your time and think about it. There's no rush at the moment, Gil. We'll be looking for outstanding candidates outside the Society."

That last bit of nonchalance was barbed. He knew that going outside the Society would not sit well with me. We were unique. Only someone who knew it from the inside should guide the institution. Casting a glance at the masthead, I didn't see too many names that fit the bill.

I would put that aside for now. Calls between Washington and Denver were increasing in tempo and duration; weekends in Denver were increasing. Here I was, in my mid-40s, falling in love with a girl not yet 30, and acting as if Indian summer would never end.

Then it hit me: Why be involved in Society business anyway? I had received more than one hint that no one should be editor for more than 10 years, the model set by MBG. If that were the case—and I already had nearly eight years under my belt—what future would I have at a Society whose chairman clearly wanted to move away from the family that had nurtured it? Why not resign when 10 years were up? I could then move to Denver and publish my own environmental magazine.

MBG knew all about my feverish new dreams and began conniving with his board buddies to bring me back to reality. I think he talked to Laurance Rockefeller over a drink, saying, "You know, Gil is having a difficult time.

He's recently divorced, Mel Payne is on his back—midlife-crisis thing. He's thinking about a new start. Maybe you can talk to him?" The next thing I knew, Dad was suggesting I call Laurance. "He's the right man, son! He'll have the best advice!"

Since Laurance happened to be in Aspen, I flew out to see him before meeting Wiley in Denver. He picked me up at the Aspen airport. I had about three hours before my Denver flight.

In a nearby roadside restaurant, Laurance deftly pricked the ill-conceived balloon of my new ambitions. He convinced me that I had the board's support, that Payne had lost his clout after the ad hoc committee fiasco, and he urged me to hang in. By the time I alighted in Denver, I had resolved to continue working on behalf of the National Geographic Society and its mission.

AT THE AGE OF 50, my brother Alec was felled by a brain tumor. War hero, talented pilot, and a man with an exuberant physical vitality, Alec was not one for the sickbed; the months following the initial diagnosis had been grueling for the family, especially for his wife, Marcia, and their two girls. MBG was so downcast, we worried about him too. Only three years earlier Alec had returned to the Naval Academy as commander of Naval Station Annapolis and had built its sailing team into intercollegiate champions.

He died in early April. The family gathered in the Naval Academy Chapel. My mother did not come. She was too old to face the stress and would handle her grief in Florida.

We took our seats beneath the chapel's dome, above the crypt of John Paul Jones, for the short but moving service befitting a Navy man. We held our emotions until the choir sang the "Navy Hymn." None of us remained dry-eyed. An honor guard carried the casket to the Naval Academy Cemetery. Alec was laid to rest on a hill above the Severn River, overlooking the Navy sailing squadron he had rebuilt into national champions.

BY THE MID-1970S the Leakey juggernaut had slowed down at the National Geographic Society. Richard Leakey was critically ill with kidney disease. On November 29, 1979, with his brother as donor, he had a successful kidney transplant. He would roar back into action with accustomed force and vigor. Even a near-fatal crash nearly 14 years later, when the engine in his small Cessna plane conked out, didn't slow him down.

The crash—perhaps an assassination attempt by someone unhappy with his anti-poaching zealotry—ultimately claimed both Richard's legs. But not, as I discovered when I visited him in a British hospital, his ardor or sense of humor. Six months after doctors amputated his left leg below the knee, he elected to have the right lower leg removed as well. He wanted to bury them together at Lake Turkana. "Two Legs in the Grave," he joked, would be the title of his next autobiography.

As always, Richard's mother, Mary Leakey, kept the flame of the family legacy burning. In 1975 she stepped out of an elevator at Geographic headquarters and, seeing two-year-old Lexi standing next to me waiting to greet her, quipped, "Already bipedal, eh?"

Mary had been excavating at Laetoli, Tanzania, about 30 miles from Olduvai Gorge. In 1978 she found the tracks of long-vanished ostriches, hyenas, antelopes, a saber-toothed cat, and hominids hidden in a deposit of hardened volcanic tuff deposited as moist ash by a prehistoric eruption. The hominid footprints—3.6 million years old—nearly match ours today. Our remote ancestors were bipedal—they walked upright—long before they fashioned tools or had evolved large brains.

That threw bipedalism back into the center of the debate over what makes us specifically human. As Mary reported in our April 1979 issue's "Footprints in the Ashes of Time," the discovery implied that "this new freedom of forelimbs posed a challenge. The brain expanded to meet it. And mankind was formed."

Years later I would sit on the terrace of Richard Leakey's house in a

Nairobi suburb, overlooking the Great Rift Valley. Its vista takes in the paleontological sites that contain the epic story of our origins—stories we could tell, thanks to a collaboration that began with Richard's father, Louis, and continued with succeeding generations.

"People don't realize that philosophical questions about our origins— ones that have bedeviled men for 2,000 years—were solved in the last 60 years through the initial cooperation between the National Geographic Society and the Leakey family," Richard said. "Then we spread it out to others. Gil, that's something you should be proud of."

I am.

SCARCELY WAS THE Laetoli report in members' hands when we were sending out next month's issue, featuring a *Geographic* article by Jane Goodall.

Most dreadfully, one night in 1975, armed guerrillas from Zaire came over Lake Tanganyika and attacked Gombe. Jane and several dozen others managed to escape, but the raiders marched three Stanford University students and one Dutch assistant back to the boats at gunpoint. It took months of negotiations to free them. That raid nearly shuttered Gombe and cost Jane her Stanford sponsorship and teaching gig. Worse, after that, the Tanzanian authorities forbade her access to Gombe except for a day or two a month. Only the Tanzanian staff could stay to keep the field observations up-to-date.

Jane retreated to Dar-es-Salaam to spend time with her son, Grub, and husband, Derek Bryceson, whom she had married after she and Hugo divorced. She also made time to correspond with her Geographic friends, Mary Griswold Smith and Joanne Hess.

I had been wanting another Jane Goodall article since the day I became editor—only I needed a new twist. By the late 1970s she could provide that angle, though it led into the dark recesses of Gombe. Jane had discovered an all-too-human side of chimpanzee life: the murderous impulses that led gangs of males to make war on rival gangs and occasionally kill and eat infants. Her shocking account, "Life and Death at Gombe," appeared in the May 1979 *National Geographic*.

In the meantime, she founded the Jane Goodall Institute. But she would continue her special relationship with the National Geographic Society, and Mel Payne and Mary Griswold Smith would serve on that board.

After Derek's death in 1980, Jane's trajectory would only be upward.

In succeeding years I would watch Jane Goodall enlist Secretary of State James Baker in her crusade to suppress Africa's bushmeat trade, fearlessly voice anti-nuclear-power concerns in Taiwan, and influence the decision of the National Institutes of Health to end the use of chimpanzees in medical research. She would receive every conceivable award—from the French Legion of Honor to Dame Commander of the British Empire to the Kyoto Prize.

Nowhere was Jane's success more evident than at a Hollywood fund-raiser many years later. I was to introduce her. It was quite a spectacle—the entertainment glitterati in their finest livery. Vainly I implored the crowd to quiet down; finally, conversation hushed, and I asked everyone to listen carefully. While the curtains remained closed, as if straight from Africa and Gombe itself, there slowly arose the increasing tempo and volume of the chimpanzee's dawn call. Soon the entire auditorium was vibrating to its cadence: *hoo-ho, hoo-ho, hoo-ho, hoo-ho, HOO, HOO, HOO, HOO, HOOOO!*

Hardly had the last hoot sounded when the place fell utterly silent; you could have heard a pin drop. Then Jane's face peeked out from behind the curtain. As she slowly proceeded to the podium, the place went wild with applause; everyone jumped to their feet cheering, whistling, stomping, and clapping in thunderous admiration.

It was amazing to consider: Our initial $1,400 research grant to Jane Goodall was the merest rivulet stemming from Louis Leakey's Society-supported work. It would grow into its own mighty stream and nourish the growth of primatology as a scientific discipline of great significance, helping to launch her extraordinary career.

DIAN FOSSEY'S TRACK was the opposite: The high point may have been in 1970, when she so famously touched Peanut's fingers. A long drop into her personal abyss followed.

In September 1970, one of Fossey's graduate student assistants at Karisoke shot two poachers in the legs. Fossey, not there at the time, condoned the assistant's actions. Her war against poachers, who snatched infant gorillas to sell on the black market and customarily killed adult gorillas to do so, was ferociously personal.

The Geographic still supported her, putting her front and center in our January 1976 PBS television special, "The Search for the Great Apes," viewed by millions. Her co-star in that film, was Digit, a young male gorilla she had grown to love. In December 1977, spear-wielding poachers murdered Digit. His body was found in the woods, head and hands removed.

That drove Dian over the edge. After the death of Digit, she waged a one-woman war against poachers who were pushed into the park from a severely overpopulated Rwanda. She spent more time tearing up snare traps, wrecking forest camps, kidnapping suspected poachers, and—it was rumored—torturing them, than studying gorillas. In doing so, she crossed a legal and psychological line.

How does a sponsoring organization like the National Geographic Society deal with "rogue" grantees? Rwanda was far away, communications difficult, and sifting fact from scurrilous fiction was tricky. The New York Zoological Society sent two employees over there to mend fences with the local population, promoting an ecotourism effort that might benefit everyone—most of all, the gorillas. Dian would have none of it, assuming they were there to stage a coup d'état at Karisoke.

Meanwhile, diplomatic cables flew as the Rwandan government, upset that Dian was practically declaring a kill-on-sight war against its citizens, complained so loudly that Secretary of State Cyrus Vance intervened.

That was the final straw. We—her sponsors and benefactors—brought

Dian home. She settled at Cornell University and began work on the book that became *Gorillas in the Mist*.

IN 1978 JOHN SCOFIELD announced his retirement. I hadn't seen it coming. John had been my associate editor for so long that I had come to think of him as a permanent fixture, an indispensable and always reliable presence.

I also saw a silver lining. Now that Mel Payne was no longer the president and had been wounded in the boardroom when his oversight committee had been killed, I had a free hand in choosing John's replacement—or replacements. I called Bill Garrett in and told him he would be the new associate editor in charge of all illustrations, layout, and design. Of course, he could still occasionally write and photograph articles.

I made Joe Judge the associate editor in charge of text. With Garrett and Judge in place, I finally felt that we had come of age as a magazine staff.

Meanwhile, there were personal matters to address. With my divorce final, I was now free to pursue Wiley.

ON JUNE 15, 1979, I stood beside the altar in the National Cathedral waiting for my bride. Then, as every head turned, I gazed at the lovely Mary Helen Wiley Jarman as she walked up the aisle, escorted by her father. In her hands was a bouquet of flowers topped by the same bit of ancestral lace worn by Mabel Gardiner Hubbard when she married Alexander Graham Bell 102 years earlier.

It was a big wedding, but one important person was missing. Knowing my mother was too frail to travel, I had taken Wiley down to West Palm Beach to meet her and, in a sense, receive her blessing.

Our big post-honeymoon trip came that autumn: China.

For the past five years we had tried to play our China card but were able to publish only small pieces on Chinese archaeology—including one on the dazzling new find made in 1974, when workers digging a well near Xi'an in

Shaanxi Province broke into the chamber holding a huge army of terra-cotta soldiers. Audrey Topping wrote that story, but her access was restricted.

In December 1978, President Jimmy Carter and Deng Xiaoping normalized relations between the two countries; staff writer Bart McDowell attended the reception. He returned with a glowing report of his warm welcome by the new ambassador, who bestowed the highest praise upon the Society.

Shortly after, Bill Garrett obtained a tourist visa and carried his cameras to China. He didn't stay long, but he traveled to Guilin Province, site of the picturesque limestone peaks so dear to Chinese landscape painters. Bill's pictures made a short article for our October issue.

By the time that went to the printer, we made an even bigger breakthrough: I would be welcome to visit China, see its cities, admire its scenic wonders, and negotiate with the Xinhua News Agency and China's Institute of Geography to publish a wide-ranging pictorial book.

Wiley and I carried roller skates on the trip, because someone told us it was the best way to the escape crowds that would press close to us out of curiosity or to try out some English phrases. Instead, I careened helplessly about the sidewalks of Beijing, Shanghai, and Guangzhou, where I flew headlong out of control and slammed into a bus, to the amusement of onlookers. Though buses were widespread, we saw few automobiles. Bicycles pedaled by people in dark gray Mao suits ruled the streets.

Wiley and I toured the Forbidden City and Summer Palace and hiked a stretch of the Great Wall (sans roller skates). We took a Li River cruise among the sculptured limestone peaks of Guilin and saw the same tableaux of immemorial China my grandfather had seen 40 years earlier: rice terraces, picturesque rafts, the reed flute cave.

But our most memorable experience was a private tour of the recently discovered imperial tomb near Xi'an, containing an entire underground army. Inside were thousands of life-size terra-cotta statues of warriors, servants, and horses pulling war chariots, buried 2,200 years ago in a gargantuan subterranean chamber. They guarded their emperor, Qin Shi Huang, who first unified China, in the afterlife. I could walk among them like a field marshal, scrutinizing their faces, no two alike.

In Beijing, Chuck Hyman of our book group and I sat down at the negotiating table. This would be no replay of those arduous hours haggling with Novosti. Censorship was not the problem; the thorny status of Taiwan and how it was portrayed on maps was. It became the subject of endless deliberations—a difficulty ingeniously solved by Chuck, who suggested differentiating the mainland and the island using two different shades of yellow, barely distinguishable but, in fact, different hues.

With negotiations completed, Wiley and I flew home.

In late 1979 the Society was invited to send a team of 30 writers, photographers, researchers, and cartographers into the remotest corners of the old Middle Kingdom.

The resulting book, *Journey Into China,* published in 1982, provided our members with the chance to see a country closed for a generation. But I had little more to do with it after my return from Beijing. It was my Indian summer, and I had eight months before leaving the editorial fold for good.

STANDING IN THE Control Center one morning, I scanned the boards for those titles that would mark my upcoming transition from editor to the president. Although I generally avoided single-topic issues, I made an exception for "Our National Parks."

Our August issue, "Mysteries of Bird Migration," was accompanied by one of my favorite map supplements: "Bird Migration in the Americas." We included a story on whooping cranes, which at one time had fewer than 20 nests in the wild. Scientists were successfully resurrecting their population.

We published a second piece on the strange life around those hydrothermal vents in the Galápagos Rift. Bob Ballard had taken me off St. Croix on a dive, which resembled a long, eerie elevator ride. We sank 5,000 feet at a rate between 60 and 100 feet a minute, leaving light behind after only 10 minutes. On the bottom he turned off the spotlights so that we could gaze at the world of tiny bioluminescent creatures, pulsing with their own lantern light. It was a sight reminiscent of Beebe's discoveries in the depths off Bermuda almost half a century earlier.

Environmental reporting was my most important new contribution to the magazine. It culminated in a yearlong effort published in February 1980 titled "The Pesticide Dilemma." Though the agrichemical industry broadcast its ire, I thought it a balanced article. And when measured by the "voting booth," I could legitimately claim success. In January 1980 our membership numbered over 10.5 million.

As 1979 turned into 1980, a team of editors assembled a special 13th issue of the magazine devoted to the challenge of energy. The installment, a comprehensive look at the subject—complete with a 12-page atlas of energy resources from fossil fuels to nuclear, solar, and wind power—would carry no advertising because it was "in the public interest." Every congress-person and senator received a copy.

I would not see it published as editor. In spring 1980 the board elected me president of the National Geographic Society, effective upon Bob Doyle's retirement in August. No surprise there; the more contentious issue was my successor as editor. I had conditioned my acceptance of the presidency on Bill Garrett taking my place—every trustee knew that. Otherwise, Mel Payne, as chairman, would try to prevent it. With Bill Garrett as editor, the magazine, I thought, would be in great hands.

On August 1, at the age of 49, I relinquished the best job in journalism and moved to the office once occupied by MBG.

Wiley, and the unborn child she was carrying, would accompany me every step of the way. I had found my soul mate. Graham Dabney Grosvenor was born on November 26, 1980—the same day as MBG's birthday.

A good omen, I hoped.

PART FOUR

THE HOUSE OF GEOGRAPHY

CHAPTER TWENTY

THE COMMAND POST

The dogwoods gracing Virginia's Blue Ridge Mountains were in full bloom as I drove up the long, winding entrance to Sweet Briar College to welcome Jane Goodall, Dian Fossey, Biruté Galdikas, and Penny Patterson. I thought that this women's college, where I was on the board of directors, would be an ideal venue for a conference on primatology, the scientific discipline dominated by so many talented women.

The Ewald Scholars Symposium titled "Hominids and Pongids (Humans and Apes)" was organized on behalf of National Geographic by Mary Griswold Smith and Joanne Hess. It was the first public forum featuring all three Trimates, plus Penny. Before the conference, Jane, Dian, and Biruté had convened in Dian's apartment at Cornell University, where she was finishing up *Gorillas in the Mist*.

I thought each of our primatologists looked a little careworn—hardly surprising, considering the challenges they faced. I was particularly concerned about Dian and hoped her health would hold up; I didn't see how she could ever return to the field. At times I thought she still showed signs of the trauma she had endured on the slopes of the Virungas.

The Trimates appeared in Sweet Briar's auditorium in April 1981. Mary Griswold Smith and I would moderate; Joanne Hess's technicians would handle the audiovisuals.

Penny Patterson, celebrated for her work with gorilla sign language, would appear onstage by herself the following day. We were afraid to put Penny in the same room with Dian, who had no love for anyone who kept a gorilla captive, and who might tear Penny to shreds.

I delivered the welcoming remarks, leaving Mary Smith to run the discussion. As expected, Jane Goodall was gracious and thoughtful. Biruté Galdikas, quiet and informative. Dian Fossey, provocative, coarse, and profane. When the young man projecting her pictures left a slide in the light of the lamp so long it began melting in the heat, she snarled so vehemently at him that I was afraid he would flee. "It's okay, Dian," I whispered. "The slides are duplicates." She continued and delivered a brilliant lecture.

I turned to gaze at the audience. Every seat was filled; it was standing room only. Young women gazed with open admiration at this famous trio. It dawned on me how much they had become role models for women in science. Four decades later, when a former student who attended was asked if she remembered the occasion, she exclaimed, "Of course! They were my heroes!"

BECOMING THE National Geographic Society president entailed a number of adjustments—not the least being my move into MBG's former office. Maybe it was that immense Persian carpet covering the floor, but it felt as though Dad had only just left. I had sat here and learned at the feet of the master. Now the office was mine—for the foreseeable future, at least.

Another change was working with a new cast of employees—especially Owen Anderson, my executive vice president. He'd joined the Geographic after returning from World War II and had come up through membership fulfillment operations. He never worked in editorial and was proud of it. A shrewd judge of character with a talent for getting things done, he was a born chief operations officer. He could be a hard taskmaster, but the stocky man with the slicked-down hair and the small eyes, which were often lost in a crinkly grin, was popular with the troops; he kept the place running.

He had learned leadership the hard way—on the battlefield. Owen had enlisted in the U.S. Army after Pearl Harbor, and in September 1944 disembarked at Normandy as an officer attached to the Ninth Armored Division. I could always confide in him; he always told me the truth, whether I wanted to hear it or not.

Meanwhile, Bill Garrett, 10 yards away in my former office, was a human cyclone, sweeping ideas and photojournalists into his orbit and spinning them back out in the form of a monthly magazine: attractively designed, informative, with gatefolds and creative map supplements. You knew he was on the ninth floor because he sucked all the oxygen out of the air; he clearly ran the editorial show. Remembering the conflict with Mel Payne, my ironclad rule was to never interfere in purely editorial matters.

Bill pushed what he called a "mini-book" approach in covering complex subjects. Rather than chase fast-breaking news, he sought to assemble coverage that was as complete and thoughtful as possible.

The Mount St. Helens eruption in May 1980 was one example. The package, published the following January, featured the work of 26 photographers, several of whom were tragically killed on the mountain's slopes. But the film in Robert Landsburg's camera was recovered. Bill published the picture taken just as Landsburg was overwhelmed by ash.

Bill and his Missouri mafia craved journalism prizes. I couldn't have cared less; I focused on renewal rate, not awards, though we won plenty. In 1980 alone, contract photographer Jim Brandenburg was named Magazine Photographer of the Year by the University of Missouri School of

Journalism. Freelancers Cary Wolinsky and Ted Spiegel came in second and third place, respectively.

Bill was on a roll. Then he made his first mistake.

The February 1982 issue included a major story on Egypt. Bill selected an image of the Giza Pyramids made by Gordon Gahan for the cover. Unfortunately, that photograph was horizontal; the cover picture was, by design, a vertical. So, without telling me or our members, Bill made it vertical. Using image editing software, he manipulated the image into a different format. I was livid.

Image manipulation is as old as photography itself. "Dodging" and "burning" and "airbrushing" and every other darkroom trick could fall into that category. You can't engrave a photograph for publication without making some adjustments, but nothing—absolutely nothing—should distort content. Cropping a photo is widely accepted, but there is an ill-defined "do not cross" line. Garrett had crossed it.

Gahan was so miffed he leaked it to the *New York Times*. They made an issue out of our "manipulation."

Embarrassed, I confronted Garrett, who insisted he had not done anything more than electronically move the camera 10 feet to the right. Nothing in the scene had been shifted—just the point of view, he argued. Anyway, it was hardly a "moment of truth" picture. To complicate matters, Gahan had paid camel riders to trot in front of the Pyramids for foreground interest. Bill would never admit a mistake. He held to his defense till the day he died.

I called the magazine's senior staff into the Control Center to say that *National Geographic* would never alter or manipulate pictures. But the damage was done. Journalism schools use that cover as a textbook case of image manipulation.

Otherwise, I kept clear of Bill's shop. My mission now was to keep pace with a changing world and steward the entire Society through the next decade and a half.

THE NATIONAL GEOGRAPHIC SOCIETY was thriving, thanks to a membership approaching 10,850,000 in more than 180 countries. The staff had grown too. That was most evident in "Breeden's empire" and television.

Bob Breeden was now in charge of all Society publications and products except the magazine. His realm, which at one point accounted for 40 percent of Society's revenues, embraced book publishing as well as educational products for children and classrooms. In 1981 the Special Publications and School Services Division produced 15 new books, 10 of them for children. Society members bought nearly four and a half million of these publications, not to mention the two million filmstrips aimed at school-age children. World had the largest circulation of any children's magazine: 1.7 million.

Breeden's staff even created a new quarterly, National Geographic Traveler: the fourth periodical on our growing shelf of publications. For years we had received letters soliciting travel advice. Breeden, who shared my recognition of the travel industry's growth, was convinced that we could parlay that into a magazine that would profile offbeat and popular destinations. We debuted our first issue in March 1984. Marketed only to members, its circulation topped a million before that year was out.

Not every Society activity now under my scrutiny was editorial or product-oriented. That 11-foot globe still spun on its axis in Explorers Hall, for instance, where exhibits attracted tens of thousands of visitors each year. There was also the photo lab, still the finest color lab in U.S. publishing, and the Printing and Engraving Division.

Most interesting were those warrens of ingenuity hidden from public view, like the custom equipment shop. When Bill Allard needed special cases to pack his cameras and film on the motorcycle that carried him down the U.S.-Mexican border, the custom shop designed and built them. When a film crew asked for a camera housing that could withstand Siberian temperatures as low as -90°F, they did that too. When the cinematographers filming the voyage of the Tigris needed an absolutely waterproof housing, the shop made an exact-fitting aluminum mold and dipped it in hot liquid polyvinyl chloride that cooled into an impermeable seal.

Our oldest activity, lectures, managed by Joanne Hess, still attracted an audience that numbered in the thousands three times a week at Constitution Hall. News Service, by the early 1980s, was becoming a modern public relations office. It produced crisp 90-second interviews with our scientists, explorers, and correspondents distributed by Associated Press Radio.

Finally, there was the powerful medium that captured a lot of attention but never made a dime for decades—television. Fortunately, that would change.

Once we established a television presence in the 1960s there was no turning back. Our popular National Geographic Specials on PBS aspired to the same quality standard as our magazine and helped redeem the "vast wasteland" that television had become. Twenty years later, 13 of the top 25 most viewed programs on public television were by National Geographic, not to mention our numerous Emmy Awards. All produced by a geographical society, not Hollywood or New York.

Compared with publishing, television had a more roguish feel, with more money thrown around, deeper expense accounts, more readiness to cut corners on content and accuracy. Dennis Kane produced our TV Specials for more than a decade. He was skilled at producing first-class programming and at navigating the shoals of contract negotiations as well as Hollywood-style wining and dining.

The opportunity to increase and diffuse geographic knowledge through new media was tempting. I began studying cable television and was so appalled that my mantra became "I have 60 channels to choose from tonight but nothing to watch!"

There was excellent news, weather, and sports; but all I could find outside that were tawdry talk shows, situation comedies with laugh tracks, movie reruns, violence, and more violence. I had no choice but to wade into this morass, if only because everybody, including my kids, were feeding at this trough. To participate in television by providing decent material evolved from opportunity to obligation.

So why not assemble a consortium of like-minded nonprofit institutions to create our own cable or satellite channel? In the meantime, the world of the National Geographic Society was bursting at the seams. We had to find more room.

The Society had grown from a handful of employees to 2,200—from several thousand members to almost 11 million. Too many of those 2,200 worked in leased space up and down the block. I justified the expense of erecting another building by pointing to our membership growth and the expansion of our products and programs.

In 1981 we broke ground on a new $330 million headquarters building between the 17th Street Edward Durrell Stone building and the original 16th Street complex. The inspired design, resembling a Maya pyramid, was created by David Childs of Skidmore, Owings & Merrill.

As the steel girders rose, a man with whom I shared my hopes and dreams would never see that building completed.

For years now we had all watched Dad start to decline. I had noticed the first signs a decade or so earlier, when the Research Committee was on a trip to Africa. He seemed more forgetful, less energetic. At first it was not alarming, but it would resurface, and I began to fear the onset of a slow dementia. It wasn't so noticeable to friends and acquaintances, or at board meetings when he showed up tanned by the Florida sun. He could be as gregarious and engaging as ever—but he didn't fool the family. Anne surely noticed too, but she skillfully covered for him.

He had slipped past 80 and was fast diminishing. All of us—Anne, Ed, Sara, Teeny, Dad's remaining sisters, Wiley, me—exchanged knowing looks and tried to prepare ourselves.

That armor has its chinks, and the blow unfailingly finds them. On Thursday evening, April 22, 1982, my brother Ed, then living in New York, was talking on the phone to MBG, who was sitting on the sofa in the living room at Hissar in Coconut Grove. In mid-conversation Dad just slipped away, never to return. He died on that sofa like a man who closes his eyes for a catnap. It was a heart attack and must have taken him gently.

We held the funeral on Monday in Washington's National Presbyterian Church and laid him to rest in Rock Creek Cemetery, in the same plot where my grandfather and grandmother are buried. At the reception, my spirits were buoyed by the scores of National Geographic family who had materialized from everywhere. Retirees I hadn't seen in years turned up. I warmly shook hand after hand as we gathered around the threshing floor of memory. The stories poured forth, prefaced by "Do you remember the time . . . ," of when MBG had done this or said that. We laughed uproariously at each tale and recalled how impulsively generous he was, how enthusiastic, how welcoming, how inspirational.

We all bade reluctant goodbyes as the afternoon shadows lengthened. MBG was gone but, for everyone fortunate enough to share the Geographic odyssey, never to be forgotten.

Hidden in the cornerstone underneath Hubbard Memorial Hall is a piece of paper, placed there in 1902 and written in an infant's scrawl helpfully guided by Alexander Graham Bell's steadying hand: "Melville Bell Grosvenor (X) His Mark."

THERE WAS NO WAY THE organization, well-off as we were, could afford to establish our own National Geographic Society television channel.

That was my glum conclusion when I finished studying the start-up costs. It only confirmed my resolution to bring together a consortium of like-minded nonprofits—National Geographic, the Smithsonian Institution, the

New York Zoological Society, Colonial Williamsburg, Mystic Seaport, and others—to pool resources; this way, we could feed quality fare to the 24-hour-a-day content beast that is a TV channel. If the Geographic kicked in most of the funding, it would be our channel, but we would have to find a way to recognize our associate institutions. In return, our partners would share interesting projects with us and give us first crack at any film material.

I took the idea to the board and won tentative approval to proceed. But the project foundered, thanks largely to my old nemesis Dillon Ripley, still secretary of the Smithsonian Institution, who insisted on establishing a governing committee to decide major issues and wanted to select and edit the films. He wanted to share control but was more than willing to let me pay for it. The idea withered and died.

I shouldn't have let Ripley poison the well. I should have just dropped the Smithsonian, even though it was one of the most prominent players.

About that time, Dennis Kane introduced me to a young man who had approached him about establishing a channel for documentary science films. I found that proposition appealing and decided to meet with Tim Kelly.

Tim had worked for Rainbow Media, which had launched Bravo and AMC, two early cable channels. He had a quiet, steely manner, and I liked him immediately. He thought the Geographic, with its visual storytelling focus, was the perfect place for a science documentary channel.

Dennis, preoccupied with the quarterly TV Specials, hired him to flesh out the idea. Soon afterward, Tim sat down with Owen and me to lay out his new vision.

We would start by acquiring documentaries; Tim had his eye on many films airing in Europe or in limited distribution. Then we would start producing our own and reel in those made by our partners, the leftovers of that "grand alliance." My original idea was not entirely dead, but Tim warned me it couldn't be composed entirely of nonprofits; we needed some commercial broadcasters as partners too.

Owen and I estimated the cost of launching a channel at $20 to $30 million.

We got shot down by the board; recent big fallouts in the Wild West cable industry predictably produced a response amounting to, "Are you kidding? This is way too risky." We shelved the National Geographic Channel idea.

After the board nixed the idea of our own channel, Tim turned to building an in-house television production arm. Our four Television Specials airing on PBS had been outsourced for years; to produce our own content meant hiring experienced film and television people and crafting a set of standards, including fact-checking protocols modeled on those of the magazine.

In addition to his initiative, I also admired Tim because he tried to find common ground between television and the magazine on projects of mutual interest. Since Bill Garrett and Dennis Kane—two oversize egos—couldn't be in the same room together, Tim would bravely march into the lion's den. In the editorial division, television was held in utter disdain.

Tim also reached out to some of the networks and negotiated a four-hour block on Sunday night with Nickelodeon, a successful children's channel, for a magazine-type feature of short documentary films. That's how we launched EXPLORER. Our first offering, on April 7, 1985, was a documentary on the finds at Herculaneum, a city buried under the eruption of Vesuvius a few days after Pompeii had suffered the same fate. We finally had a presence in the fast-growing world of cable television and could start building a staff to produce quality content.

ONE DAY GARRETT came into my office to talk about a magazine cover he had envisioned. Bill wanted to put a hologram on the April 1984 issue, still nearly a year away.

A hologram? That might cost millions! Bill explained that it would accompany an article on lasers and demonstrate our ability to stay on the cutting edge of imaging technology. The American Bank Note Company had produced an eagle hologram for the cover of its recent annual report for the same reason: to demonstrate its ability to mass-produce 3D images like the ones they had pioneered on credit cards to foil counterfeiters. No major magazine had done this. It would be another first.

I approved it, giving Bill the same deal Mel Payne had given me: Trade off editorial pages to help pay for it. It was extraordinarily complicated. That image fitted into its allotted cover space with only a 1/32-inch margin for error. The holograms were heat-stamped onto the covers, but the foil often failed to adhere, and an improved adhesive backing had to be developed before the entire run of 11 million covers was sent to the printer in Corinth. I hoped being the first magazine to do this was worth it. Although a visual genius, Bill was never a master of finance.

Between those covers, the only thing I was now in charge of were the advertising pages. I had been rigorously schooled by Dr. McKnew never to let the advertising tail wag the *Geographic* dog. GHG, MBG, and I kept ads confined to the front and back of the book, and never depended on advertising's fickle revenue stream for major funding; we were membership-driven. Advertisers always wailed about being locked outside the sacred precincts of the editorial feature well, but those were inviolable precepts.

Then Bill Garrett had a brilliant idea. He inserted one-page editorial components into the advertising sections, including updates to past stories and "Earth Almanac," briskly paced paragraphs detailing new developments in conservation. Their popularity ensured millions of eyeballs focused on the adjacent ads. Bill also gave me the long-sought President's Page and introduced Members Forum, a space dedicated to reader response. We never shrank from printing critical letters.

I was also willing to undertake what MBG would have abhorred: Putting time and shoe leather into recruiting and keeping quality advertisers. I spoke at advertising luncheons, forums, and the Detroit Economic Club, pitching the *National Geographic* as an ideal advertising vehicle. Our greatest success—and certainly the longest-lasting one—came early in my tenure as president.

In early 1981, three people came together to produce a brilliant concept. One was Karen Altpeter, a young picture editor who had recently joined the staff from *National Wildlife;* she proposed we profile an endangered or threatened species once a month. The second was Garrett, who brought her to me; and the third, myself, enthusiastic about an environmental-themed campaign. We refined the concept immediately.

Dai Iwai, our advertising guy in Tokyo, suggested Canon as the perfect candidate and made the first outreach. I flew to Tokyo and struck an agreement with Ryuzaburo Kaku, Canon's CEO. We instantly connected. The rest is history. "Wildlife as Canon Sees It" became the longest, most successful advertising campaign in *National Geographic* history.

It became Karen Altpeter's baby. Locating images taken with a Canon camera of a different endangered species was task enough; ensuring that she also had the lens used, focal length, aperture setting, film type, and shutter speed was equally important, because the series was also a mini-lesson in wildlife photography.

Canon provided camera equipment, which we seeded among our research grantees. They were required to use Canon cameras and lenses in some out-of-the-way places to ensure an adequate stream of publishable images. I suspect thousands of aspiring wildlife photographers discovered Canon, a leading brand in the field today, through those ads.

From the first page in January 1982 featuring the giant panda until today, more than four decades later, hundreds of rare and imperiled fellow creatures have been photographed and profiled in a series unmatched in global scope and its intimate portraiture.

That endeavor was a triumph. But I also made a mistake that still keeps me up at night.

For decades the only way to join the National Geographic Society was to be nominated, theoretically, by another member; every issue had a bound-in membership nomination form showcasing sketches of photographers in the field working on Society membership–supported grants. By the 1970s that page reliably produced between 300,000 to 400,000 new members each year, and cost us practically nothing at a time when actively soliciting a new member could cost $20 to $30 each. But in 1982 I unwittingly dropped it.

I didn't do it intentionally. I don't even remember doing so, but I must have let it be turned into another advertising page. Gone were the profiles of scientists in remote locales working on Society projects. Gone was the reminder that your membership dues contributed to this sponsorship. "Join the adventure" is not quite the same thing. It's an advertising jingle, not a vision of our mission. Every time I visited the doctor or dentist in the old days, I would check the *National Geographics* in the waiting room; sure enough, most of the nomination forms were torn out. I would joke we should place free magazines in doctors' offices everywhere.

Garrett had included an On Assignment page among the advertising pages, which showcased a given issue's contributors at work behind the scenes. It was smart and well designed. Maybe the nomination form looked tired in comparison. What pains me most is that killing it amounted to a sin against the very idea of membership so sacred to me and my forebears. The Society, after all, was the membership, from which all blessings flowed.

ON TUESDAY, JUNE 19, 1984, President Ronald Reagan dedicated our new building. The pink granite and glass structure, stepped like a Maya temple, was an eye-catching addition to our headquarters complex. The 500,829-square-foot edifice housed new audiovisual studios, photographic labs, cartographic quarters, and specialized equipment workshops—in short, the latest and best in publishing and broadcasting technology that three years of careful construction could support.

Although we had declared it a special holiday for our now 2,400 employees, 1,200 of them showed up at headquarters to celebrate the occasion, watching on closed-circuit television in the new cafeteria.

As the new 400-seat Gilbert H. Grosvenor Auditorium filled up with dignitaries, Chief Justice Warren Burger and other trustees mingled with members of President Reagan's cabinet, senators and representatives, members of the diplomatic corps, Society officers, and press.

After the presentation of the colors by the Armed Forces Color Guard, an invocation, and my welcoming speech, the Great Communicator himself surveyed the assembled dignitaries and, to a rumble of laughter, asked, "I wonder who's watching the store?"

He turned to me, recalling the occasion when he jokingly accused me of creating one of his biggest problems in his move to Washington. "Gil, I have hundreds of *National Geographics* at the ranch, and I don't know how the hell I'm going to haul them all to the White House.'" More laughter. Then, with impeccable timing, the president looked around the cavernous room and said, "I guess you have trouble storing your old *National Geographics* too."

That brought down the house.

After admiring the new space we had provided for our future, guests could visit the newly refurbished Hubbard Memorial Hall and the mural-size paintings adorning the grand marble staircase that had been there since 1928. N. C. Wyeth had executed the series, called the "Romance of Discovery," featuring Balboa, Columbus, and Richard E. Byrd. The restored colors were so rich they looked almost gaudy.

The old, vaulted meeting room with the enormous sandstone fireplace at the top of the stairs had held our library and then our dusty archives. I had it restored and turned into our new boardroom; I couldn't wait to leave all that whizzing and clacking drapery on the ninth floor of the Stone building. Although we needed permission to shut down 16th Street so a crane could hoist that long table of burled elm and walnut through one of the tall windows, it was worth it. That table and portraits of Society forebearers now stood in a room worthy of its tradition and high purpose.

I hoped everyone appreciated the dome crowning the new building's lobby, decorated with stars positioned as they appeared in the night sky at 8 p.m. on January 13, 1888, the evening the Society was founded.

As the real stars emerged that evening, I was full of hopes and dreams, convinced our sails were trimmed and our course well set.

CHAPTER TWENTY-ONE

MY $125 MILLION DINNER

As Barry Bishop and I sat together in my office one autumn day in 1984, we confronted an even steeper uphill climb than his Everest ascent.

We were plotting to reshape the landscape of geography education in the United States.

Why was I so adamant about geography education? Imagine viewing our planet from 500 miles above through the lenses of an imaginary, instrument-laden satellite, launched 60 years ago. Call this satellite Geographos—Greek for "geographer."

Geographos would be equipped with sensors that could detect vegetation changes, ozone depletion, carbon dioxide emissions, temperature changes, water distribution, and more. The growing mountain of data and its 60-year-old baseline could help monitor the pulse of the planet: a medical metaphor that suggests our blue-and-white home spinning in a black void looks and acts like a self-contained ecosystem, if not a single organism.

Is Earth healthy or diseased? Think of a doctor analyzing medical records, calling up baseline information from a patient's first visit. Twenty years of X-rays of a 55-year-old smoker can track a lung lesion better than a single image.

The analogy is obvious. Geographos would transmit observations homeward, where geo-physicians would compile data and check it not just against those 60-year-old baselines but also against calendars derived from Antarctic and Greenland ice cores, tree rings, and fossil seashell rings dating back 800,000 years.

The symptoms? Expanding deserts, rising temperatures, devastating storms, acidifying oceans. Diagnosis? Planet Earth is middle-age and overstressed, and suffers from an autoimmune disorder derived from a superfluity of *Homo sapiens* in the system. In my simplified scheme, this diagnosis would spur the geo-managers to remedy the disorder.

In sum, geography is key to understanding the world.

BARRY HAD SHOWN ME THE results of a recent poll of 2,200 North Carolina college students—utterly appalling. Only 12 percent of those tested could name all the Great Lakes; in 1950, according to a *New York Times* survey, 46 percent of college students could do so. Only 27 percent of the North Carolina undergraduates knew that Brazil was the country through which the Amazon primarily flowed; in 1950, 78 percent of students got that one right. Few knew in which country the city of Manila was located. Many could not even name three countries located between the Sahara and South Africa. So it went, one dismal example after another.

Here was clear testimony to the decline of geographic instruction in the United States. Much of my previous preaching had fallen on deaf ears; now we had the evidence. But instead of feeling elated, I felt angry and embarrassed. We had been working for nearly a century to increase and diffuse geographic knowledge, but we had failed to help students understand the world geographically.

Barry and I had been striving to join forces with professional and academic geographers to improve geography instruction—a top-down approach. We now realized the problem—and solution—lay somewhere in the 13 years between kindergarten and grade 12. We needed a bottom-to-top approach as well; we had to insinuate ourselves into the classrooms and motivate teachers in those classrooms.

I was determined to remedy the situation.

At Barry's behest, I went to see Kit Salter, a professor of geography at UCLA who had formed an alliance of California-based professors, teachers, and administrators to expand the role of geography in secondary-school education.

On a spring afternoon, I sat in Salter's office, listening to him explain how he could take the same visuals and use them to teach either a kindergarten class or a Ph.D. course. I remember one: the Diablo Canyon Nuclear Power Plant, built practically on top of geological faults like the nearby San Andreas. With National Geographic's photographic collection, we could use visuals to teach across the spectrum too. That evening he invited me to dinner at his house.

The dining room was about 10 feet square, and the kitchen was so small that the refrigerator lived on an annex porch. Kit's wife, Cathy Riggs-Salter—a geography teacher in a local public school—served coq au vin at a table so tight that all the plates clattered against one another whenever anyone shifted in his or her seat. She called it their "plate tectonics." I was instantly charmed.

After I opened a bottle of wine I had brought, I began recounting my ambition to align the Society with geography educators to reestablish the subject at all grade levels. I brought up our new National Geographic Kids Network, developed in collaboration with the National Science Foundation and Technical Education Research Centers, which hoped to link more than 40,000 classrooms around the globe, so that school children could share results of common scientific experiments.

Sometime between the first bottle of wine and the second, Kit outlined his alliance of California geography teachers. It was built around the "five themes of geography": location, physical and human notions of place, shaping the landscape, human movements and interactions, and how regions form and change. He told me how exciting it was for high school geography teachers and college professors to talk to one another, which seldom happened.

If Kit could do this in California, could the National Geographic Society do something similar on a national scale?

We batted around the idea of a national network of geography teachers harnessed by the National Geographic Society. Kit reminded me that geographers were a far-flung lot, working too often in isolation. All the more reason, I replied, to form an alliance encouraging them to communicate.

I might have spent $25 on those two bottles of wine. But the ultimate cost of dinner in that tiny house, I like to joke, was probably more than $125 million. Because that is what we ultimately spent on the Geography Education Program we created.

IN JUNE WE FLEW KIT SALTER to Washington to meet with me, Barry Bishop, and Susan Munroe from our Educational Media Division to work on the Geography Education Program. We'd start at the local level; the alliance would be a coalition of state-based networks, each with their own particular needs. We'd start small, with seven states—adding seven more each year. The National Geographic Society would provide financial support and supply educational materials.

Teacher training in geography would be crucial. I volunteered our new headquarters complex to host our first Summer Geography Institute in July 1986. Seven teachers from seven states would spend four weeks with us, taking a crash course in geography to learn how to best teach it. They would return home and hold training seminars for teachers in their own state to spread the gospel of geography. In seven years we covered all 50 states.

THE NOVEMBER 1985 ISSUE now in members' hands was stunning. The cover featured another hologram—this time of a small skull some three million years old found in South Africa in 1924. The skull, called the Taung Child, was the type specimen for *Australopithecus africanus,* one of the earliest branches on the human evolutionary tree, and loomed on our cover in a decidedly eerie way. The accompanying story, "The Search for Our Ancestors," was an extensively researched, stunningly illustrated compendium of paleoanthropological knowledge. It was supplemented by " the story of how Kamoya Kimeu, an eagle-eyed Kenyan fossil hunter, had spotted a fragment of a skull in the desolate hills west of Lake Turkana (formerly Lake Rudolf), within sight of the Leakey kitchen tent. The team found an almost complete *Homo erectus* skeleton, the first recovered of such antiquity—1.6. million years old.

"Lake Turkana Boy," around 12 years old, remains a sensational find; those sublime deserts stretching away on all sides from the "Jade Sea" still hid secrets. Only those with special eyes who could read the land and hear the bones singing could pry them open. Kimeu, who had been chief of Richard Leakey's "Hominid gang," could read the land and hear those songs. Best of all, more discoveries lay ahead.

IN LATE DECEMBER 1985 Dian Fossey was murdered in Rwanda. After finishing *Gorillas in the Mist,* and against all advice, she had returned to the Virungas. There someone, still unidentified, cleaved her skull with a panga knife in her cabin in Karisoke.

The next decade was shadowed by genocide and war in Rwanda. I sat on the board of the Dian Fossey Gorilla Fund and remember when we heard the distressing news. The camp and Dian's cabin had been looted and destroyed.

Yet both the park and the gorillas were saved. Two years later, her gravestone, with "No one loved gorillas more," was erected on that Karisoke hillside. Actress Sigourney Weaver would make *Gorillas in the Mist* there, and the story of Fossey's self-sacrifice would move millions of people worldwide.

Contributions would flow in, saving the park and its famous inhabitants. To this day, that foundation fights to save gorillas from destruction.

FINDING A HIGH POINT TO 1985 is easy: the discovery of the ocean liner *Titanic*, which famously sank in 1912.

On September 11, 1985, our new Gilbert H. Grosvenor Auditorium was packed to capacity to hear Robert Ballard announce the world's poorest-kept secret. He had discovered the resting place of the doomed ship—arguably the worst disaster in maritime history. The wreck had eluded searchers since it disappeared off the coast of Newfoundland in 12,500 feet of water.

Bob used *Knorr,* the Woods Hole research vessel. We secured the English-language magazine rights, and our own Emory Kristof was aboard as the pool photographer for the *Geographic.*

The real sponsor was the U.S. Navy, which had funded development of *Argo,* the sophisticated camera sled that Kristof and his team had helped design and that could search as deep as 20,000 feet. The Navy wanted Ballard to use it to explore and map the wrecks of two nuclear submarines lost in the 1960s: the U.S.S. *Thresher* and the U.S.S. *Scorpion. Titanic* was a training exercise. The allotted time to search was rapidly coming to a close when *Argo* piped up images of a debris field. In a now-famous moment in undersea exploration, a ship's boiler came into view—and soon after, the famous liner itself. Word leaked out on ship-to-shore radio the next day; pandemonium ensued.

By the time our official press conference was held, pictures leaked by the media had appeared on front pages of newspapers and on television. In our auditorium, Ballard would describe how the ship broke up on the way down, landing in two sections; how the seafloor was covered with fine china plates; and that the numerous boots and shoes strewn about were the only human remains.

Bob Ballard became a household name after "How We Found Titanic" was published in December of that year. The "magazine of record" again.

OUR CABLE PRESENCE ON Nickelodeon was hardly six months old when Tim Kelly told me that he had stepped into an elevator at a cable television conference and met Ted Turner. When Ted learned that Tim was from National Geographic, he exclaimed, "I love National Geographic! You come on up here with me."

Tim followed Ted to his suite, drank beer, and was harangued by one of America's biggest media moguls about "that little tiny channel." He wanted us on his channel, WTBS: the first "superstation," now reaching nearly 40 million viewers a day.

This was a huge opportunity. We invited Ted Turner to Washington. He paced around the room declaring how much he loved National Geographic—but if we didn't sign on, he warned, "I'm going to bury you!" In his next breath, he said, "I believe in the environment. I try not to breathe too deeply, and I drive a little car."

Turner's media success aside, I especially admired his triumphant defense of the America's Cup in 1977. "Real sailing," MBG would say.

We structured a deal similar to Nickelodeon's: two hours of programming each Sunday night. He would pay for it, a sum in the multimillions; we would still own the content. A very generous deal for us.

EXPLORER debuted on WTBS in February 1986. Now we could build our team, hire the best filmmakers, and take the field time necessary to produce outstanding work. We returned to the *Titanic* with Ballard, who took *Alvin,* his three-person submersible, down to personally inspect the wreck. That film scored the highest ratings achieved in cable at the time.

The WTBS agreement was a dream deal, but my bond with Ted was really forged over sailing. The first time I went to Atlanta to confer with him, I was ushered into his office—but stopped short at a display case. There stood the actual America's Cup, the 1843 silver ewer—the world's oldest sporting trophy.

How could that be? The America's Cup was kept at the New York Yacht Club. "Had a fellow rummage through the silver vaults of Garrard & Company—the official crown jewelers—in London," Ted volunteered when he caught me gawking. "He found its twin. Bought it on the spot."

I didn't ask how much. Who was I to judge? After all, I was forking out hundreds of millions for my own passion: geography education.

At that very moment, we were hosting our first Summer Geography Institute at Society headquarters for those seven teachers from seven states who would spend several weeks of intensive teacher training with us. They convened in the same auditorium where Bob Ballard had held his *Titanic* news conference. They ate lunch in our cafeteria, sitting with our writers, photographers, editors, visiting scientists, and explorers. When possible, I would join them, introduce myself, and ask where they were from and what steered them to geography. I wanted everyone to interact. They were now part of the Geographic family too. All expenses paid, and all they had to do was promise to run at least three staff-development workshops in their own school districts. We eventually had teachers from all 50 states attending, and if each kept that promise, they would be disseminating their new skills to more than 3,000 fellow teachers every year.

We also handed out six million maps to every school in the country; maps and the fundamental themes of geography were our tools. I wanted those initiatives and the establishment of a foundation to be the signature event of our centennial. As part of that run-up, President Reagan proclaimed the week of November 15 "Geography Awareness Week."

On January 13, 1988—our 100th birthday—we presented our centennial gift to the nation: the National Geographic Society Education Foundation, underwritten by $20 million in Society money plus an additional $20 million in matching funds promised by the board.

The grass was beginning to grow.

CHAPTER TWENTY-TWO

APOGEE— AND FALL

I f Bill Garrett had one dictum that defined his editorship, it was "f/8 and be there!" Be at the heart of the story and don't leave until you have the goods in hand.

How typical, then, that this man with the sharpest eye for pictures would retrieve perhaps the most famous 35mm slide in our history—one pushed to the side by a picture editor who didn't like the intensity of the young girl's gaze. Garrett knew at once it was the cover shot. And that's where that icon of icons, the "Afghan Girl" with the penetrating green eyes, landed: on the cover of the June 1985 *National Geographic*.

With the possible exception of the "Blue Marble" planet Earth image, it is surely the most recognized photograph in our magazine's history. The name and fate of this young girl living in a Pakistani refugee camp remained a mystery until 2002, when Steve McCurry, who'd made the image, returned to Afghanistan and found her living with her husband and three children. In my opinion, the cover image of Sharbat Gula, the "Afghan Girl," epitomized Bill's editorship, just as the "Blue Marble" had epitomized mine. One spoke to the human condition; the other, to our fragile planet.

Despite the successes—and there were many—as the late 1980s wore on, membership stalled. Had we reached our sweet spot? Spending also became a concern.

In principle I have always agreed to spend whatever it takes, but always kept an eye on the balance sheet. Take our underwater exploration symphony in those late 20th-century years. It went by the unmusical title "integrated surface-to-bottom photographic coverages."

In, say, the Caribbean's Cayman Wall or California's Monterey Bay, a navy of alien-looking humans and their machines would enter the water all at once. Ace underwater photographer David Doubilet, in fins and face mask, would stalk the sunlit shallows; strange-looking camera sleds and remotely operated vehicles, or ROVs—many designed by Emory Kristof—brought light to the deeper, darker reaches of the same shelving banks. Our television division might be involved. "Shark Lady" Eugenie Clark, supported by our Research Committee, would be in charge of the scientific program.

A bizarre underwater world became a fantasyland of strange creatures never seen alive in their own element. Discoveries were made; I was unfairly accused of not thinking this important. When a Woods Hole barge overturned in a storm and we lost hundreds of thousands of dollars' worth of photographic equipment, for example, I approved its replacement. But the budget, which invariably went into overdrive, could be stretched only so far.

During his tenure as editor, Garrett expanded the range of stories, including offbeat topics like an article on the sense of smell that came with a survey, complete with scratch-and-sniff strips. A million and a half members responded, making it the largest scientific sampling of its kind. I sometimes wondered if Bill wasn't playing more to the New York photojournalism community than to our membership. That "Sense of Smell" article opened with a picture of women smelling men's armpits. A photograph in a story about a sunken World War II troopship depicted a row of urinals now flushed by Pacific waters.

I wondered how our members would react. We had enough problems in the Bible Belt whenever we published articles on human evolution.

Since our membership was now plateauing near 11 million each year, but not growing as it did during the 1960s and '70s, I didn't want to lose members if we could help it.

When it came to Bill's slate for our centennial year, I found three things worrisome. One was the February issue, entirely devoted to Australia's bicentennial. I shared MBG's reservations about single-topic issues; if you're not interested in Australia, you probably wouldn't even open that issue. A second worry was December's planned cover, which would be transformed into one huge hologram: An arresting picture of an exploding glass globe on the front would symbolize the shattering of our fragile Earth, while a McDonald's advertisement, similarly sculpted by lasers, would be on the back. It would be colossally expensive and technically challenging to produce.

My third worry was personal and professional. In our September issue, Bill and Joe were reopening the vexed question of whether or not Robert E. Peary reached the North Pole on April 6, 1909. The National Geographic Society had sponsored him, and GHG proved one of his staunchest supporters. My grandfather had been an admirer and close friend of Peary's.

Hardly had Peary returned to the expedition vessel, the *Roosevelt*, in April 1909 when he heard that his erstwhile companion in exploration, Dr. Frederick Cook, claimed to have reached the pole a year earlier. That forced Peary's supporters to challenge Cook's navigational data, ultimately deemed fraudulent. But the verification of proof was soon turned against Peary. He couldn't pony up sufficient navigational data either.

Naval officers particularly disliked the arrogant and aloof Peary, who had come up through the U.S. Coast and Geodetic Survey rather than the Navy proper. They went after the man, challenging his claim to the pole. Congress got involved, and hearings dragged out through 1911 and 1912. Since no one could prove it one way or another, he was reluctantly awarded the palm.

GHG remained steadfast in his support. That's why, on my 1979 trip to the North Pole, I carried Peary's 1909 expedition flag in my pack.

Two things launched this reevaluation. One was the 1973 publication of the book *Peary at the North Pole: Fact or Fiction?* Author Dennis Rawlins, an astronomer and longtime Peary debunker, challenged Peary's claim as fraudulent and castigated the Society for its complicit role in being the first to hail Peary as conqueror of the North Pole. The second was the December 1983 "docudrama" *Cook and Peary: The Race to the Pole.* It was seen by an audience of millions who loved Richard Chamberlain as the dashing Cook, who reached the pole first, and loathed Rod Steiger's scheming Peary, who sought to steal the glory. The show was fiction, and I wrote a blistering President's Page telling members how misleading it was.

That got Joe Judge interested in solving the polar puzzle. Joe, a knowledgeable historian, was already on a quest to discover where Columbus first stepped onto the New World, in anticipation of the upcoming quincentenary celebration of the discovery of America. Working with Luis Marden, they replotted Columbus's track across the Atlantic by reinterpreting logbook entries and using new navigational software. They concluded that Columbus first landed on tiny Samana Cay in the Bahamas, and not on San Salvador, generally credited as his landfall.

Joe convinced Garrett that we should take on Peary and the North Pole. I think Bill saw an opportunity to burnish his credentials as the courageous editor of *National Geographic* willing to overturn decades of Society support for a dubious hero. They went to Peary's descendants and persuaded them to release the explorer's restricted diaries, hoping to finally settle the case.

I wasn't going to override the editor. I felt that a fair and impartial review of the diaries and other papers in the Library of Congress would probably exonerate Peary—at least to the extent that he and his companions had ended up within range of what we now know to be the GPS-determined North Pole.

Once the family agreed to open the papers, Bill and Joe asked Sir Walter Herbert to investigate them and write up his conclusions for the Geographic.

Sir Wally, a famous British Arctic explorer in the old vein, had crossed the ice cap from Alaska to Norway via the North Pole in 1969, making him the first person since Peary to reach 90° N by dogsled, even if others had reached it by snowmobile. I could not see how he would stay impartial in judging Peary. If Peary's polar claim fell, it would make Wally Herbert the first explorer to reach the pole by muscle and dog power alone. Sir Wally's verdict, not surprisingly, was that Peary missed the pole by some 60 miles, having veered west of his intended path because of shifting ice. Yet, Herbert, too, failed to provide proof.

What really galled me was Garrett's decision to publish the story during our centennial year, when we were being honored for our century of support for research and exploration. I thought he was too anxious to confess our "errors" while we held the spotlight. I could only hope the press wouldn't blow it out of proportion.

False hope, it turned out.

When the story broke with Sir Wally Herbert's assessment, the headline in the *Washington Post* story by science editor Boyce Rensberger screamed: NATIONAL GEOGRAPHIC REVERSES, AGREES ADM. PEARY MISSED NORTH POLE.

The *New York Times* ran a story with a similar headline. Inevitably, I knew, newspapers all over the world would be playing it up.

Rensberger's article mentioned Dennis Rawlins, "whose book depicts the National Geographic Society as a collaborator in perpetuating the Peary fraud." Rensberger had Sir Wally weigh in on Rawlins: "Basically, what Rawlins is saying is correct."

Most maddening of all was Bill Garrett's quote: "Nothing is new . . . It's just that it's never all been put together in one place before. Slowly, we're trying to clean up old wives' tales that don't hold water."

I was angry. We were approaching the climax of our centennial celebrations, and Bill and Joe were tarnishing the Society's reputation without valid information.

FINE WEATHER AND FAIR WIND, and I'm at the helm of *White Mist* once more, sailing the waters of the Bras d'Or Lakes on a fine August afternoon. The crew is my family, and the destination a favorite cove or beach or perhaps just a destination unknown. Summers at Beinn Bhreagh are always rejuvenating, always restorative.

I had bought *White Mist* from Dad's estate and mostly kept her in the Bras d'Or. We'd make occasional forays across the Cabot Strait to Newfoundland or over to Prince Edward Island.

Aunt Mabel still held court at The Point. I was down in Burns Cottage. Teeny was now entrenched at Killich, the house once owned by Casey Baldwin, Alexander Graham Bell's business partner. Our family vacations often overlapped; it was about the only time I saw her those days. I was happy that she would attend our centennial banquet in November and promised her a seat at the best table.

But I couldn't leave the Society behind. That summer I was increasingly worried about stagnation in our membership. We were still at nearly 11 million—a huge number by any standard—but our renewal rate, once the pride of the publishing industry, was starting to slip. One likely reason was the explosion of special interest magazines, which were pulling readers away from general interest ones. I had only to look at my own coffee table. It was piled high with *Fine Woodworking* and practically every yachting and sailing magazine then published. People obviously chased their interests and dreams.

We were also oversaturating our membership with books and products. So was every other publisher. Breeden's empire was still strong, but for how much longer? Our purchased lists—magazine publishers bought subscriber lists from other organizations hoping to increase their circulation—were not producing as abundantly as they had before.

Throughout those August days, I was trying to avoid an unpalatable course of action: The need to trim staff and expenses.

Before climbing into the car for the journey back to Washington, I gave Teeny a final heartfelt hug and told her I'd see her in November.

REHASHING THE PEARY CONTROVERSY at the expense of the Society was painful, but the source of escalating friction between Bill Garrett and me was the December cover, which was bogged down in production. As the culminating issue in our centennial year, the issue's editorial focus was "Can We Save This Fragile Earth?"

The cover photograph—a bullet-shattered Steuben crystal globe, symbolizing the destructive impact of humans on the planet—was a technical tour de force by staff photographer Bruce Dale. But the hologram production and printing of it was a fiasco that tested our limits. Garrett was responsible for editorial content, but I was responsible for producing the magazine and delivering it to members. I doubted that any hologram company could complete such a gigantic undertaking—more than 10.5 million covers, front and back—in our time frame.

In retrospect, the process just wasn't ready. Our quality-control managers were constantly rejecting inferior covers, pushing everything further and further behind schedule. Costs had already exceeded projections. When I would ask Bill how late we were, he'd wave his arms. "Don't worry, don't worry," he'd mutter. Worry I did, because the production people reporting to me didn't share his confidence. At one point I urged Bill to postpone the hologram cover; he assured me they would make up lost time.

Those delays caused that issue to run late, and the image—well, it looked so-so. Missing your publication date has a huge impact on advertising revenue: Advertisers don't have to pay that month's rate. It was a double whammy: An exorbitantly expensive cover was now augmented by a loss of advertising dollars.

All was coming to a head in September 1988, when the article on Peary was out and Bill was airily dismissing "old wives' tales."

I had prepared myself for a volley of telephone calls from reporters about the apparent about-face on Peary. But I remember only one call that mattered.

On the night of Friday, September 30, I received word from Cape Breton Island that a drunk driving a truck had crossed the median on the Trans-Canada Highway and struck the car driven by Teeny. Dick, her husband, had been in the passenger seat and had been seriously injured; the drunk had been killed, and Teeny . . . Teeny died en route to the hospital. In stunned disbelief I booked the first flight to Baddeck I could.

My mother and father and brother were gone, and now Teeny, the last of my nuclear family, was dead. Teeny, seven years my senior, had been my confidante. Teeny was the one who taught me sailing, who urged me to follow my instinct and join the Geographic, who scolded me when I didn't spend enough time at home with Wiley and the kids. Gone—in a random moment of senseless violence.

I RETURNED TO THE OFFICE on Monday, October 10. The next day, my assistant, Joyce, announced that Boyce Rensberger of the *Washington Post* was on the line.

I picked up the phone. "What can I do for you?" I asked cautiously.

"You believe in publishing about 'the world and all that is in it,' right?"

"Right," I echoed back. Trap! I thought. Don't step into it.

Then he cut to the chase. "What do you have to say about the 'slip'?"

The slip? What was he talking about? A ladies' undergarment? The place where I moored my boat at the marina? After some initial confusion, it turned out that he was referring to a piece of paper found in the Robert E. Peary Collection in the Library of Congress.

Dennis Rawlins claimed that he had found a slip of paper confirming that Peary had actually missed the North Pole by 121 miles—and knew it. The slip contained sextant readings from a navigational sight Peary claimed to have taken at the pole.

Rensberger wanted a comment. I warned him that Rawlins had an ax to grind and was widely recognized for trying to defame Peary. "Oh, I know all that," he responded impatiently. "But this time it's different: Rawlins has hard evidence. The slip proves that Peary was a fake."

Rensberger mentioned in an offhand tone that the story was coming out in the *Post* the next day.

Did it ever. PEARY'S NOTES SHOW HE FAKED CLAIM blared forth from page 1 in a type size, in my imagination, reserved for the attack on Pearl Harbor. The lengthy piece mentioned the Society in less-than-flattering terms and ended with the possibility of Peary's claim being officially disavowed.

Only a few weeks earlier, Sir Wally Herbert had concluded that Peary probably missed his goal and was carried by currents some 60 miles to the west of the pole. Now Rawlins was placing him 120 miles to the east!

It's one thing to declare Peary probably failed to reach the North Pole, but quite another to say he was a fraud and imply that others—including GHG and the National Geographic Society—had aided and abetted him.

I called in Robert Sims, our director of communications. Bob, a former Naval officer from the Pentagon, had been Defense Secretary Caspar Weinberger's spokesman. I asked him to find a group of navigational experts to work on what was essentially a navigational issue. "We have a hell of a mess. Fix it," I told Bob. If anyone could do that, Bob Sims could.

Sims was back in my office sooner than expected. In suburban Maryland he had located the Foundation for the Promotion of the Art of Navigation, founded by retired naval officers concerned that the growing reliance on GPS was eroding the knowledge of navigational techniques so necessary to the operation of ships and aircraft. The foundation's president, Rear Admiral Thomas Davies (Ret.), had also designed a sun compass for Admiral Byrd, so knew a thing or two about polar navigation.

Would the Navigation Foundation thoroughly analyze all the available navigational data from Peary's 1909 expedition? We'd pay all bills—but the final judgment must be the foundation's and it must be unbiased.

Davies agreed, and he set to work with three of his colleagues, all former naval officers and expert navigators.

When the Navigation Foundation issued its interim report on Peary, barely a month after it had been hired, it demolished the so-called smoking gun: the slip, the scrap of paper supposedly proving Peary a fraud because the "sextant readings" scrawled on it were far off the mark. The slip, Admiral Davies announced, contained no such sextant readings. Those scrawled numbers were the serial numbers of Peary's chronometers. Rawlins's latest charge against Peary was flicked away.

If that put me in a good mood, it was quickly dispelled. During a quick trip to Hong Kong, a friend commented that the anniversary issue with the hologram was "the strangest-looking cover. It looked like a mirror. What was it?"

It was only the first of many complaints from members in Asia. After looking into it, Owen and I discovered with mounting anger that thousands of substandard covers had been essentially dumped there, apparently with Bill Garrett's knowledge. I called him into my office.

Bill was never a man to admit wrongdoing and didn't then either. He knew I was furious. He also knew I couldn't fire him over this, if only because the production people had been evasive about it as well. I worried our friendship had been frayed beyond mending.

IT WOULD TAKE A YEAR for the Navigation Foundation to wrap up its investigation on Peary and produce its 240-page final report. It looked at Peary's "practical navigation"; he had a proven history of accurate dead reckoning, even across vast distances in whiteout conditions. Matthew Henson, his assistant, was just as able and fast, if not faster.

At the pole, Peary took 13 observations of the sun. He marched 10 miles in what amounted to the cardinal directions, increasing the likelihood of crossing the elusive spot. He also recorded wind speed and direction, and hours and distance traveled. "We were impressed by the absence of even a single inconsistency under the most rigorous scrutiny," Davies reported.

Our sleuths used another technique that proved the point: photogrammetric rectification—analyzing the shadows cast in photographs and working back from those shadows to calculate the angle of the sun and thus a line of position on Earth.

Using this method, they subjected seven photographs taken by Peary at the North Pole to analysis. In those photographs where shadows cast by the men could be clearly read, the experts concluded that the place where Peary and Henson were standing was somewhere between four and 15 miles from what we now call the geographical North Pole.

The most conclusive arguments were the deep-sea bottom soundings, used in making maps of seabed topography, which never lie. The Arctic Ocean floor in 1909 was terra incognita. Peary carried two drums spooled with 6,000 feet of steel piano wire, plus three 20-pound lead plummets. Providing the Coast and Geodetic Survey with soundings of the seafloor was part of the scientific justification and funding for his expedition.

The soundings could not be faked because no one in 1909 could even guess at the hidden abyssal topography. I was particularly interested in eight of the soundings—96, 110, 825, 580, and 310 fathoms, plus three "no bottoms reached" in the vicinity of the pole. They indicated a rise, a plunge, another rise, then a fathomless plunge. Could those be matched to what we know of Arctic bathymetry today? They could, because the Navigation Foundation compiled a map, using data from the Defense Mapping Agency, the Office of Naval Research, and Soviet and British sources.

The fit of soundings to topography was remarkably exact, verifying most of the dates that Peary logged for each location and most of the distances he claimed to have traveled.

Vindicated by a map!

When we published the findings reversing our reversal in the magazine, Bill and Joe reacted with seeming nonchalance. Quod erat demonstrandum, Bill concluded in his Editor's Note.

ON THE EVENING OF NOVEMBER 17, 1988, some 1,500 guests converged on the Sheraton Washington Hotel for our centennial banquet and awards ceremony.

I had given considerable thought to the 15 honorees to be awarded a special Centennial Medal and Steuben globe for their contributions to geography and the Society. Each would represent an important field closely associated with us. For cartography, I called up Brad and Barbara Washburn. For mountaineering proper, there was no more famous name than the conqueror of Everest, Sir Edmund Hillary. Oceanography? The man who gave us the key to the silent world, Jacques-Yves Cousteau.

Space exploration? The first American to orbit Earth, Senator John Glenn. Deep sea exploration? The man who discovered new biological communities in the Galápagos Rift and found the *Titanic*: Bob Ballard.

Photography? That pioneer of deep-sea imaging and inventor of the strobe flash, Harold "Doc" Edgerton.

Then there were disciplines we helped found or foster. Although we did not originate the travelogue, we popularized it through our lectures—Thayer Soule was the best of the best. Paleoanthropology? Louis Leakey revolutionized the discipline. So we recognized Richard Leakey and his mother, Mary, for continuing the legacy. Both were deserving on their own. For field-based observational primatology, we honored Jane Goodall.

When it came to classical archaeology: Kenan Erim for his work on Aphrodisias. Nautical archaeology? We had been the principal popularizer of founder-architect George Bass. Wildlife conservation? The nod went to the silver-haired twins, Frank and John Craighead.

In closing, I reminded everyone, "In our first 100 years we were discovering the wheres of our planet. In the next 100 we will discover its hows and whys."

OWEN AND I COULD FORESEE THE palmy days drawing to a close. Our membership hovered near 11 million; our staff was the largest in our history. We were improving geographic instruction in schools. After six years of work, more than 35,000 copies of our new *Historical Atlas of the United States*, produced under the direction of Bill Garrett, had been sent free to every secondary school in the country, a million-dollar centennial gift to the nation.

We were doing great, but we could sense trouble. I sent a memo to the staff saying that every division at the Society would have to tighten its belt. Not through layoffs but rather staff reductions by attrition, early retirement, transfer, and consolidation. If we acted early enough, we could avoid any layoffs for at least the next five years.

When no one at the magazine wanted to hear anything about belt-tightening, I sent Owen to visit a young picture editor I had targeted as a potential editor of the magazine. Although born in the United States, Robert W. Hernandez had been living in Cuba with his parents when Castro's revolution erupted in 1959; he and his family became émigrés to the United States. Before he landed at the *Geographic,* Rob was a sailor and had worked in conservation in the Arctic. He was so quietly competent that he soon rose to number two in the Illustrations Division, second only to Tom Smith.

Owen sat down in his office. "Hernandez, what do you want for next year's budget?" he asked.

Rob looked blankly at him.

"Budgets, budgets. What do you want?"

"I don't know," Rob said uncertainly. "I've never seen a departmental budget."

Owen had just plumbed the depth of financial ignorance at the magazine. If the golden boy for both me and Bill at this time looked blank at the mention of budgets, we had problems.

"Well, how much do you plan to spend next year?" Owen probed, enumerating the salaries of all the picture editors and photographers and estimating how many weeks and months they would spend on the 61 stories needed for next year.

Rob just sat there. "Owen, I have no idea. Nobody has ever sat down with me and told me even the basics of what we do from a financial perspective, how much each story should cost, how much in salaries, how much in expenses, how much in equipment, how much of this and that. How can I tell you whether I want more or less? Of course I want more because more is always better than less but . . ." He trailed off.

Rob's underlying assumption was that he could spend anything he wanted.

It was going to be an uphill climb.

WHATEVER RESERVATIONS I HAD about the magazine—and they were few—I was glimpsing a brighter outlook for our television efforts. EXPLORER on WTBS was reliably winning Peabody Awards every year, partly because nobody else could afford such high production budgets. Our TV programming never made a penny for us in all those award-winning years. Still, it brightened our brand for millions of potential members to see.

Then the Discovery Channel in Silver Spring, Maryland, began running into financial trouble. I called Dennis Kane and Tim Kelly into my office and asked, "'Hey, guys, why don't we try to hook up with Discovery? Together we could dominate the documentary area."

"Everything they produce is a bunch of shit," Dennis replied.

"Yeah, but they have great potential, and we should talk to them," I countered.

But Dennis remained stubbornly opposed. Maybe he realized he wouldn't have had the authority he enjoyed at the Geographic.

I should never have let the matter drop; I think we could have forged a partnership with Discovery and created a good deal for us both. Kelly agreed. It could have made us the leaders in documentary television.

Today Discovery is a media giant. We lost an important decade in the creation of our own television channel. But my focus was print media, and I relied on the TV guy for advice. He had said no.

About that time, Dennis Kane decided that greener pastures could be found in commercial television and left. Picking his successor was a cinch. Tim Kelly was promoted to chief of our television division. He was only 32 years old, but I had full faith in his judgment.

Many years before, Dr. McKnew told me that should I become the Society's chief executive, I had an obligation to identify not only my successor but also "my successor's successor." In Tim Kelly I thought I glimpsed the latter.

NEITHER BILL GARRETT NOR I handled our growing disagreements well. Bill had been testing my authority for the past few years but was so uniquely talented that I kept telling board members that I could work out our differences. Still, there was no pause in the flood of expense requests signed: "Approved, WEG."

Then, in January 1990, membership dropped by nearly a million.

Losing close to 10 percent of our membership was a huge blow. Garrett shrugged it off with no effort to trim costs. I called him into my office. I appealed to our mutual love and respect for the *Geographic,* but he turned away. I reminded him that the bylaws stated that the president was CEO, responsible for the institution, its mission, and its employees. Pushed to the edge of exasperation, I opened the magazine's masthead page and put my finger on it, saying, "Look, Bill, there's my name. It's above yours and it's in a bigger font!"

Privately, board members began telling me I should fire him for insubordination; Owen had been urging me to do so for at least a year. Behind the scenes, Owen sent Al Hayre, Society treasurer and a board member, to Bill, suggesting that Bill toe the line and accept my cost-cutting campaign. His response, Al reported: "The board would never fire me." He was wrong. As CEO and board chairman, I could.

Bill argued that cutting editorial didn't make sense. After all, the magazine provided 60 percent of revenues. What he didn't mention was that his expenses exceeded income. Breeden's net revenues were keeping us profitable.

About this time, Bill convened an in-house "Committee on the Future" and made Rob Hernandez chair. Bill and I met with Rob in my office and said that we wanted the input of young staffers. We wanted a strategic plan for the future.

Rob ran with it, canvassing the entire staff, not just those at the magazine. He held confidential town halls division by division, including the business side. The report stunned both Bill and me. Neither of us—or Bob Breeden, for that matter—escaped criticism. "The three-way cold war between Bill Garrett, Gil Grosvenor and Bob Breeden . . . has the staff confused and deeply dispirited," the committee wrote in private to Bill. Like kids listening to quarreling parents, they just wanted it to stop.

I hadn't realized how obvious our rift had become.

Garrett hated that report and thought Hernandez was deliberately trying to undermine his authority. He turned on Rob, pushing him to the sidelines. Bill was sure his staff loved him—which by and large it did, sometimes to the point of downright worship—and wouldn't countenance the fact that many also thought he had an insufferable ego.

One day in March 1990 I entered a conference room to address the magazine's senior staff about the need to trim staff and finances. I was barely halfway through when Bill rotated his swivel chair to face his staff and ostentatiously feigned falling asleep. He was clearly challenging me.

Stunned by his behavior, I finished and stalked out without taking any questions. Later I heard that after my departure he said something to the effect of, "Don't worry about all that. Gil's on another one of his tangents. Reducing expenses and staff doesn't apply to the magazine."

That was his last antic. I consulted every board member, except Bill. Every one of them approved firing him. I did not consider this a victory but rather a defeat; I had failed to convince Bill of the gravity of the situation. I remain perplexed by his refusal to learn from the demise of *Look, Life,* and the *Saturday Evening Post,* all crashing at or near their peak circulation.

I think Bill believed that if he produced the best possible magazine—which he did—nothing else mattered. Financial awareness did not resonate with him. With a growing circulation, we could have tolerated money issues. With a static or falling base, ignoring finances is fatal. To protect the financial stability of the National Geographic Society, I would fire anyone who stood in my way. Even Bill Garrett.

On Thursday, April 12, 1990, at our board meeting, we swept through routine business. Before adjourning I held the Executive Committee behind. One final time, I laid it all on the line and repeated my issues with Bill. One final time the board concurred—unanimously. Bill would be fired on Monday.

The intervening weekend was something of a blur. I knew there would be collateral damage. Joe Judge was next in line to be editor. But he was so joined at the hip with Bill that I couldn't see him working out in the role. So I'd run the possibility of his leaving past the board. I worried about my friendship with Lucy Garrett and their sons—particularly Ken, who had already embarked on a promising career as a National Geographic photographer.

Monday: Owen has laid most of the groundwork for a 3 p.m. meeting with Bill. Then Bill is in my office. I'm telling him that he's out and telling him why. I have a shard-like memory of Bill's face as he sits there, registering emotions ranging from surprise and confusion to anger, then a hint of panic. He is saying something, not pleading but remonstrating, maybe even trying to strike a deal, man to man, friend to friend. It is no use. A facilitator sweeps him up and takes him into a small room, closing the door. People on the ninth floor are staring, starting to realize that something big is blowing up. I know that word is spreading like wildfire. Meanwhile, I am walking straight into Bill Graves's office.

I tell Graves that he is the new editor of *National Geographic*. I have picked him because he is Geographic family; his father was GHG's right-hand man in the 1920s and '30s. Bill is a talented wordsmith, not a picture man, but is nearing retirement. I know he will never pretend to be anything other than a caretaker editor.

Bill Garrett is not allowed to return to his office. He is escorted down the elevator to a waiting car. Out walks the best picture man ever to have crossed this threshold.

I'm now in the Control Center, telling the magazine's senior staff that Bill is no longer editor and that I have named Graves to replace him— saying this in an atmosphere so heavy with hostility that I can cut it with a knife. A knife they want to turn on me. Questions are shouted. "Was this your idea or Bill Garrett's?" Howard Paine asks. "Mine," I respond pain- fully. I turn on my heel and walk out.

Once again, I'm making that thousand-mile walk to my office. There I sit, drained of emotion. I remember only one visitor. One of my oldest Geographic friends, Joanne Hess, still running lectures and audiovisuals, is comforting me with words, honest words, true words. She is telling me that I will take this one to my grave. I know she is right.

PART FIVE

A BETTER STEWARDSHIP

CHAPTER TWENTY-THREE

STORM CLOUDS

t was a relief to escape the office for a vacation; the press coverage of the Garrett firing was brutal. The *Washington Post* made Bill Garrett the martyred editor, me the ogre CEO, and my assistant, Joyce Graves, the Lady Macbeth who put me up to it to crown her new husband, Bill Graves, editor. That really angered me. I could take the calumny from the press, but to accuse Joyce was outrageous.

Staff morale at the magazine plummeted. Also quitting was a relatively new addition: Charles McCarry, the editor Bill had brought in to attract talented freelance writers. He resigned in sympathy. Tom Smith, chief of illustrations, was gone within a few days, refusing to consider a senior position in Breeden's group. Graves wanted his own man and had promoted Bill Allen, a talented picture editor, to associate editor for illustrations. Mary Griswold Smith would never forgive me for supporting that move.

When Graves assured the staff there would be no radical changes in editorial direction, I hoped that things would calm down. Although Joyce had warned me about Bill's unpredictable temper and explosive rages early in their marriage, I had not paid much attention.

A YEAR LATER, IN MARCH 1991, I lost my right-hand man. Owen Anderson retired as executive vice president at the age of 70. Because he was so indispensable, I had convinced him to stay on for five more years, but he left when the health of his wife, Lois, began to seriously deteriorate. His managerial instincts were superb. Most of all, he had an uncanny ability to understand what really motivated an employee and a can-do approach to solving problems. He was exacting and empowering. When he retired, his responsibilities were distributed among no fewer than six senior staff.

Together we had kept an eye on the gathering storm clouds and agonized as membership continued its slow slide. We were losing on average 200,000 members a year: a 2 percent decline. Though we vowed never to chase circulation, we'd gain some back because the tally was made each January 1, when we dropped members who hadn't paid their annual dues on time. We kept sending them the January, February, and, once, even the March issues, hoping they'd renew; at least 50,000 of them usually did.

When Owen retired, we were just under 10 million for the first time in years. We still had a huge membership and one of the highest renewal rates in the magazine industry at 83 to 85 percent—but even that was slowing. When your circulation increases by 300,000 to 400,000 a year, it's easy to make money, innovate, have a large photographic staff and the best lab in magazine publishing, and other perks. Static circulation paints a different picture.

I was sitting on the Marriott Corporation board when the hotel chain was growing by leaps and bounds. There was a banker on the board who kept warning Bill Marriott: "No tree grows to heaven. You must budget your finances for zero growth. If you don't, you will have trouble when that inevitably happens." I didn't pay enough attention to that advice because at the time the Geographic was also surging. Now I remembered it.

Not that we were in bad shape. We were making money to support education, research, and exploration, and had hundreds of millions stashed in the bank. It was just new, this retreating tide. GHG and MBG had seen only growth. Until now, so had I. During my editorship, membership increased by nearly four and a half million. In the 1980s we plateaued at just under 11 million. By the early '90s, membership was nine and a half million.

Fortunately, Breeden's empire was still going strong. Our books, other magazines, and educational media were reliably gobbled up each year. Still, I had lost Owen Anderson, my right-hand man, in early 1991; I would lose my left-hand man by the end of the year. Bob Breeden, 65, was retiring. I really enjoyed working with Bob; he clearly understood and supported my belief in focus group testing, particularly among our relatively homogenous membership.

For nearly 30 years, ever since MBG tossed him the White House guidebook, everything Bob touched had turned to gold. He had over 100 million copies of his books out there: one of the most highly successful, if unheralded, book publishers in the business.

Breeden made only one mistake, toward the end of his career. He grew enamored of an accountant's tactic: not writing off part of the cost of a new book's expenses on the initial press run. Though postponing it makes the initial bottom line look better, the practice tempts larger print runs. Sooner or later, inventory costs would balloon, Owen had warned me. Even as Breeden was retiring, our warehouses in Gaithersburg, Maryland, were bursting at the seams with overstock. What to do?

We held an inventory clearance sale in late October 1991 and notified members living within a 40-mile radius of Gaithersburg. More than 10,000 people arrived, overwhelming the 500-space parking lot. We cleared over $200,000 in that one weekend alone. But excess inventory plagued us for years to come.

In the meantime, my own retirement loomed, four years hence. That meant grappling again with succession.

If I could have done one thing differently, it would have been to train a successor in the same way I had been trained: through exposure to every facet of the editorial and business departments. But a business-editorial training course wasn't feasible, and Tom McKnew was long retired. I was also motivated by the master's insistence that I pick both my successor and my "successor's successor."

Tim Kelly might fit that bill; his natural history unit was producing exceptional footage for use in television films, and he was already making a deal with the Imax Systems Corporation of Toronto to jointly produce films for giant screens. But Tim lived in Television Land, while the Society still revolved around print. More than once, he had attempted to bridge the gap with the magazine. He had yet to receive a warm welcome from editorial, particularly Bill Garrett.

Going outside might mean hiring someone who wouldn't appreciate or understand our uniqueness as an institution. At that time, though, I thought I had no choice but to look for a successor amid the hardball world of companies that operated for profit.

The first recruit from that world promised to be a perfect fit. Michela English had been a vice president in charge of business development for Marriott and walked through our doors in late 1991, around the same time Bob Breeden retired. She had attended the Yale School of Management and was smart and financially savvy, while still idealistic; she also had a sly sense of humor. I sat her on the next highest rung on the ladder to my perch, making her a senior vice president alongside Bob Sims, my director of public affairs and major confidant. Michela also sat on the board of trustees, as well as on the Education Foundation board. I was certain she had a bright future.

Although only in her early 40s, Michela could be entrusted with Breeden's empire: books, *Traveler* and *World* magazines, Educational Media, and the rest. She had a lot to learn about publishing and media, but I felt confident she'd come up to speed quickly. And she did.

In the meantime, I had to keep the Geographic in fighting trim, maintaining a steady balance sheet while discharging its mission to increase and diffuse geographic knowledge from as many platforms as possible. Owen used to look at me with that mischievous glint in his eye and say, "I'm sure glad I don't have your job."

"It's not just a job, Owen," I told him once, with a sigh. "It's a legacy."

IT MUST HAVE BEEN 1991, probably at a Goodall Institute event held at our headquarters, when Jane first asked me about my efforts to promote geography education. She seemed particularly interested in our grassroots approach. She had been visiting schools in Tanzania and talking to students and teachers. Sooner or later, our conversation turned to the environment, and she broached her dream for Africa. Why not establish a network of young people willing to undertake environmental projects—planting trees or cleaning up garbage—as a public service? Maybe harness a network of locally based groups through the Tanzanian school system.

Jane envisioned loosely affiliated local chapters, public service projects boosting environmental awareness, and coined a great name for it: Roots and Shoots. In many respects, it mirrored our Geography Education Program; engaging the school system was the key. There, I could offer advice.

"Jane, it's brilliant!" I said. "But you must spearhead this venture yourself. You cannot delegate leadership. You cannot rely upon school officials alone to invigorate and maintain the project."

When Jane Goodall sets her sights on a task, she's tenacious in seeing it through. Starting in Tanzania, Roots and Shoots soon spread over Africa, then around the world. Thousands of local chapters operated in more than a hundred countries, most of them affiliated with schools or churches. All promoted a better stewardship of the planet.

The program has been a spectacular success; Jane works tirelessly to promote it. Whenever I'd see her, we graying crusaders would swap stories about our parallel projects. We both prized the time spent with young people, their teachers, and their counselors.

Yet as National Geographic's CEO, I had to be seen to be effective. I had to prove to everybody that I was behind the venture 100 percent. Teachers are dedicated; I had to match them, dedication for dedication, and share in their victories and defeats. This was driven home during that first 1986 Summer Geography Institute, after "Pomp and Circumstance" played at their graduation. Most everyone marching across the stage had tears in their eyes, and mine started welling up too. I quickly turned away—I couldn't be seen that way.

Then it hit me. Yes, you should be seen this way! That proves you are genuinely with them in this crusade, not just some figure who descends from on high to scatter a few rhetorical crumbs. After that, I tried to never miss an opportunity to show up in the name of geography education.

After the success of the video game *Where in the World Is Carmen Sandiego?*, we devised something similar for young kids: Teddy bears that traveled around the world, thanks to commercial pilots and flight attendants willing to send postcards to the kids: "Mr. Bear is now in Hong Kong" or "Cuddles has arrived in London and will visit Piccadilly Circus!" This way, children could plot their protégés' progress on maps and remain engaged with geography.

One evening, after a tiring business trip to Tokyo, I had hardly settled into my plane seat for the long flight to D.C. when a flight attendant gave me a teddy bear to carry home. Whether by chance or whether my name was recognized on the passenger manifest, I would be the one to return the globe-trotting bear to the school in Minnesota it called home.

When I returned to Washington, I flew out to that primary school in Minneapolis. The principal, teachers, and students had spent hours preparing for my visit, plastering every classroom with geography posters and maps gathered by a graduate of our summer training course in Washington. They just wanted to show their appreciation. I walked through those doors, past a gauntlet of students, teachers, and administrators, clutching that teddy bear. A couple of hours later, when I walked out those doors, tears of pride rolled down my cheeks.

It's hard to explain my commitment to the Geography Education Program. I didn't ask to be born a Gilbert Grosvenor in the National Geographic Society's founding family. But for this cause, I found both a pressing national need and an ability to impact change, thanks to my legacy and my Geographic family. I threw my weight into it, trying to do the most good. This was the battlefield I chose.

Within six weeks in the late summer and early autumn of 1990, the last lions of the old Geographic slipped away. Thomas McKnew died in August at 94; and in early October, Mel Payne followed, at 79. While the loss of the old guard was hardly a surprise, the swiftness of Payne's death shocked me. Suddenly, I became the village elder. How could that be? Their ghosts began to haunt me. McKnew's whispered, "Succession. Succession. Succession." Payne's murmured, "The golden era is over."

One or the other had always been present at every board meeting I had ever attended; it was strange to pull up a chair at that table when neither was present. Everyone rooted in the 1940s or '50s was dead or retired. Those of us from the '60s were approaching 60 or gliding right past it. Like me. Like Tom Abercrombie.

Sitting in the cockpit of *White Tiger,* the boat we jointly owned, Tom and I would sip wine and gaze up at the stars. Tom had lost a step or two: normal for a field man passing 60. When he and Lynn finally secured the permissions necessary to retrace the old 1,600-mile "frankincense trail" across the Arabian Peninsula, she was the assigned photographer and he, the writer. Tom didn't like that, but the days when he could handle both words and pictures of an assignment were over. Tom's summation of his own career was appropriately reflective: "One never seduced by a foreign culture will never appreciate the fetters of his own."

Trimming the Geographic oak meant trimming staff: The cost of salaries, benefits, and pensions was always a significant burden. I remembered that morning in MBG's old 16th Street office when Dr. McKnew told him of a budgetary shortfall that would require cuts to staff and how MBG's response—"Why don't we publish an atlas instead?"—solved the problem.

Increasing revenues, rather than cutting services, wasn't so easy now. Our members were saturated with our mailings and not rising to the promotions as avidly as they had in the past.

Around this time I was told that if I wanted someone to address our financial challenges, I should consider the publisher of the Baltimore Sun, who had done just that.

J. Reginald Murphy, a native Georgian, had been editor of the Atlanta Constitution and the San Francisco Examiner before taking on the Baltimore Sun's problems as publisher and CEO. I thought his blend of front-office financial and publishing expertise, mixed with a keen understanding of journalism, was exactly what we needed.

He was 59 and not sure he wanted to work until 65; he'd had a heart attack, so didn't need additional years of stress. He would be a "short-termer," someone without deep ties to the Society who might put it through a crash fitness program and modernize the fulfillment operation. He also loved to play golf and was slated to become president of the United States Golf Association in 1994. I agreed he could do that concurrently.

In 1993 Reg Murphy joined the Society as executive vice president, a position synonymous with chief operating officer. He was now number two in the hierarchy. Though disarming on first acquaintance, there was something flinty and unyielding behind the folksy manner. Michela English was dubious; she cautioned that he might not be the right fit for us. I assured her that Reg was a short-termer. Perhaps I should have listened to her more closely.

As expected, Reg pared down the staff, advising me that a mass early retirement of long-term employees was unavoidable. In 1994, 146 of 180 eligible employees opted to take a very generous package. It meant that practically everyone I had worked with since the 1950s and '60s was packing up. Tom Abercrombie, Dean Conger, Bart McDowell, Bruce Dale, Emory Kristof, Jim Blair, Charlene Murphy, Mary Griswold Smith—scores of those who had been young when MBG was our guiding star.

All that institutional memory, loyalty, and dedication went out the door. Some editorial types were still furious with me about firing Garrett and replacing him with Bill Graves.

Nearly 64, Graves was a caretaker editor, around only long enough for a successor to be identified. Unlike Garrett, he enforced budgetary discipline with an iron hand and saved us millions.

But I didn't pay enough attention to the warnings of his wife, Joyce, my executive assistant. Graves was subject to volatile mood swings. I never witnessed it myself but was told that when he was agitated, the veins in his neck would pop out and throb; red-faced with rage, he would let everybody and anybody have it. I regret picking him, but felt I had little choice at the time.

With ample time, I chose his successor more carefully. Bill Allen, Graves's associate editor for illustrations, had come up through Breeden's empire. He had worked with books and *World* magazine before moving to the flagship magazine, where he had displayed editorial and administrative competence, along with tact and poise. Those qualities were important at this juncture. Had I not been forced to make an instant decision after firing Garrett, I like to think I would have chosen him in the first place.

The year 1995 welcomed a new editor. It also welcomed expansion of the magazine's reach.

IN MY MIND, HAD BILL GARRETT followed a normal retirement path, Rob Hernandez had the inside track in the race to become editor of *National Geographic*. That retirement, of course, never happened. Garrett had sidelined Hernandez, leaving him in limbo, and Graves willingly left him there.

Rob was too talented to be wasted. I began having breakfast with him once or twice a month. At one of these sessions, he put down his knife and fork and said, "Gil, I have an idea. I truly believe that the magazine has international potential beyond the English language."

At that time, no more than 20 percent of our membership was outside the United States, and most of that was in Canada, the United Kingdom, Australia, and New Zealand. Even when he worked for Garrett, Rob had the portfolio "foreign editions" assigned to him but never really opened it. Now he was making a serious proposal.

"It's a modern global age, and furthermore, I think this brand deserves a bigger theater in which to play."

"I think you're right," I replied. "I've been thinking about this for years; go explore it."

In fact, I'd appointed a small committee to explore the concept, but the idea had languished. Though *Reader's Digest* had been highly successful with foreign-language editions, I was still haunted by the failure of *Life en Español,* which contributed to the demise of its parent magazine.

I slipped Rob out from under Bill Graves and reassigned him to Michela English, where he could flourish.

For at least a year and a half Rob studied printing and publishing in countries around the world, as well as different models of partnership. How do you manage quality control through every stage of the process? Would the membership model still work? Soon he had a proposal we liked and presented it to the board.

We started with a Japanese edition.

Japan was the most literate nation in the world and, like Germany, had a reputation for producing high-quality products. Michela and Rob pitched a partnership with Nikkei, Inc., Japan's leading publisher of newspapers and magazines to the board: a 50-50 joint venture, each party contributing five million dollars in capital. The plan was approved, and we flew to Tokyo for the formal launch of our first "local-language edition," as we called them.

In bookstores, in exhibitions, and even on the side of the Sony Building, the June 1985 cover photograph of the beguiling Afghan Girl was in full view.

Rob and Michela were happy; the original projections were for 88,000 subscribers the first year, but the actual number was almost twice that, topping 160,000. I was disappointed; I'd hoped for something closer to a million because of our heavy promotion. In Japan, though, magazines weren't so much subscribed to as purchased as a single copy at a kiosk. The American-style fulfillment system might not work there or in other countries.

Nevertheless, we were launched into a global arena—and, thanks to Rob Hernandez's vision and Terry Adamson's legal expertise, would ultimately publish the magazine in 33 local-language editions, subsequently managed through licensing agreements. That Japanese edition marked the beginning of a transformation from a National Geographic Society into an international geographic society.

Tim Kelly was thinking across borders too. While his natural history unit was producing footage of never-before-seen animal behavior, Tim was also trying to convince Ted Turner to air programs on a dedicated channel with us. But by the mid-1990s Ted was caught up in his merger with Time Warner, a mega-cable player; he told Kelly we had probably missed our window. Tim positioned our television division as a key player in the global entertainment industry. That meant strategic partnerships and joint ventures with for-profit companies: a major shift for us.

Through the years, the Society had held fast to its nonprofit status because the scope of our activities was educational. With the eventual exception of advertising revenues, we were exempt from corporate income taxes because we made no profit, plowing income back into our mission-oriented educational programs or banking it for a rainy day.

Every year as president, I had our accountants assess the viability of our nonprofit status. Every year it came up aces. But the media world was changing so swiftly, and our need to keep pace was so critical, that we looked into the idea of setting up for-profit taxable subsidiaries we would fully own. Tim Kelly couldn't negotiate big deals hampered by not-for-profit restrictions.

In 1995 we spun off our television efforts into a wholly owned taxable subsidiary called National Geographic Television, Inc., with Tim Kelly its president. He now had a free hand for dealmaking.

We also began discussing an even bigger version of such a subsidiary—one in which we might incorporate not only television but also maps and videodiscs. That way, we might better protect our nonprofit, educational core: our journal, publications, classroom products, and mission-oriented activities.

This was the genesis of National Geographic Ventures, Inc.—which, in addition to television shows and products like maps that we could now sell in bookstores, also included our infant NG Interactive. The World Wide Web was two years old, and we were late to that game.

Tim was too busy with television to head up the proposed new Ventures. I would have to go outside. Michela English told me she knew someone and set up a lunch for us to meet.

I instantly liked John Fahey. He was in his mid-40s, bright, optimistic, cheerful, and well-spoken. He had worked at Time Warner for two decades, most recently as chairman, president, and chief executive officer of Time-Life, Inc.

There was no little irony in hiring a man from Time-Life, but Ventures needed someone with experience in publishing a wide range of products for the open market. Fahey had that experience. Since my retirement was only a few months away, it was really Reg Murphy's decision. At the January board meeting in 1996, Murphy was elected to succeed me when I stepped down the following May.

My short-term successor was now in place.

NOT THAT I WOULD BE MOVING all that far. As chairman of both the Education Foundation board and the board of trustees, I would be shifting GHG's bound volumes to an office only one floor up. I would come in a day or two a week, largely to help the Geography Education Program and its outreach. We had also established a development office to fundraise for the program. I could meet and greet potential donors.

Nevertheless, an era was closing. Five generations of my family had built and nurtured the place. For the last three decades, the board made it clear that the Grosvenor succession had ended.

Certainly, my younger siblings and my children could apply there, but I doubt they'd be hired. As it turned out, they chose different paths, choosing to work, variously, in art, journalism, and medicine.

At 63, I first announced my imminent retirement to the board of trustees. I half expected someone to protest, to urge me to stay on a few more years. Silence. I reminded them a year later that I would be leaving when I turned 65. Silence again.

When I became president, I vowed to leave the Society in better shape than I had found it. That was easy when circulation was booming; it wasn't so easy now.

Nevertheless, we did well. In 1995 *National Geographic, Traveler,* and *World* accounted for about half the Society's $422.6 million in revenue; the rest came from books, educational media, atlases, and investment income.

Membership seemed to stabilize at around nine million, still off from its peak. The flagship magazine still had the fifth largest circulation in the country, and television soon became profitable. By the end of that year, we had total assets of nearly $730 million and absolutely no debt, no mortgages, and a fully funded retirement program. For GHG, MBG, and me, it was always pay-as-you-go; we never borrowed a penny, even during our building-construction years.

Though it was painful, I did reduce staff. That year we had the first layoffs in the history of the Society. Reg Murphy managed its details, which largely hit the service departments—back then, mostly young people who could seek other careers. Senior workers were given generous retirement packages. And Murphy was negotiating the sale of the Membership Center Building, the fulfillment center in suburban Maryland, which would cut more employees loose when we outsourced those activities.

The resignation of one person in particular saddened me. Only weeks after Reg was anointed my successor, Michela English gave notice. She had accepted an offer to be president of Discovery Enterprises.

I was devastated. Clearly the biggest mistake of my career was not pushing her with the board to succeed me as president and CEO while I still had the clout of my office and a board familiar with her talent. I am confident that as CEO she would have led the Society through difficult times. Ironically, my judgment was prejudiced by the same "youth stigma" that had plagued me in my early career. I also remember her reservations about Reg when he was first being considered. How prescient she was.

On April 1, 1996, John Fahey became the first president and chief executive officer of National Geographic Ventures, Inc. Everyone wanted to meet him because he exuded such an air of confidence and optimism. A new day was dawning; the internet was having its first wave of success, and most media pundits declared with confidence that the future of publishing was digital. National Geographic's website would launch in June, and Fahey seemed just the ally to lead us into the new era.

The *Washington Post* covered the changing of the guard at *National Geographic*, quoting John as saying: "There's a faction here that just wishes things were the way they were 20 years ago. But consumers have changed, the competition is more acute. We've reached a point where we need to be more aggressive." The comments didn't bother me but provoked a grim chuckle from some of the senior staff.

But another comment did give me pause. Sitting in his office, I remember him breezily saying, "Print media is dying." I was glad *National Geographic* magazine wasn't being included in the new Ventures—yet.

May brought the inevitable last toast before I stepped away from active service to the Society I had loved so much. Time to put the glass down and enter a new phase of life.

CHAPTER TWENTY-FOUR

A HIGHER AND A BETTER USE

Even before I turned 65, I began planning for retirement. I fantasized living on Maryland's Eastern Shore in a tree-shaded old clapboard house in St. Michaels: workshop in back, sailboat bobbing at the end of my pier. Occasionally I'd break my reverie and ask my wife, "Wiley, you've been so patient all these years. It's your turn to live your dream." Then I'd return to my charts of the Chesapeake Bay.

"Are you serious?" she once responded.

"Of course, dear," I answered, before resuming my perusal of sailing catalogs.

A month or so went by. I came home one evening to find Wiley surrounded by flyers featuring 10 horse farms for sale out in the "horse country" of Piedmont, Virginia. "I thought we might go out and look at these," she said. Uh-oh, I thought.

One weekend we did, and nine out of the 10 were easily dismissed. But when we turned into the gates of one place, located in Fauquier County near the Blue Ridge Mountains, a beautiful red fox jumped across the driveway. It was a sign, a blessing, a benediction. That vixen had such a burnished look about her pelt, she appeared more copper than red. We promptly fell in love with that farm.

The brick house, spacious and comfortable, stood on a hill with an unobstructed view of the mountains. The property embraced 140 grassy acres not too far from Interstate 66, the main commuter highway from Front Royal to Washington.

We christened it Copper Fox Farm, moving there from McLean soon after I retired. There was enough room behind the house for me to indulge in my latest hobby, propagating exotic azaleas. It was the perfect place for Wiley to realize her long cherished dream of breeding horses, particularly pintos. Many of her horses won prizes, and a few fetched a good price. Ted Turner, who owned ranches in Montana, even bought one for Jane Fonda, his wife at the time.

One summer we visited Ted's Montana ranch and saw him at his most ebullient. He promptly drove us all over the vast expanse of shortgrass prairie to show us his bison herd. His interest in bison, he told me, began when he read about them in *National Geographic* as a boy.

Meanwhile, back home, I tended my azaleas. I built four long hoop houses and wrapped them in plastic to protect the plants from freezing in winter. I was soon propagating upwards of 1,200 azaleas at a time. My goal was to have one variety after another blooming from the first of April until the Fourth of July.

I was incredibly happy puttering away with my plants, no more so than when I piled 52 blooming plants into my Prius and took them into the Geographic, where I sold them to the staff for a nominal sum.

That was a bonding moment with the Geographic family. Staff would come down to the parking garage, pick out their plants, and we'd catch up. After my retirement, it was the only easy way I could greet people who had worked there for decades. Not long ago I saw an e-mail thread: 240 former employees were discussing the azaleas they had gotten from me. I'm glad they're flourishing.

Wiley and I would spend summers on Beinn Bhreagh, where we had built a log house high on the hill, not far from The Point. From its spacious windows I enjoyed an unsurpassed view of Baddeck Bay, the Little Bras d'Or Lake, and the village of Baddeck. There was always a sailboat heeling in the breeze that I could watch. I had sold *White Mist*—the upkeep on a fine wooden boat was too much—and had downsized to a 38-foot fiberglass sloop I named *Dragonfly*, which was moored within my sight.

Yes, place is important to me. And those two places—one new to us, the other as old and cherished as my very being—would be the two poles between which we lived out our retirement years. A third was downtown D.C., where I often drove in to chair a board meeting, sometimes having had no sleep the night before; mares have a habit of foaling between midnight and three o'clock in the morning. A quick shower and I would hit the road, groggily happy.

The first time I returned to the office after retiring was in response to an invitation to join a meeting about Tim Kelly's latest television venture. I assumed I had been included as chairman of the board. Crossing the courtyard to the M Street Building, I encountered Reg Murphy. He greeted me and asked where I was going.

"I'm responding to a memo to attend a television meeting," I answered.

He stopped and looked me in the eye. "No need for you to go to this meeting. You're not involved." He turned and walked away.

Okay, I told myself. He's the CEO now.

To his credit, Reg was doing exactly what we had planned: Trimming the Geographic oak. Over the next few months, he would complete the sale of the Membership Center Building and clear warehouses full of inventory. Fulfillment and membership services would be outsourced, and 350 employees—more than 25 percent of the workforce—were let go.

Reg downsized the staff with a will. I couldn't criticize him, because I had spent my last five years doing the same thing, mostly through attrition.

But I was chagrined to learn that six key staffers in the Geography Education Program were on the list.

Aside from that decision, though, Reg left geography education to me. "This is Gil's program. I'll let him run it," he told Bob Dulli, the dedicated staffer who actually directed it. That was troubling too; this was a National Geographic Society program, not my hobby horse.

Reg was also looking to invigorate Society membership. He wanted to welcome younger readers into the fold; advertisers preferred a younger demographic, he said. I was concerned about alienating our older members—the ones who gave all those gift memberships to nieces, nephews, and grandchildren. Reg even considered ending the annual membership cycle—January to December—in favor of the month-to-month renewal format practiced by other magazines. This didn't allow for the significant December boost from holiday gift memberships, which sometimes amounted to 40 percent of our annual renewals, and I was glad when the notion was abandoned.

Murphy, thankfully, turned to more constructive projects. On December 4, 1996, he and Bob Wright, president and CEO of NBC, announced a partnership to create and develop the National Geographic Television Channel for the global marketplace—firmly marking the dawn of a new era at the organization, which would align with the new direction of the larger media landscape.

That was Tim Kelly's achievement; he had done all the legwork to establish National Geographic Television's first branded distribution service. Although we started making money producing content, owning rights, airing it on EXPLORER, and selling it on tapes and discs, Tim foresaw the day when that model, supported by Ted Turner's generosity, would no longer work. When Ted rebuffed Tim's idea of establishing a channel together, he looked at alternatives, winding up at NBC, then owned by General Electric.

NBC gave Kelly not just a warm reception but an actual deal. It was expensive to launch in the United States, so we would first target Europe, Asia, and Latin America. The National Geographic Channels International would be a three-way partnership consisting of the Society, NBC, and Sky Broadcasting in the U.K.

Tim was careful when it came to content. He spent months negotiating protections and controls to ensure quality. NBC backed him because it, too, had a brand image to protect.

Hardly had the new channel started growing in Europe and Asia when Reg was grooming his own successor. In February 1997, John Fahey became the Society's executive vice president and chief operating officer, as well as a member of the board of trustees.

Reg was ready to get out. He had trimmed budgets and wanted to resume his golf game, adhering firmly to his short-timer role. On December 11, 1997, I chaired the board of trustee meeting that elected John Fahey the Society's 16th president.

The Society inevitably began to change. As National Geographic's commercial endeavors grew, business necessarily began to trump editorial.

That began before the year I retired, when a member of the board—the chairman of our compensation committee—tried to push through an executive bonus plan. Some argued that without a bonus plan, we'd never attract outside talent.

I had enough clout then to fight it; I didn't think bonuses were appropriate for a nonprofit organization, even though they had become necessary to attract outside talent. In my opinion, too many executives think about their bonus first and their staff second, provoking resentment. It widens the gap between the haves and the have-nots. And it risks decision-making becoming bonus driven. At one of the first board meetings after I stepped down as CEO, that committee chairman pushed the executive bonus plan through the board.

In 1998, for the first time in a century, *National Geographic* went back on the newsstand; soon our books were in bookstores, and you didn't have to be a member to buy an atlas. While this was considered necessary to compete in the changing marketplace, I felt that Geographic membership lost its magic and uniqueness.

I hoped that it wouldn't prove too damaging. But I worried it would destroy the incentive to renew membership if you could just pick up the magazine at the grocery store. The language of Society executives—and its growing numbers of vice presidents—changed. Members became "subscribers," and a new buzzword—"eyeballs"—proliferated as we chased television viewers and digital users.

As CEO, John was focused on the new channel, which he hoped to launch soon in the United States.

Overseas, the National Geographic Channel had been a runaway success, but debuting in the States would be prohibitively expensive without partnerships. NBC was still our primary partner. But British Sky Broadcasting, another participant, didn't have much of a presence in this country. So NBC sought a controlling interest in Fox Broadcasting Company—one of many media assets controlled by Rupert Murdoch's News Corporation.

Domestically, the National Geographic Channel would be owned by the Society, NBC, and Fox; together we would pool several hundred million dollars to buy our way into the big-money cable television world. Fox put up most of that; we contributed 21 percent, which gave us a 28 percent equity stake because it was our name and library of films.

Having our own domestic channel would inaugurate a new era. No more Television Specials produced with WQED and broadcast on PBS. EXPLORER would be uncoupled from WTBS, still a part of Time Warner, since we needed help filling our 24-hour programming schedule. That upset Ted Turner; he loved National Geographic and was proud to host us on his superstation. It was also hard for Tim and me; Ted was one of the best partners we ever had.

The channel was all set to go when, at the last minute, General Electric, NBC's parent, pulled out. As a triumvirate, we were safe—nobody could completely control us. But without NBC, we were left alone with Fox, which had a reputation for sometimes questionable programming decisions.

Tim and his cohorts scrambled to shore up our quality controls against Fox's programmers. Our team and an outside law firm worked for months, ensuring that we had the ultimate right to select and approve content, to fact-check everything, and to veto programming not congruent with our mission. Tim thought we built up enough quality controls. Reality suggested otherwise.

I FOLLOWED THIS CLOSELY AS CHAIRMAN because I thought we might be skating on thin ice. Every outside producer we had ever dealt with had bridled at our fact-checkers. Television was a more slippery medium than magazine journalism. Fact-checkers forced producers to be accurate; that's one reason why we'd won so many Emmy Awards. We were getting the stories right. People believed what we said.

Though the contract clearly gave the Geographic editorial control, John seemed reluctant to enforce it. He appreciated accuracy, but in the end it was entertainment first; mission programming came second—a frequent cause of friction with Tim. John was just more realist than idealist. And his realism told him to stay on the good side of Fox's executives.

As the date of the launch approached, a pricey television studio was built in Explorers Hall. Out went our enormous freestanding globe, relegated to storage. The new studio would be located on the corner of 17th and M Streets so that people on the sidewalk could be seen waving and smiling, like they do on the *Today* show.

On the morning of January 1, 2001—when everyone else was sleeping off their New Year's Eve toasts—the staff of the National Geographic Channel U.S. was clinking champagne glasses as the United States became the 113th country to join the 100-million-household international cable network Kelly and crew, in partnership with NBC and Sky Broadcasting, had built in only four years. Tim's dream had finally come true. But he still had to reckon with Fox.

When the studio cameras started to roll for the opening salvo of the daily news program *NG Today,* John Fahey was the first guest. "Our mission has not changed, but the way we gather and disseminate information of the natural world is greatly enhanced by this channel and broadcast," the Society's newest president said. "The founders would be proud of what we're doing."

MOST OF THOSE RETIREMENT HOURS I spent at headquarters were devoted to the geography education crusade. One of our most notable successes was the idea of a geography bee, originated and implemented by Mary Lee Elden. Alex Trebek, the legendary host of *Jeopardy!,* served as moderator of the first National Geographic Bee in May 1989. As it turned out, Alex became so dedicated that he returned year after year for a quarter century to host the bee.

Another success involved the College Board. For years, Bob Dulli had been trying to establish an Advanced Placement exam in geography: a milestone in the quest for academic legitimacy. Incomprehensibly, the College Board, which develops and administers the tests, kept rejecting us—and our geography.

Finally, Bob, who was still running geography education, invited its development director, Robert Orrill, to Washington to spend two days with our Geography Education Program, using all the right maps, atlases, and other props. Orrill finally got it: Geography was not only back in the curriculum; it was the "renaissance discipline" of the day. Within two months, the College Board approved an Advanced Placement exam in human geography—a huge triumph for the Geographic and for Dulli.

Then, a major blow struck the nation—and the Society.

On September 11, 2001, I watched the endless replays of those jets hitting the World Trade Center from a hotel room in San Juan, where I had flown for a geography project. Toward evening, one of my colleagues came to my room. Her news broke my heart: Joe Ferguson, Bob Dulli's chief lieutenant, and Ann Judge, the beloved head of our travel department, had been escorting three local teachers and three excited elementary students on an educational field trip to California's Channel Island National Marine Sanctuary when their plane, American Airlines Flight 77, was flown into the Pentagon.

Ann and Joe made things happen. They were smart and personable and touched everyone they encountered with their own zest for life. And now they were gone.

A few weeks later we held a memorial for Ann and Joe across the street at the Mayflower Hotel. The staff crammed every nook and cranny in the large room to watch the audiovisual show depicting our fallen comrades' lives and loves, joys and sorrows. I could hardly deliver my remarks I was so choked up. John Fahey was just superb. Always so good on his feet, he rallied his troops with the deftest of touches and somehow instilled the old ardor back into spirits at a time of deep mourning. He was every inch a leader on that memorable day.

IN DECEMBER 2010, I stepped down as chairman of the board, though I retained a seat there. In most respects the National Geographic Society had been completely transformed since I retired as president 16 years earlier. Our successful century-old nonprofit organization had become a global media company.

Although I was the last of my family to serve as editor, president, and chairman, I would not be the last Grosvenor to help steer the Society into the future. In 2009, Dr. Alexandra Grosvenor Eller—my daughter, Lexi— was elected to the board: the sixth generation to sit at that table. I was obviously delighted. Lexi, who had graduated from Princeton and sailed through medical school, was much smarter than me, and would have her own ideas. The legacy was as important to her as it was to me. But she could think for herself, and we both resolved to never discuss pending board issues. We still don't.

In many ways, change was for the better: Every issue of *National Geographic* was available in digital form. The magazine was published in at least 30 local languages; it was still placing high in national awards. Our television efforts had earned more than 120 Emmys. *Traveler* was a frequent winner of Lowell Thomas Awards, and *National Geographic Kids*—the rebranded *World*—had been voted Periodical of the Year several times. Nearly 150 million people used the National Geographic website. The Society's Explorer-in-Residence Program was booming, its television channels truly international, and its affiliation with Lindblad Expeditions, a cruise line specializing in remote places, a success.

One of John Fahey's best decisions was to promote Chris Johns to editor after Bill Allen retired in 2006. Chris was a terrific field photographer. John, spotting his potential, fast-tracked his rise through the magazine. As editor in chief, Chris put together a special issue on Hurricane Katrina and one on Africa, accompanied by an "Africa: The Human Footprint" map supplement. He would do the same with Yellowstone National Park a few years later. In 2008 he was awarded Editor of the Year at the American Magazine Conference for his leadership.

Rob Hernandez and Terry Adamson, our executive vice president and chief legal counsel, were the driving forces behind our local-language editions; they helped create a Society with new revenue sources and market opportunities. Sadly, Rob never got due credit and eventually left to take a position at Disney.

SEISMIC TRANSFORMATIONAL SHIFTS in the industry were afoot. Across the media landscape, magazines struggled to stay profitable during the economic downturn of 2008 and 2009. At the same time, social media, powered by the rise of the smartphone, was rapidly changing the way the world shared and communicated information, and streaming video put a television in everyone's pocket. *Gourmet* folded in 2009; flagship Time, Inc., properties, including *Time* magazine and *Sports Illustrated,* were spun off and sold in 2018. Others struggled to retain ad sales and readership in an increasingly noisy digital world, where every piece of "content" competed with its counterparts for readers' attention and eyeballs. The age of 12-month assignments in distant lands began to feel like vestiges of another era.

Membership was still tapering off. By 2010 the National Geographic Channel was becoming the financial engine of the Society. Unfortunately, much of its content struck me as tawdry and sensationalistic.

Tim Kelly still had a few cards up his sleeve. When he noticed that one of Fox's many channels was lying dormant, he saw an interesting opportunity—thus creating Nat Geo WILD. In January 2005, while attending the Sundance Film Festival, Tim viewed a film made by a team that had overwintered in Antarctica. It featured penguins with corny voice-overs. Tim bought it and rescripted it. The film became *March of the Penguins,* which won the 2006 Oscar for Best Documentary Feature.

Meanwhile, I recognized fewer and fewer faces in the halls. Sometimes I'd forget the newfangled ID badge and was refused admittance to the cafeteria. But I'd always show up whenever I was needed. I'd shake hands, introduce people—anything to help the cause.

I took satisfaction in our achievements. The Education Foundation, which I had envisioned as a 10-year effort, had lasted three decades, thanks in part to the support of President George H. W. Bush. We managed to get geography declared a core discipline in U.S. schools: a huge deal. We enabled geography standards to be written and adopted by every state. We created endowment funds dedicated to geography education in half those states. And each year, some 193,000 kids take the Advanced Placement exam in human geography. Finally, each new National Assessment of Educational Progress in geography shows improvement in students' grasp of the subject—though we still have far to go.

WHEN I STEPPED DOWN AS board chairman in 2010, I had done so not only because I had little clout left, but also because it paved the way for Tim Kelly to become National Geographic's 17th president. John, who had stepped up to the chairmanship, wasn't thrilled about that but acquiesced; finally, my "successor's successor" was in place. Or so I thought.

I began the long glide into contented old age. But contentment was elusive when it came to National Geographic Society matters. The year 2012 was especially rough.

It culminated in an auction of treasures from our archives. Administered by Christie's and dignified with the title "The National Geographic Collection: The Art of Exploration," dozens of paintings commissioned for our articles and books over the years were yanked out of cabinets and sold to the highest bidder. They included Else Bostelmann's glowing depictions of the strange creatures William Beebe had glimpsed in the black abyss, many of the bird portraits GHG had commissioned from painters like Allan Brooks and Louis Agassiz Fuertes, and Tom Lovell's highly praised historical scenes, including his much reproduced "Surrender at Appomattox," which went for $80,000.

Prints by famous photographers, including Margaret Bourke-White and Ansel Adams, were trundled out and put under the gavel. Even things that should have mattered to the Society as an institution—a Norman

Rockwell—like painting of a man and his grandson in an attic reading stacks of old *National Geographics*—were boxed up and sold. Everything was scanned, and we retained reproduction rights. But it still felt as though we had been ransacked.

Pierre Mion, the artist who created all the NASA visualizations and with whom I had worked closely, was so incensed by the sale of his painting of Apollo 11's lunar module that he quit talking to me. I found it particularly upsetting that some frames from the space collection were probably sold too, because those had once been entrusted to us by NASA for safekeeping: a brutal irony.

The auction made nearly four million dollars, the vast majority from the sale of four lots. Three were paintings by N. C. Wyeth—one a superb depiction of dueling pirates on a Caribbean beach redolent of the romance of history and geography we had tried so assiduously to cultivate. Three paintings that made our headquarters so unique a place: gone.

The fourth was Alexander Graham Bell's set of Edward Curtis's 20-volume *The North American Indian,* one of only 222 in existence. That had been entrusted to the National Geographic Society by Bell himself, who had been such a pivotal president. Gone, the gavel banging down for nearly a million dollars. Many of my cousins were incensed.

I remained on the board. While on a trip to Albania in 2012, I got a call from John, letting me know that there would be a special board meeting about succession. I told him I'd jump on the first plane to Washington. "Oh, no," he replied, "We're not going to do anything right now." I called in to the meeting; the connection was terrible. A few days later, Tim resigned; the official announcement was issued on September 18.

This left John as chairman and CEO—with the office of president of the National Geographic Society unfilled for a little over a year. In January 2014, Gary Knell—formerly CEO of the Sesame Workshop, producers of the beloved children's show *Sesame Street,* and most recently CEO of NPR—came aboard to fill that role.

In October I lost a final boardroom battle. I argued strenuously against airing a docudrama on the assassination of Osama bin Laden, *Seal Team Six,* two nights before the election between Barack Obama and Mitt Romney. I thought it amounted to a covert Obama endorsement, and at all costs, the Geographic must remain nonpartisan. Postpone it, I urged. No one supported me. The film aired—and the media took note.

On the drive back to the farm, I realized the time to stay home had arrived. Sixty years to the day since I started working there, I officially retired from the National Geographic Society board of trustees.

Over the years, many Geographic compatriots had started slipping away. After a telephone call in the first week of April 2006, I knew that the road to Shady Side would never feel the same; Tom Abercrombie had unexpectedly succumbed to routine heart surgery at the age of 75. He slipped away just like that, although I imagine that Azrael, the Islamic "angel of death," had a tussle for his soul. Other hands would have to finish building the 24-foot skipjack in his workshop and complete the memoir he had undertaken. As I absorbed my loss, I was reminded of his favorite line: "If life is a journey, why not take the high road?" Inshallah, my friend.

A decade later, on a summer morning in 2016, another telephone call: Bill Garrett had died of a stroke.

I hadn't seen much of him since the firing, though Ken Garrett, Bill and Lucy's son, had steadily worked for a reconciliation between us. Ken was by then an established *National Geographic* photographer specializing in archaeology, so I'd bump into him in the halls. Finally, 13 years after that dark day in 1990, he persuaded Bill and me to reconnect. Our two families met at Ken's house to share lunch, watch a football game, and celebrate his 50th birthday.

I vividly remember a rendezvous—perhaps our last—about two years later. Wiley and I had been on a Baltic cruise aboard the *National Geographic Explorer,* one of the ships run by the National Geographic–Lindblad partnership. We were disembarking in St. Petersburg, Russia, at the same time a new set of passengers was embarking for the return cruise. Both groups mingled in the large dining room in a nearby hotel, which became so crowded that the only empty chairs were at the table at which Wiley and I were sitting. Suddenly, we saw Bill and Lucy Garrett being escorted over to those last two seats. The total surprise on their faces could only have mirrored that on ours. For a moment I thought that someone had stage-managed this. But no, it was pure serendipity.

We talked, we laughed, we caught up on each other's lives. Once more, I saw a sight I thought I would never see again: that sly, gap-toothed grin so prominently on display in the old days. Well-met in a faraway city, we were amiable again—once more, if only for that fleeting hour, friends.

THE SECURITY LINE AT THE Halifax, Nova Scotia, airport is usually not very long. I was in a somber mood before I even entered it that day in September 2015—despite the prospect of flying to St. John's, Newfoundland, to board the *National Geographic Explorer* to cruise the shoreline of that island province.

There was only one person ahead of me in line when I reached the table where you put your carry-on items into containers to be x-rayed; a 50ish woman whom I had never seen before glanced at my travel-stained National Geographic knapsack, looked straight at me, and asked, "What happened?"

Taken by surprise, I was speechless. But her question only further darkened my mood.

When I arrived at St. John's, my driver, a young man supplied by the cruise ship whom I knew from previous trips, stowed my bags and, climbing behind the wheel, turned around and asked, "What happened?"

I could hardly speak. I was amazed that enough people would find the previous day's news as immensely sad as I did.

It had been a glorious afternoon in August 2015 when the sun sparkled across the Bras d'Or Lakes. Reflected light shimmered on the surface.

The breeze was much too fresh for small sailboats; I could tell that by watching a 30-foot sloop from my hilltop window. For one thing, it carried way too much canvas. Its skipper must have been inexperienced, because he seemed oblivious to a particularly ugly puff of wind streaking toward his vessel. I wanted to shout, "Round up! Take in sail! Reef the main!" from my quarterdeck. But I was a mile away.

Then my telephone rang; the spell was broken. "Hello," I answered, annoyed at the intrusion.

It was the office, calling to tell me that the Geographic was expanding its partnership with 20th Century Fox into a "broader relationship." The deal, which had been struck by Gary Knell and approved by the Society's board that August, was that our organization would contribute the television assets, the flagship magazine, *Traveler,* books, maps, and the travel program; in exchange, Fox would contribute $725 million to the National Geographic Society's endowment, which, with the new subsidy, would stand at one billion dollars.

I was speechless. I didn't understand. Then it began to sink in. I asked if we would be equal owners. The answer was no: Fox would own 73 percent of the new entity; the National Geographic would own 27 percent.

I could not believe what I was hearing and asked how this new alliance would be governed. Under the agreement, I was told, the partnership's board of directors would manage the new joint venture.

For the first time since its founding in 1888, the Society and its magazine would be divorced from each other. Our world-renowned institution was being split asunder. Our board of trustees had ceded ownership to a bottom-line-driven, for-profit company. As majority shareholder of the new partnership, Rupert Murdoch would now, in effect, own National Geographic Partners, Inc.

Stunned, I walked down the hill, away from the telephone call that had shattered my sense of legacy, my heritage. I sought the sanctuary of *Dragonfly*, moored nearby.

To Gary Knell, John Fahey, and the board of trustees, this was simply a business decision based on the current media landscape and their best projected analysis of where the organization might be in 10 years' time: Sell it now while it is still worth something.

THE DEMISE OF THE National Geographic Society my family had known and nurtured for five generations was the greatest blow to befall me yet; what takes a century to create can be demolished in a fortnight. Sure, the media landscape had changed; sure, these decisions had clearly been difficult to make. But bereft of its publications, I feared the Society would drift rudderless while the magazine, books, and products were sold down the line, from one buyer to another, marked down each time as the value lessened. There is surely a higher and a better use for such a Society as ours.

By now the day was ebbing. As if to cheer me up, a classic Baddeck sunset painted the western sky, framed from below by the evergreen balsams of the Margaree Mountains. When shadows crept across the lake and engulfed *Dragonfly*, it was time to row ashore and face reality.

A few years have passed and I'm still deeply saddened. Now the day approaches when I will cross over the bar. I don't look forward to the encounter with the shades of GHG and MBG. They'll greet me with the one question I still can't answer.

"What happened?"

NO TREE GROWS
TO HEAVEN

've been ruminating over the collapse of civilizations lately: a popular
pastime these days. Ah, the transitory nature of human endeavor and
the folly of pride—I know it well, archaeology being among the most
abidingly popular subjects in *National Geographic* magazine. Squatting
on my haunches at excavations in a hundred places, from Angor Wat to
Xi'an to Olduvai Gorge, I've nodded solemnly as archaeologists explained
to me why this palace was deserted or that city, which once stretched 16
miles from gate to gate, lay beneath six feet of earth by the time the 20th
century opened. History's long parade of empires—one after another—
were born, flourished, conquered, either dramatically collapsed or carried
on, transformed by the experience of challenge and response.

It is hard for me to resist the comparison, for I'm sitting in my office
high on the hill of Beinn Bhreagh, flipping through an archaeological atlas
we published years ago, paging past one vanished civilization after another.

Those pages reminded me of why I think the Society occupied such a
unique spot in 20th-century American culture. At one point, during the
1980s, only *TV Guide* and *Readers' Digest* had larger circulations than the
journal of a geographical society. That says as much about the U.S. reading
public as it does the quality of that journal.

I will take the latter fork, for I believe that the wide-ranging influence of the Society stemmed directly from its core principles—the Society's leadership, its staff, and the loyalty of its membership.

First and foremost, the Society was founded to promote the "increase and diffusion of geographic knowledge." It would do so primarily through its official journal, the *National Geographic* magazine. It was among the last of the more than 100 geographical societies founded in the 19th century, one of the few established without government patronage. And it would depend upon membership to fulfill that mission.

Mission. Magazine. Membership. On that three-pointed cornerstone everything else was built. Editorial principles, a Washington-based headquarters, and a balanced board of trustees—this completed our genetic code, our DNA. We stayed loyal to that code for the rest of the 20th century. The magazine's "symphonic" mix of articles, with something that appealed to every member; MBG's diversification efforts with the atlases, globes, books, and television specials, and his recruitment of professional journalists; even my own efforts to steer in a more environmental direction, expand our television presence, and especially promote geography instruction in our nation's schools—all sprang from loyalty to that code. I believed that evolutionary changes were absolutely essential but that revolutionary changes were often fatal.

The staff was characterized by its loyalty, longevity, and continuity. The Cartographic Division alone had two father-son teams lead it—Albert and Newman Bumstead, and then Jim and Dick Darley—each family devoting nearly seven decades to serving the Society. The high quality of our cartographic products owed everything to this continuity, coupled with the unrelenting commitment of the editor. The same holds true for the photo lab, the photo engineers, the men and women in charge of printing and engraving, and other unseen parts of the Society so crucial to the magazine's reputation for excellence.

Our peerless editorial research department, led over the decades by a formidable trio—Margaret Bledsoe, Ann Wendt, and Lesley Rogers—who among them had probably at least a hundred years of service, deserve all the credit for "According to *National Geographic* . . ." as a byword for veracity. It was driven home to me by that unlikely source, South Africa's ambassador Pik Botha, roaring, "But you don't understand. People believe what you write!"

Every department boasted leaders who served for three decades or more, exemplifying a tradition of quality and craftsmanship handed reverently from one generation to another. The pride in workmanship resembled a medieval guild and, I believe, explains the success of the National Geographic Society.

Above all, I salute the membership. Their loyalty made it work, setting everything else in motion. In exchange for modest annual dues, everyone received 10 issues and four map supplements a year, in addition to the opportunity, available only to members, to purchase our books, globes, and other geographical products.

It was proverbial that no one threw the magazine away. Printed in the trim size and stiff spine of an academic journal, they were designed for easy shelving; soon those shelves would accumulate hundreds of issues, supplementing the encyclopedia and unabridged dictionary as a home reference. That explains why a half million members bought slipcases to store their magazines and indexes to find information. "The gift of learning" was easy to bestow.

Membership meant more than mere subscription. It had a cachet that won loyalty. A man once walked across the island of Sri Lanka just to show me his framed membership certificate. Ernest Hemingway's short story "Homage to Switzerland" is about two strangers waiting for a train who discover that each is a member of the Society.

In *It's a Wonderful Life,* George Bailey, played by Jimmy Stewart, holds up a copy of the magazine and exclaims, "I've become a member of the National

Geographic Society!" It sounds corny, but membership mattered. It mattered to collectors, too, who salted away every publication and product we ever released. And it certainly mattered to the gentleman who placed the following personal ad in the *Denver Post*: "SHEILA: Please return my National Geographic Collection. You may keep the engagement ring."

Our logo, a golden rectangle, reminds me of the golden ratio of the ancients—the 3-to-2 ratio of the Parthenon's facade and in the trim size of our cover.

Alas, no tree grows to heaven. We made mistakes—all of us who once led the place did so. I have a trunkful to atone for myself. The board of trustees has its share too. It should never have broken up the unique position of "president and editor" and made the president rank higher than the editor, allowing the money person to dominate the content person. I should never have had to fire Bill Garrett; I should have been able to persuade him to support, not fight, the crucial need to downsize, to reduce spending and staff in the face of falling circulation. But I failed in repeated attempts to do so.

I'll acknowledge that in the digital revolution, my successors faced a tsunami the likes of which we never before experienced. I'll acknowledge the skill with which they steered the Society through the storm that had sunk so many print publications. I acknowledge their good ideas, and I applaud their achievements, including those of Society CEO Jill Tiefenthaler.

Some people think I might find a healing balm in Disney's acquisition of National Geographic Partners, part of the package of media assets Fox jettisoned in 2019. They point out that Fox was never a good fit for us, and I agree. Disney, founded by a perfectionist when it came to providing quality content, gives me reason for great hope.

Though I never met Walt Disney, MBG did and admired his energy, charm, and charisma. The friendship between MBG and Walt Disney was a mutual-admiration society. MBG even published a story, "Walt Disney: Genius of Laughter and Learning," in 1963. The Disney studios were bursting with old *National Geographics;* our pictures of wildlife, cultural attire, and landscapes gave Disney animators a sense of how an animal or foreign culture looked and helped sculpt a realistic model for their films and theme parks.

I am frequently reminded by friends that while the *Saturday Evening Post* and *Life* fell by the wayside long ago, *National Geographic* survives—survives in incarnations different from anything GHG might have imagined. National Geographic Partners boasts the world's most popular Instagram account, has chalked up another Academy Award for the documentary *Free Solo,* and still publishes the magazine in 33 local-language editions. And National Geographic, per se, enjoys perennial status as the most trusted brand in media.

These days, with my limited vision, I just look at the magazine. Bill Allen, Chris Johns, and Susan Goldberg—all former editors—are only the most recent in a long line of talented men and women who have helped make our journal so successful. There is still plenty of geography, as well as deeply researched articles and innovative features on a variety of interesting subjects. They are always accompanied by well-designed gatefolds, page maps, illustrations, and photographs. I was particularly impressed with a series of articles on the warming Arctic, always an interest of mine; similar packages on pollution, plastics, food, and water; and special issues on Hurricane Katrina, Yellowstone National Park, and Mount Everest that would have made Barry Bishop proud. All have kept readers informed on critical issues facing our planet. The "magazine of record" is still alive and well.

Most important of all, geography itself remains—and that was the point. Greater, more widespread geographic literacy: the increase and diffusion of geography broadly conceived.

"History is about the past, Gil," Alex Trebek once said to me. "But geography holds a key to the future."

I have thought about that often. History, too, helps predict the future. But much of its ability to do so is predicated in geography, in the physical circumstances of peoples and nations. Geography helps us understand that asteroid impacts and volcanic eruptions are likely in the future, because we see abundant evidence of past occurrences. Global struggles between haves and have-nots are important issues that must be addressed if we are to achieve planetary harmony, and geography has a role to play in seeking these solutions.

Despite those who view the world with hopeless dismay, I still believe that industrial societies can be resilient and adaptive. We can adopt the can-do attitude of Dutch engineers who have been diking out the sea for centuries. We can preserve vast tracts of forest and sustainably harvest only necessary timber. We can plant trees in towns and cities designed to accommodate the surrounding natural habitat. We can harness cleaner energy sources. We can be parsimonious about water usage. We can set aside vast tracts of coral reef and other marine biodiversity hot spots in the ocean.

Looking out the window, I see a storm brewing over the Bras d'Or Lakes, a small dark cloud hanging above the southwestern horizon, above the gentle mountains some 20 miles away. Like many squalls, it will grow quickly and spread across the sky.

A deep rumble is followed several seconds later by lightning. The show is about to start. My window is higher than that eagle's nest in the balsam fir tree below me and I have the perfect seat.

Outside, the air hangs heavy and sticky. Birds sense the change and vanish. Dark cat's-paws of fresh strong wind dance across the water. More deep rumbles, more lightning flashes.

A curtain of rain now spreads across the horizon, heading toward the village of Baddeck. It quickly enshrouds the lake, climbs up the hill to Beinn Bhreagh, and slams against my windows.

I stand up and leave my office. The squall will abate soon, moving north. We might get a rainbow out of this one, I think. Wiley is already putting on her walking shoes, and I hunt for mine, for we both know that the end of a storm in this blessed corner of the world is a glorious moment to be alive.

Once again we climb to the top of the mountain to a spot near the graves of Alexander and Mabel Bell; as if by magic, birds reappear and the sun breaks through. Once again we gaze out over the Bras d'Or Lakes, taking in that sublime panorama of headland and island, those long green slopes glistening in the soft northern light. Once again, hand in hand, we breathe in the spicy scent of wet balsam and prize each pristine drop of moisture adorning every blade of grass. For all things change, but Earth abides, always returning, full circle, to the dew-fresh morning when the world is young.

ACKNOWLEDGMENTS

When the task of acknowledging the help and support of many friends and former colleagues finally was upon me, my thoughts naturally turned to our dedicated and long-serving National Geographic family. The influence of my father and grandfather is by now so obvious I need not further elaborate on them. Were it not for Bud Wisherd, I might never have joined the Geographic staff. And if Bob Sisson had not taken a literally wet-behind-the-ears neophyte under his wing on that railroad bridge, I might not have stayed 60 days, much less 60 years. Franc Shor, Tom McKnew, Tom Abercrombie, Donna Grosvenor, John Scofield, Bob Breeden, Owen Anderson, Alex Trebek, Joe Judge, Bill Garrett, and Richard Leakey—I remember them all so vividly, and I see them in my mind's eye every hour of every day.

But they have now all sailed over the horizon, and my task is now to thank as warmly as possible such remaining friends and colleagues as Rob Hernandez, Tim Kelly, Chris Johns, Michela English, Kenny Garrett, Bob Dulli, Dick Boehm, Kit and Cathy Salter, Joe MacInnis, John Fahey, M. J. Jacobsen, Mary Lee Elden, Karen Sligh, and Mike Ulica—each of whom gave generously of their time to converse with me about our favorite subjects, the National Geographic Society and its magazine.

Lisa Thomas, the publisher and editorial director of National Geographic Books, was unfailingly enthusiastic about my writing a memoir.

Bright, calm, and soft-spoken, Lisa leads a conference with grace and confidence. She is a great talent. Hilary Black, executive editor at National Geographic Books, was a perfect fit for me. I really appreciate her style. Hilary instinctively knows when to cajole, when to soothe, and when to just listen. When she issued deadlines, I was highly motivated to comply. I particularly wish to thank these two women for their sensitivity working with this legally blind, crotchety 90-year-old author.

For six years I talked with Mark Jenkins almost every day for an hour, discussing my life's experiences. Mark was a great listener. I truly appreciate his contribution to this book. His knowledge of Geographic lore and research skills were invaluable to me.

Cathy Newman, for many years a most distinguished writer on the National Geographic staff, skillfully edited the text down to size. I am most grateful for Cathy's sensitive cuts—well, most of them! Any verbose author could benefit from Cathy's skills.

I appreciate Adrian Coakley's photo-editing skills and his willingness to consider a photographer's favorite images, which are not always the most appropriate.

After working with Renee Braden for more than three decades, she still amazes me with her ability to remember and retrieve any image among the multimillion photographs under her supervision. She will always remain a favorite among our Geographic family.

Deborah Grosvenor, a very successful literary agent, agreed to take on my project. Deb's advice has been fantastic. Were it not for her unceasing efforts, this undertaking would have failed.

I wish to acknowledge Helen McGuire for her secretarial and computer skills. These past four years she has made my life so much easier.

Most important of all to me, I wish to acknowledge the tremendous contribution my wife, Wiley, has made to this book. Not only has she been my partner for more than 40 years, but she has guided me through these past six years, helping me cope with my vision issues. More than once, Wiley successfully deterred me from abandoning this memoir. "Remember, Gil, once you're gone, future historians will write from hearsay." If that failed to persuade me, out came the clincher: "You owe this memoir to your Geographic family and your forbears." That's my Wiley! She can always cut to the chase. Now that the book is finally closed, I thank her from the bottom of my heart—where she dwells forever.

INDEX

NATIONAL GEOGRAPHIC SOCIETY

Using the power of science, exploration, education, and
storytelling to illuminate and protect the wonder of our world.
Join us at natgeo.com/impact

GIL GROSVENOR'S WORLD

CANADA

NORTH AMERICA

UNITED STATES

Jasper National Park

Florence

Yellowstone National Park

Denver

Wild Acres

Copper

Fox Farm

New Haven

Gibson Island

Washington, D.C.

Baddeck, Cape Breton Island

Deerfield

Guysborough

Island of Newfoundland

R.M.S. *Titanic* discovered

Cape Canaveral, Cocoa Beach

Bermuda (U.K.)

ATLANTIC OCEAN

Nuestra Señora de *Atocha* wreck, Florida Keys

Silver Shoals

DOMINICAN REPUBLIC

Fort Shafter

Hawai'i (U.S.)

PACIFIC OCEAN

TROPIC OF CANCER

EQUATOR

Galápagos Rift

Galápagos Islands (ECUADOR)

ECUADOR

PERU

Apurimac River

Machu Picchu

BOLIVIA

Paramaribo

SURINAME

SOUTH AMERICA

Andes

Andes

ARGENTINA

Península Valdés

TROPIC OF CAPRICORN

Pitcairn Island (U.K.)

N

W   E

S

South Georgia Island (U.K.)

ANTARCTIC CIRCLE

SOUTHE

ARCT

ARCTIC CIRCL

UNITED KINGDOM

London

Brielle

Madrid

PORTUGAL   SPAIN

Ponta Delgada, Azores (PORTUGAL)

Casal

MOROCC

North